Children at the Center

*Transforming Early Childhood Education
in the Boston Public Schools*

Betty Bardige
Megina Baker
Ben Mardell

HARVARD EDUCATION PRESS
CAMBRIDGE, MASSACHUSETTS

Paperback ISBN 978-1-68253-202-7
Library Edition ISBN 978-1-68253-203-4

Library of Congress Cataloging-in-Publication Data

Names: Bardige, Betty Lynn Segal, author. | Baker, Megina, author. | Mardell,
   Ben, author. | Boston Public Schools. Department of Early Childhood.
Title: Children at the center : transforming early childhood education in the
   Boston Public Schools / Betty Bardige, Megina Baker, Ben Mardell.
Description: Cambridge, Massachusetts : Harvard Education Press, 2018. |
   Includes bibliographical references and index.
Identifiers: LCCN 2018011680| ISBN 9781682532027 (pbk.) | ISBN 9781682532034
   (library edition)
Subjects: LCSH: Boston Public Schools. Department of Early Childhood. | Early
   childhood education—Massachusetts—Boston. | Early childhood
   education—Curricula—Massachusetts—Boston. | Education,
   Preschool—Massachusetts—Boston. | Education,
   Preschool—Curricula—Massachusetts—Boston. | Learning, Psychology of. |
   Group work in education.
Classification: LCC LB1140 .B289 2018 | DDC 372.210974461—dc23 LC record available
   at https://lccn.loc.gov/2018011680

Published by Harvard Education Press,
an imprint of the Harvard Education Publishing Group

Harvard Education Press
8 Story Street
Cambridge, MA 02138

Cover Design: Endpaper Studio
Cover Photo: Peter Hershey © 2018 Boston Public Schools

The typefaces used in this book are Adobe Garamond Pro and ITC Legacy Sans.

Contents

Chapter One

Children at the Center

In 2014, Boston's new mayor, Marty Walsh, sent a letter to the city's four thousand kindergarteners:

> My name is Marty Walsh, and I am the mayor of Boston. You live in Boston and are some of its youngest and most important residents. As Bostonians, you have the right to share your opinions about the city.
>
> I hear you are learning about structures as part of the construction unit. I have a question for you. *"What suggestions do you have about construction in our city to make Boston fairer and a more interesting place for children?"*
>
> I know you know a lot about Boston. You know about buildings you see and your houses and your schools. It is important that constructions such as parks, buildings and roads be fair and interesting.
>
> This is a big question, so take your time in answering it. Talk to your classmates, your teacher and your family. Do research to get ideas. Write your ideas and please make a model to help me understand your ideas better.
>
> I look forward to learning about your ideas and seeing your model.

This unusual invitation was not an idle request, nor was it divorced from the work and learning the children were doing every day. It has become an annual tradition.

Walsh's message to Boston's young children and their families is: *You are valued citizens of this community. We take you and your ideas seriously, and we believe you are capable of great things.* That message is at the heart of the Boston Public Schools' (BPS) early childhood programs, which have increasingly been built and continuously improved based on a set of nine core principles that reflect both democratic values and current scientific thinking about how children learn and develop (see "Boston Public Schools Department of Early Childhood Core Principles").

More than a decade ago, Boston made a daring bet—that it could build and sustain a high-quality, whole-child focused, intellectually engaging early education program that would significantly lower the city's persistent achievement gaps by locating that program within its public school system. That bet is clearly paying off. Approximately 65 percent of the 4,300 four-year-olds who will enter Boston's public kindergartens in 2018 have been educated in public school prekindergarten classrooms.[1] Another 250 are attending free, eight-hour, year-round community-based programs that follow the BPS curriculum, receive money from the school department to enhance teachers' salaries, support both teachers and directors with training and coaching, and offer comprehensive services to children and their families. Following the more than 2,000 children in BPS prekindergarten (K1) classrooms in the 2008–2009 school year, researchers documented gains in vocabulary, preliteracy skills, and early mathematics that were the "largest found to date in evaluations of large-scale public pre-kindergarten programs."[2]

Boston's Public Schools and community-based early learning programs reflect confidence in the curiosity, creativity, and capability of its youngest learners—and of their teachers. They place children at the center, offering a rich and engaging curriculum that allows time for exploration, play, research, and conversations that lead to broader connections and deeper understandings.

At their best, the classrooms are filled with joyful, purposeful activity. With instructional and curricular support, the children work together in fluid groups, learning from each other and pushing and building on each other's ideas. Mayor Walsh's trust and confidence is borne out in the ways they interact with their teachers and with each other, and in the ways in which their teachers interact with each other, families, and administrators.

> ### Boston Public Schools Department of Early Childhood Core Principles
>
> 1. Schools must promote our democratic society and support children's and teachers' sense of citizenship though multiple connections to families and community.
> 2. Young children are curious, active learners who are capable of high-level thinking processes, empathy, and taking multiple perspectives.
> 3. Strong relationships are at the center of powerful learning experiences.
> 4. Early learning programs must support children's physical, intellectual, language, and social-emotional development, along with their curiosity, creativity, persistence at challenging tasks, and academic learning.
> 5. Flexible, hands-on curricula that align with prior and future experiences foster mastery of learning standards and achievement of twenty-first-century goals.[3]
> 6. Basic literacies, knowledge, and higher-level skills can be furthered through pretend play, projects, extended conversation, and thoughtful instruction.
> 7. Because young children learn and develop at different rates and exhibit a wide range of interests, strengths, and learning styles, teachers need the time, flexibility, information, and resources to tailor learning experiences and engage all children, including dual language learners and children with special needs, as full participants in the classroom community.
> 8. The adult and child learning environment are connected and mirror one another through respectful processes of inquiry and differentiation.
> 9. Varied assessments provide data to inform instruction and drive change. Teachers and families participate along with administrators and specialists in interpreting findings, evaluating their implications, and shaping resultant decisions.

Teachers are learning along with the children—discovering and building on each child's capabilities, interests, and questions as they work to "make learning visible" to the children, their families, and within the wider community.[4] Coaches and specialists support teachers in this quest, listening to ideas and dilemmas, sharing suggestions when requested, and collaborating in examining and interpreting data to see where programs, lessons, and pedagogy might be adapted or improved.

This vision has been a decade in the making, and infuses the work of the Boston Public Schools Department of Early Childhood (DEC). Its implementation has shaped an increasing percentage of Boston's early education settings—especially the growing number that are housed within its public schools. And as the program is shared, the DEC is transforming early education programs in Massachusetts and beyond.

In the DEC's curriculum, many conventional dichotomies—such as play versus academic rigor, teacher-led instruction versus learner-driven exploration, inferential learning versus direct instruction, breadth versus depth, and a focus on head (intellectual concepts and skills) versus heart (social-emotional development and engagement of passion) become synergies rather than choices or compromises. Throughout this book, you'll see examples of teachers, coaches, and administrators wrestling with these balances and affirming integrative possibilities. You'll also see how a content-rich and intellectually challenging curriculum offers platforms for engaging and productive play, and how questions and discoveries that arise from play drive academic learning. You'll see teachers joining learners' projects and offering instructional supports—both direct and inferential—that build knowledge and skill or suggest new approaches. You'll see the choice, adaptation, and redesign of curricula so that children, teachers, and families can make wide-ranging connections and explore them in depth. And you'll see how engaging empathy, passion, kindness, and friendship foster efficient intellectual and academic learning, while engagement of reflective and analytic thinking enhances empathy, self-understanding, and prosocial behavior.

You'll also learn how a curriculum and instructional program that begins with the assumption that young children are capable of higher-order thinking, empathy, and taking multiple perspectives can build both sequentially acquired "basic skills" and enduring foundations for skilled reading and mathematical understanding. (See the appendix for a discussion of the rigorous research that documents these impacts and continues to shape key program decisions.)

Walking into many of Boston's preK and kindergarten classroom, you may think you are in an elite private school or at a university lab school. You might see four- and five-year-olds tackling complex ideas and thinking in sophisticated ways: observing closely, analyzing, theorizing, representing, looking again, comparing, debating, citing evidence, considering others' perspectives, synthesizing, and coming to consensus. You may see them working both independently and collaboratively, asking each other for help, pausing in their play to include or help another child. You might witness extended play episodes where children construct and act out sophisticated scenarios with convincing role-appropriate language and tone. You'll likely notice teachers recording children's dictated words, conversations, and learning processes. And you'll see children engaged in artwork, storytelling, reading and writing, and mathematical reasoning and problem solving, often at a surprisingly complex level. Yet these classes are not designed for an elite group, but instead for a typical urban demographic: multiple languages, a diversity of backgrounds, and many children with identified special needs, with most of the students eligible for free or reduced-price breakfast and lunch programs.

Boston's early childhood programs, like many across North America, have been influenced by the pedagogy and practice of the renowned municipal preschools in Reggio Emilia, Italy. Articulated by Loris Malaguzzi, the Reggio preschools' leader and founder, the Reggio philosophy challenges educators to see children as competent learners in the context of their peer group. This view of the child concurs with Piagetian perspectives that see early childhood as a unique and foundational period of development with distinctive learning styles, but differs from their view of development as "largely internal and occurring in stages."[5] Like Lev Vygotsky, Malaguzzi believed that social learning precedes and supports cognitive development.[6] He emphasized the role of an environment where teachers and children co-create learning.

In Reggio-influenced classrooms, teachers intentionally arrange learning materials to engage children and probe as well as challenge their thinking. Children engage with each other and their teachers as they investigate the materials and create art that represents their ideas. Malaguzzi saw children as competent and creative thinkers who represent and explore their developing knowledge in "a hundred languages" of movement, play, visual arts, storytelling, music, construction, hands-on experimentation, and discussion in collaborative as well as individual endeavors. Interpreting these ideas in Boston, BPS teachers not only "listen to" and support these languages, they engage with the children, as well as with families and colleagues, in more fully understanding the communications, reflecting on the learning, and deciding where to go next.

The brief stories and classroom-visit chapters presented throughout this book illustrate this dynamic process as it occurs in Boston classrooms and in the parallel and supporting worlds of coaching, administration, and family engagement. Teachers go beyond surface learning, beyond the casual "good job," and push to develop deep understanding of children's thinking, questions, and curiosity.[7] Likewise, coaches and administrators join teachers in probing their thinking, practice, and ongoing learning, using formative and summative data—along with documentation that makes children's learning and learning processes visible—to ground their reflections, deliberations, and decisions. Unless otherwise noted, these exemplars are transcriptions of actual events, with children's names and identifying details changed to protect their privacy.

Our classroom visits offer evidence of how the child is situated as both capable and connected; how networks of relationships weave together opportunities for belonging and participation. They portray some of the ways in which Boston applies Malaguzzi's ideas, integrating them with related ideas from progressive educators, scientific research, and recommendations of leading professional organizations such as the National Association of the Education of Young Children (NAEYC) as well as with state and national education standards, local expectations, and the learning opportunities that its families, communities, and physical environments offer.

Picture yourself as the child to whom the mayor of your city makes an authentic appeal for help. In asking for your class's ideas and expertise and the results of your research, adults assume that you are a competent individual learner, a member of a classroom community, a family, a school, and the larger community—and that you are able to find those answers. These are sizeable expectations for small children, and for those who teach and care for them or make decisions that affect their welfare. They reflect a view of the child as eager to learn: rich with wonder and knowledge, strong, capable, and resilient.[8] In this view, the child possesses great potential, which it is the teacher's privilege to perceive and empower.

But what of children who don't exhibit these characteristics, or whose development or abilities may have been compromised by illness, trauma, or other adversities and who may face greater learning or behavioral challenges? In Boston, as in Reggio Emilia, such children are deemed to have "special rights" rather than "special needs."[9] Like all children, children facing challenges are entitled to good care and quality teaching because of who they are, not because of what they need or what they can or can't do.[10] They are valued members of their communities—friends and classmates whose unique personalities, strengths, and interests enrich learning for others. As with all children, the teachers' role in fostering friendships, supportive relationships, and social-emotional growth is as important as their role in fostering academic learning. At the same time, children who need more time to learn, adapted modes of instruction, therapeutic supports that facilitate their full participation in a group project, or help from other children have the right to these accommodations.

All children are seen to benefit from the inclusion of children with special rights. They learn early that individuals differ in learning pace and style and that working, playing, and learning together is natural.[11] Learning projects are sufficiently open-ended to engage all children, and for all children to enjoy and learn from their own and each other's engagement. Children who learn better in substantially separate groups have the same rights to respect, care, and kindness—and to joyful, developmentally appropriate learning experiences that facilitate their development in all domains.

Boston might be expected to lead the way in early education. It was the site of the first English-language kindergarten in the United States, founded in 1860 by Elizabeth Peabody, a pioneering teacher who became a tireless advocate for the kindergarten movement.[12] Boston is the home of Wheelock College (now part of Boston University), one of a handful of early education schools that have shaped the field; other historic leaders, including Lesley University and Tufts University's Eliot-Pearson School, are in neighboring cities. Boston is also the capital of a state that has made relatively large investments in programs for young children and whose students have repeatedly scored at or near the top in both reading and math on the National Assessment of Educational Progress (NAEP).[13] Yet, like many urban systems, Boston continues to face challenges of residential segregation, large numbers of students with high needs, aging infrastructure, and policies and systems designed for an earlier era and for older children.

The process of building an early education program, continuously improving quality, scaling up and building institutional supports for successful efforts, addressing the diverse needs of children and their families, and keeping all stakeholders engaged has been neither easy nor straightforward. Again and again, the small team that took on these challenges relied on their core values that put children at the center and on their initial but continually evolving strategies of creating developmentally appropriate settings; offering a high-quality curriculum; building teachers' skills through professional development and coaching; building principals' skills as early childhood leaders; engaging families; and using data, documentation, and collaborative interpretation and response to drive ongoing improvement.

Boston's early childhood programs remain a work in progress. Curricula, materials, and teaching tools create learning possibilities for children, but it is the messy, deliberate, demanding, and often exhilarating daily work of supporting children's learning that turns possibilities into realities. Similarly, getting teachers the supports they need—not just curricula, teaching tools, and educational materials, but also appropriate environments, data systems, professional development, coaching, wraparound and family engagement efforts, and administrative policies—involves negotiating multiple relationships and systems.

The United States has many excellent preK programs that are grounded in the science of early childhood development and learning; some school-based preK programs that have achieved significant academic results; and a few examples of child-centered, "developmentally appropriate," play-based programs that have been incorporated into urban public school systems. Other cities have developed public school–based programs for three- and four-year-olds. In fact, nearly every school district in the country offers (or funds) public education for all three-, four-, and five-year-olds with identified special needs—in self-contained classrooms or in classrooms that include peers whose development falls within the typical range, as appropriate. But Boston may be unique in building a high-quality, play-based, intellectually engaging, and demonstrably effective program that is reaching upward, downward, and outward to create meaningful and sustained change in the ways that the school system and its community and parent partners engage and educate *all* of their young children.

Many school districts have built programs for four-year-olds in the same way they added kindergarten—from the top down. For instance:

- Oklahoma introduced universal, school-based, academically oriented preK by moving school down a year. A study in the Tulsa public schools demonstrated that all income subgroups showed significantly strong academic gains when compared with a control group who remained in community care because they had missed the age cut-off by a few days. Socioeconomic gaps narrowed, and dual language learners showed particularly strong gains.[14]
- Montgomery County, Maryland, built on Head Start programs already operated by the schools, strengthening their academic components and expanding them to all four-year-olds in neighborhoods with concentrated high needs, in a successful ten-year attempt to substantially narrow gaps in high school completion and college readiness between rich and poor areas of the county.[15]

New Jersey school districts with concentrations of children from low-income families added three-year-old and preK programs to fulfill a court-ordered mandate. The state provided both oversight and supports, including financing, professional development and coaching, and evaluation. Community-based childcare, preschool, and Head Start programs were brought under their school districts' umbrellas, but retained their identities. When implementation began, only 15 percent of programs (both public and private) were of "Good to Excellent" quality, as measured by the widely used Early Childhood Environmental Rating Scale (ECERS-R). Eight years later, nearly two-thirds scored in the "Good to Excellent" range and none were rated as "Poor." A longitudinal study showed gains through the fifth grade (when compared with children of similar background who had not participated), especially for children who began at age three.[16]

There are also a number of early childhood programs that have proven effective at scale—many espousing principles similar to those that have animated Boston's effort. These include:

- Reggio Emilia, Italy, established its renowned early childhood programs after World War II, as a way to rebuild the community. The programs have continued to grow and improve and have received worldwide acclaim. But until relatively recently, they have had only limited connections with the K–12 schools that their graduates attend.

- HighScope, a Michigan-based organization that built the renowned Perry Preschool Project and tracked its graduates for forty years, has disseminated its curriculum, professional development offerings, and child assessment measures both nationally and internationally.[17] Michigan's state-funded Great Start Readiness Program, for children from low-income backgrounds, is built on the Perry Preschool model. In a matched comparison study with a quasi-experimental design, HighScope found that its graduates maintained a significant edge not only at kindergarten entry, but in second grade, fourth grade, and middle school, and in their rate of high school graduation. Michigan significantly expanded the program in 2012; assessments have consistently shown that both original and expansion sites have maintained the quality—and pedagogy—that led to its documented success.[18]

- Head Start, our nation's signature early childhood program, was informed by the Perry Preschool model and has been shaped by the efforts of families, teachers, researchers, and varied administrative teams. The program has developed over the years, sometimes with inconsistent quality or variable or seemingly not sustained outcomes. Recent efforts to strengthen systemic quality have improved individual programs and led to favorable and sustained child outcomes.[19]

- Educare provides enhanced facilities and staffing for children from pre-birth to age five and their families in Early Head Start and Head Start programs. The Educare model relies on data utilization, embedded professional development, high-quality teaching practices, and intensive family engagement. Strong national and site-based leadership continuously supports these practices and also forges local partnerships with other family-facing organizations. A series of site-based and programwide studies have documented the power of this model to foster ongoing family engagement and to prevent achievement gaps at school entry and through grade 4.[20]

Clearly BPS is not alone in viewing young children as eager, physically active, capable learners whose innate curiosity drives their efforts to understand their world and their place within it. Neither is it alone in building programs that respect young children's developmental agendas and their individual and collective proclivities. The DEC and its partners are also not alone in recognizing that the curiosity and creativity that seem to come naturally to young children are as important to cultivate as literacy and math skills, or in intentionally building the warm relationships and mutually engaging interactions that are key to high-quality early education programs. And they are not unique in seeing play-based education as the most effective route to academic rigor for young children and in using academic content to enrich play. But Boston has been a pioneer in building a program grounded in these beliefs, values, and practices within an existing public school system.

Today, Boston's preK programs attract visitors from throughout the nation and around the world.[21] Their reputation for results is spreading, backed by both outside research and the classroom quality and child outcome data that the system regularly collects to inform instruction and policy. In 2016, the *Atlantic* published an article, "What Boston's Preschools Get Right," that described Boston's as "one of the best free, public school programs in the country," touting the program as "student-centered, learning-focused, and developmentally appropriate." It featured Mary Bolt, a ten-year veteran of Boston's preschool program, who described the program this way: "The curriculum is so fun, they don't realize it's rigorous. Kids tell parents on Saturday that they want to go to school. If we were drilling them and doing worksheets, they wouldn't be saying that.[22]

The core principles that drive BPS programs for four-year-olds (and some three- and five-year-olds as well) have not only transformed virtually all of its kindergarten classrooms, but are percolating upward to first and second grade, and outward and downward to influence community-based early learning programs and "Play to Learn" groups for toddlers and parents. Instead of building an education program from the top down, as many school systems do, Boston is rebuilding its from the bottom up.

The following chapters provide an inside look into Boston's public school early education programs and how they came to be. You will meet key members of the DEC, who have worked along with outside authors to tell their story and make their learning visible.

As tour guides, we will describe not only what Boston did, but how. We will explain choices, early results, and evidence of success—but we'll also reveal the internal challenges, barriers, and occasional changes of course. We tell the story of how a small team built a multifaceted early childhood program that began to drive change within the schools and community. This essentially chronological story will be punctuated by vignettes that show the program in action. We'll eavesdrop in classrooms, witness family and community events, attend a DEC staff meeting, and talk with teachers, coaches, administrators, and researchers as they reflect on their work. As in the historical chapters, we point out the highlights, looking through multiple lenses of child development, educational theory, research, and policy. We provide context and explanation as needed, and will hopefully address the questions that you may be asking. We'll delve deeply into practices that have been key to Boston's success, including strong curricula, a push for schools to achieve NAEYC accreditation, and professional development. An appendix describes how data and research have been used to inform resource allocation and to drive systemic change.

The principles that have guided the journey repeatedly manifest themselves in the DEC's decisions, directions, and culture, as well as in the teaching and coaching practices you'll see on your visits. To aid you in following the story, we call them out in the endnotes and occasionally within the text. So let's begin—with an extended visit to a classroom that showcases the DEC's core principles in action.

Chapter Two

The Colorful Café

A Visit to a K0/K1 Inclusion Classroom

with Melissa Rivard and Jodi Doyle Krous

The classroom community you are about to enter is an unusual one. It is one example of what can happen when a dedicated and creative teacher is able to build on the supports of a strong curriculum, thoughtful and aligned professional development experiences that integrate with reflective coaching, and supportive family, neighborhood, and school communities. This story emerged through Melissa Rivard and Jodi Doyle's implementation of a Reggio Emilia–inspired process of using documentation to reflect on and make decisions about teaching and learning while it is underway; make the children's activities and thinking visible to them in ways that support their ongoing learning; and share their learning with others.[1] The events are accurately transcribed, but we've changed the children's names. As you read this story, you will be able to see numerous illustrations of the DEC's core principles.

On a Sunday afternoon in June, more than sixty invited guests—siblings, parents, grandparents, aunts, and uncles—gather at a long table covered with checkered tablecloths, surrounded by colorful paintings and strings of lights hanging from the brick walls that line the school playground. They are here to celebrate the opening night of The Colorful Café—a real restaurant that emerged from the playful imaginings and diligent work of a group of sixteen preschoolers, their teacher Jodi Doyle, and the many colleagues, parents, and community members who joined Doyle in supporting their vision.

This project began five months earlier in the art studio and dramatic play areas of a combined K Zero (age three to four) and K1 (age four to five) inclusion classroom at the Eliot Innovation School, which serves children of diverse backgrounds in Boston's North End, a neighborhood known for its food and festivals. Five of the children in Doyle's class have special rights, having been diagnosed with developmental delays.

Doyle is in her fourth year of teaching. She holds a master's degree in elementary education, with licenses in early childhood, special education, and teaching English as a second language. She has explored the Reggio Emilia approach in her BPS professional development courses and workshops and in coaching sessions with Marina Boni—an experienced Reggio-inspired teacher and literacy expert who has been a key shaper of Boston's Department of Early Childhood since its inception. Doyle's full-time paraprofessional partner, Christopher Breen, enables her to work with children individually or in small groups and, on occasion, to take a group outside of the classroom.[2]

Neither the children nor their teachers knew a few months ago that they would create a restaurant. They were just beginning the *Opening the World of Learning* (OWL) curriculum unit "World of Color."[3] With a strong focus on building oral language, this open-ended unit would engage them in exploring color not only in the art area, but across the full spectrum of activities you would expect in a preschool classroom: active and dramatic play; music and dance; storybook reading; storytelling and book-making; building with blocks and other materials; sorting, counting, measuring, and beginning to explore mathematical concepts such as order, comparison, pattern, volume, and proportion; assembling puzzles; conducting science investigations and experiments with light sources, prisms, and filters; and writing. As they worked, played, and helped each other, they would hear and use rich, descriptive language in conversations with each other and with adults.

Mixing Colors

As Doyle sets up the art area for the World of Color unit, she reflects on the interests and skills of the children in her class and the challenges that will intrigue and engage them. She pours paints into small containers and adds empty containers into which children can pour and mix the paints. She also sets out paper plates for color-mixing palettes and makes sure that all the materials are visible and within easy reach. She positions the easels side by side so that children can view each other's work.

Doyle wants the children to use these materials independently, to make choices about what to do and how to do it, and to learn together, building on each other's ideas. These social-emotional and citizenship goals are important for all of the children, and especially so for those with special rights. At this point, four months into the school year, all of the children know how to put on their smocks, bring paints and paper to the easels, and clean up when they finish their work.

Today Doyle puts out every color she has, not just the primary colors the curriculum guide suggests. Her coach has encouraged her to take her cues from the children, and Doyle thinks that a less formulaic approach might be more fun for her group and support more exploration. Once the children's interests are sparked, she can engage them more deeply in figuring out how to combine colors to make new ones.[4]

The excitement Doyle observes as she begins to talk with the children about color seems to confirm this hypothesis. Children shout out questions that they immediately test out, "What does white do? What does black do? How did you make that brown?" Over a period of weeks, the studio fills with colors that the children have invented.

As the explorations continue, Doyle notices that although some of the children have moved on to other endeavors, a group of six girls repeatedly clusters in the art studio during Choice Time (also called "Centers"), a major daily time block. They seem particularly passionate about mixing new colors to use in their paintings. To encourage project-based learning, Doyle invites the girls to create a collection of colors for the whole class to use. The group instantly embraces this idea.

After days of watching the girls experiment—mixing until they happen upon a color they like—Doyle wonders if challenging the girls to replicate a particular color might push their thinking. While other children are working independently or with Chris Breen, Doyle asks the girls to bring their recent paintings out to the hall and spread them on the floor. The girls have been so prolific that their lined-up paintings stretch all the way down the hall. Doyle asks them to pick a few paintings with their favorite colors, and then select one color to try to replicate. The girls keep shouting, "I love this one!" but finally settle on a shade of pink. Doyle prepares a table with paints, plates, and brushes and sets up a video camera to record the process. She asks the girls to tell her how to make that exact color, and follows their instructions.

During the session, the girls struggle to re-create the color. They appear to be simply guessing, pointing almost randomly at colors to combine. When Doyle reviews the video, she notices something else. The girls were shouting, "Use this one." "You need more of that one." They weren't using any of the descriptive language they had been working on to indicate which colors they wanted. Doyle decides to work more with the girls on developing precise language before revisiting the activity.

A few days later, Doyle reconvenes the group during Choice Time. She places the containers of paint that they have recently mixed on the table. She then opens her laptop and shares a few minutes of the video so the girls can see themselves as they attempted to instruct her:

DOYLE: What did you notice?

ISABELLA: You didn't know what to do.

DOYLE: What do you mean, I didn't know what to do?

SOFIA: We have lots of shades of pink and purple.

AVA: You didn't know which paint we were saying. We were saying, "This paint, that paint, this paint, that paint."

DOYLE: So how could we fix that problem?

SEVERAL GIRLS, SHOUTING AT ONCE: By saying the colors!

Doyle points out that many of the colors look similar, and selects one shade of purple to use as an example. She asks, "If I wanted this color, what other words besides 'purple' would I have to use so you would know which one to give me?" Isabella responds, "Every color is different." She picks up two containers of purple paint and puts them side by side. "Those two are different." Then she points to another two, "Those two are different." Ava interrupts her and points to two of the purples and says, "But these two are the same." Other girls chime in, still using imprecise language as they point to matching and different colors.

Doyle interrupts. "This is the same thing that happened last time. You keep saying, 'This one and that one.' I'm confused. How do I know which paint you are talking about?"

Isabella begins again with a similar tactic, pulling two of the containers of purple paint toward her, saying, "Miss Doyle, this one looks like this one but this one is a little darker and this one is a little lighter." She then points out another pairing, "And that one's darker and that one's lighter." Doyle points out that she is starting to hear some words that are helping to clarify, "I heard the word 'purple' and I heard the words 'dark' and 'light.'" Ava continues in this vein and points to one of the other purples, "And this one is sparkly." Doyle asks, "So I could say that I want a sparkly one?" Camila points to two containers of paint, one pink and one purple, "But these are both sparkly, so I wouldn't know which one if you only said sparkly." Doyle points to the pink one and asks, "What would I have to ask for if I wanted that one?" Camila responds haltingly, "The pink sparkly one."

Doyle gets a roll of masking tape and a marker and suggests that they label each color. She picks up a container and asks the group what that paint's name should be. The girls throw out ideas, "Colorful purple." "Rainbow purple." "Colorful purple plain, because it doesn't have any sparkles in it." The girls have a hard time agreeing, so Doyle suggests coming back to that color and moves onto the next.

Doyle puts the container of pink paint in front of Mia, a child with developmental delays who has been paying close attention but has not yet said anything. Doyle suggests to the group that they let Mia have a turn, and the girls turn their attention to her. Mia says quietly, "It looks like my socks." "Should we call it 'Socks'?" Doyle asks.

Camila offers another suggestion. "We could call it 'Piggy Pie,'" she says, referring to a picture book by Margie Palatini with pink pigs on its cover. The group loves the idea, including Doyle, who, knowing the answer, prompts "Why did you say 'Piggy Pie,' Camila?" The group shouts in chorus, "Because Mia loves *Piggy Pie!*" Doyle acknowledges that *Piggy Pie* is indeed Mia's favorite book and turns to Mia, "Are you okay with that?" Mia nods emphatically.

The group sounds out the words together as Doyle writes the letters on the masking tape, and they agree to take turns putting the labels on the containers. Soon some girls are asking if they can do the writing. The group huddles in closely, sounding out the words for their friends as they work to form each letter.

Ask yourself Jodi Doyle's question: What did you notice?

- *You may have tuned in to Doyle's thought process as she considered how to set up activities that would intrigue the children and engage their thinking. Being a "reflective teacher," she engaged in the ongoing work of "closely observing and studying the significance of children's ongoing activities."[5] Doyle used the video to assess the children's understanding so that she could plan the next steps—and she helped the children to use it to "drive change" in their own behavior as well.[6]*

- *You might have been struck by the way the girls worked together, giving everyone a chance to participate, respecting and building on each other's ideas—demonstrating empathy and perspective-taking along with curiosity, active learning, and an eagerness to experiment.[7]*

- *From an academic perspective, the wider mix of colors and Doyle's questions and suggestions prompted the children to use richer and more creative language than you might hear in a typical lesson on combining primary colors. It is also impressive that preschoolers are sounding out and writing words or watching classmates do so with such rapt attention, and that there is a seemingly seamless integration of physical, intellectual, language, and academic learning experiences.[8]*

- *From a social-emotional vantage point, you can see how smoothly the group functions and the genuine friendship among all of the girls. Strong relationships among the children and adults lend power to the learning experiences that the teacher offers, orchestrates, observes, and builds on.[9]*
- *You may be wondering how these young children have learned these skills. What else happens in this classroom?*

Bringing It to the Whole Group: Thinking and Feedback

Remembering that her initial invitation to the girls was to mix a set of paints for the whole class to use, and seeing that they were mixing only variations on pink and purple, Doyle decides that it's time for the group to bring their work to the whole class for feedback. She gathers the class for "Thinking and Feedback," a routine developed by the Department of Early Childhood and used throughout its programs. As she usually does, Doyle reminds the children who have difficulty with speech that they can use their picture boards and friends for support.

As you read the following episode, ask yourself:

- *What do you notice about the children's use of language?*
- *What does their teacher do to support their conversation?*
- *How do the classroom routines support all of the children and enable those with language delays to fully participate in the language-building conversation?*

Doyle asks Sofia to explain what the group is working on. "We've been mixing paint together to make colors because the easel runned out of color so we made colors," Sofia answers. Doyle leads the group through the first step of the protocol—looking and thinking. The group sits quietly, looking at the containers of paint in the center of the rug. After a minute, Doyle asks, "What do you notice about this paint?" Landon looks at his picture board and says, "Pink." Doyle prompts him to form a full sentence from this observation, "I notice that it is pink." Several children follow with similar observations.

Next Doyle asks if anyone has any questions for the group, reminding them that these are "*Why did you . . .*" or "*What did you . . .*" kinds of questions.

With a big smile, Michael indicates that he has a question, and Doyle encourages him to use his picture board. Michael turns to a friend next to him, so Doyle adds, "Or you could use Noah." Michael points to an image on the board and Noah says, "Paintbrush." Doyle asks if Michael's question is about whether the girls had used a paintbrush. He smiles and nods. Another boy asks, "Why do they have those papers on them?" referring to the masking-tape labels. The girls explain that they tell the names of the colors.

Finally, Doyle asks the whole group if they have any suggestions for how the girls could make their work even better. The group immediately focuses on the need for different colors. Ava points to Mia's rain boots as an example: "Mia's boots are like rainbows." Many of the children were wearing their rain boots, so Ava's idea prompts others to call out colors they see on each other's feet. Orange. Yellow. Red. Green. Blue.

Doyle encourages the children to take it further, "An idea that I'm hearing is that you can look at things around you and be inspired by their colors. When you saw Mia's boots, you noticed all the colors. What are some things that you see inside or outside and would love to paint?"

CAMILA: Some branches and some flowers and some leaves.
NOAH: People.
MAISHA: Colorful flowers.
DAVID: I like to paint dogs.
JACOB: I like to paint with red.

After the class offers their suggestions, Doyle turns to the paint-mixing group and asks what they think they need to do next. Without hesitation, Sofia exclaims, "We need to investigate colors!"

You may have noticed that some of the children use full sentences with mostly conventional grammar to make statements, offer explanations, and ask questions, while others communicate with single words or pictures. Yet as a group, they engage in meaningful dialogue. You may also have noticed a couple of examples of quite sophisticated vocabulary, with children spontaneously using words like "investigate" and "colorful" that they may have learned from the curriculum.

The teacher started the conversation and used prompts and questions to move it along. You may have also noticed that the children seemed familiar and comfortable with the Thinking and Feedback protocol, eagerly responding to prompts to explain what they've been working on, share what they noticed, ask both "what" and "why" questions, and make suggestions.

If you had watched the conversation, you might have seen how customized picture boards enabled some of the children to participate in the discussion by pointing to pictures of words they wanted to say. You would have observed the teacher's active listening, her attention to subtle cues that a child had something to say, and how much time she gave children to observe, think, and respond.[10] You might also have seen children looking to each other for help and showing genuine interest in each other's ideas. And you would certainly have noticed the enthusiasm with which Sofia and her friends embarked on their "investigation."

Stepping back to look from a systemic perspective, note how the teacher draws on her own expertise and knowledge of the children and supports provided by a flexible, research-grounded curriculum and a well-resourced classroom as she tailors learning experiences to engage all of the children as full participants in this community-building conversation.[11]

The Color Investigation

Doyle is excited by Sofia's idea of a color investigation and immediately begins discussions with colleagues about how she might follow through and build on that idea. They think about places in the community where the children might go for inspiration and ways for them to capture the colors they see. Spring is still around the corner, so none of the neighborhood gardens are in bloom and the farmers market hasn't opened yet. But a local flower shop whose owner Doyle knows seems like the perfect place for a field trip. Doyle chooses a time when some of the children will be working with specialists and Chris Breen can supervise the rest in quiet Choice Time activities.

The group sets out on a cloudy March day. Doyle has brought several cameras, cast-offs donated by parents and colleagues at her request. She shows the girls how they work and tells them to take pictures of colors that inspire them to paint.

Barely out the door, the girls start pointing excitedly at colors, many of which would have escaped Doyle's notice. Walking alongside the corroded iron fence of the schoolyard, Isabella points to a patch of gray where the black paint has peeled away to reveal the metal underneath. Doyle encourages her to take a picture, then asks the group, "What colors do you think we would need to make that gray?" Camila shouts, "I know! Because I've made that before. We would need some black and . . . " She stops to think, then adds, a bit less confidently, "Some blue. That would help."

During the same photographic "pit stop," Mia notices something on the ground and squats for a closer look. It's a small yellow caterpillar crawling over dark brown mulch. Doyle hands Mia the camera and, seeing her struggle, reminds her which buttons she needs to push. Meanwhile, all of the girls have huddled around to see, wanting to take their own photographs of Mia's find. As it begins to dawn on Doyle that this five- or six- block walk could take more time than she planned, she establishes the rule that the person who first notices a color gets to take the picture.

The children walk right by a candy-apple red door. Doyle tries to get them to notice it, but they are focused on Sofia, who is pointing to the white dome of a church and on Camila and Maisha, who have each found a different shade of blue. Doyle commends them on remembering that their classmates asked for more blues and whites.

Continuing to search for blues and whites, the girls notice different shades. While taking a close-up photograph of a light blue car, Camila turns to notice the exact same blue on a vending machine on the other side of the sidewalk. In response, Maisha points to different blues that she sees, including the one in Sofia's rain jacket. Maisha takes a picture of Sofia's sleeve, then one of the car, and then shows Sofia the two different blues in the LCD panel of the camera. "See? Cool, right?"

As they approach the flower shop, Doyle checks in to make sure the girls are still clear about their purpose. "What are we looking for?" The girls respond in unison, "Color!" Mia zeroes in on a bouquet of white and lavender flowers, but the camera won't take the shot. She looks for Doyle, who is busy assisting someone else. She turns to Camila instead. Camila can't figure it out either, and calls out to Doyle, "She needs help!"

Dee, the store's owner, welcomes the children. Doyle, keenly aware that they've entered an enticing space filled with fragile objects, helps Camila photograph an ornate gold pot. "What color is this, and how do you think we could make this color with paint?" asks Doyle. The group recognizes the color as gold but struggles to come up with ideas about how to make it. Camila suggests, pointing to Dee, "Maybe we could ask her?" She does, but Dee doesn't know the answer. Perhaps remembering their purpose for coming to the shop, Camila reassures Dee, "Well, we can take the picture to our school and try to make it." After the girls have photographed nearly every flower in the cooler, Dee reminds them, "I want to know how to make that color. I hope you'll come back to teach me when you figure it out." The girls promise, shout "Thank you!" to Dee, and make their way back to school.

Back in the classroom, Doyle faces a dilemma. Showing the girls all seventy-five photos they took and asking them to choose their favorites would be time-consuming and potentially overwhelming. Yet she wants to allow them to choose. Again, Doyle turns to a colleague. They look through the photos together with an eye toward both assessing the children's understanding of the investigation's purpose and giving the girls a good variety of photos to choose from for the next step. As they sift through the pictures, Doyle and her colleague are struck by the degree to which the girls remained focused on their task—to find not only colors that inspired them but also ones that their classmates had specifically asked for—and by the number of photographs that revealed colors and objects that Doyle wouldn't have chosen. They select fifteen images, representing a wide range of colors and subject matter and the girls' unique points of view, for Doyle to print and share with the girls the following day.

During Choice Time, Doyle gathers the girls on the rug to talk about their images. She lays the photos out in front of them, and immediately the girls begin to sort them by color. When Doyle asks why they put together the ones that they did, Ava points to a group of four and replies, "Because they all look pink at the same time." Through this process of sorting and selecting a favorite image from each category, the girls agree on six images with new colors they would like to try to make: a sunflower (yellow); Sofia's light blue sleeve in front of a red brick wall; a fragment of a gray cement plaque; the gold pot in Dee's shop; a box of orange candles; and a bright pink celosia flower.

Doyle had been thinking that the purpose of the investigation was to find new colors to mix for the class, but she now realizes that the girls wanted to make paintings of the photographs they chose. While it hadn't been her intent, she seizes the opportunity to involve the whole class in observational painting and color mixing. Breaking the class into small groups, she begins showing other children the girls' photographs and asking which image they would like to paint.

Notice how the adult environment mirrored the one that Doyle was working to create for the children. Her documentation of the girls' work provides data that helps her assess both their learning and her own instructional strategies. She reflects alone and with colleagues on what she notices and where to go next—before asking the girls to do the same. Doyle becomes intrigued by colors along with the children, and, like them, she considers multiple perspectives as she makes choices. And all of them wonder how to make gold.[12] What else did you observe?

How-to Books: Sharing What We Are Learning

As the children become more skilled at mixing the colors they need, Doyle asks them to pause and reflect on what they are learning so they can share their learning with each other. She introduces the idea of "how-to" books, which she knows her students will be repeatedly asked to create as part of Boston's K2 (kindergarten) curriculum. Knowing that some of the children will be going to kindergarten next year (others will stay with her), Doyle decides to ask the children to create "how-to" books about aspects of painting in which they feel they are becoming expert. The books will become a shared resource for the classroom; creating them will help the children develop their sequential thinking and communication skills.

DOYLE: We've done a lot of paint mixing. What do you feel like you are experts at now that you could teach the other kids?
CAMILA: Painting colors.
EMILY: How to mix paint.
MAISHA: How to mix colors and make different blues.
MIA: Gray. Sofia likes gray.

ASHLEY: How to make magenta.
AVA: How to make colors lighter.
ISABELLA: Yeah! We can do that!
SOFIA: How to be an artist.

By the end of the conversation, the group decides to work in pairs or trios to make the following books: *How to Make Light Blue*; *How to Make Dark Red*; *How to Make Gray*; *How to Make Magenta*; *How to Make Sunflower Yellow*; and *How to Be an Artist*.

Doyle leads each of the groups through a similar process. First, she sits with each group and asks them to explain the steps to her. She writes down the children's words verbatim and, when they've finished, reads it all back to them, asking if there is anything they want to add. Each small group then shares their first draft with the whole group so they can get feedback that will improve their book and communicate their ideas more clearly. As a whole group, they test out the instructions in the book to make sure they work, making additional suggestions and corrections as they go. And finally, they illustrate them.

In this next episode, Doyle calls on a specialist to help her work with Mia, who seemed to be struggling more than the others with the concepts of color mixing, proportion, and experimentation.

Doyle meets with Carrie Ann Tarzia, the speech and occupational therapy specialist, who helps her develop a plan for supporting Mia in grasping the concept of mixing two colors to get a color that is like both but may be closer to one than the other, as well as in using words to communicate what she knows. They decide that Doyle should use some visual supports to talk about color and give Mia specific choices about which colors she might mix, rather than posing an open-ended question. Doyle works with Mia individually while the rest of the class is in a language lesson.

Doyle begins, "Remember how you told me that you wanted to make gray for Sofia?" Mia nods. Doyle draws two squares on a white piece of paper in front of Mia and says, "When you make gray, there are two colors that you need." Doyle then puts out six small paper squares, each with a different color circle on them—gray, yellow, blue, red, black and white. "I want to know what two colors you need to make gray," picking up the square with the gray circle and placing it directly in front of Mia.

Mia concentrates for a moment, then chooses the blue swatch. Doyle picks it up. "You think you need blue?" She places it in one of the empty squares she has drawn, then asks, "What other color do you need to make this one?" as she points to the gray. Mia points to the red swatch. Doyle is conflicted about whether to tell Mia the correct answer or to try to support Mia in discovering it for herself. She switches strategies and tells Mia that one of the colors she needs is white. She asks again, "Which other color do we need? Which one looks like gray?" Mia says, "blue," and points to the corresponding swatch.

Doyle tries another strategy. Thinking it may be helpful for Mia to see an example of making a color lighter, Doyle suggests that they try it to see what happens. Doyle leads Mia through the process of mixing the color she has selected—blue—with white. Then they do the same with the black. Doyle asks Mia to paint each of the colors on the gray swatch and Mia sees that it is the white and black mixed together that makes gray. Doyle moves on to the next step while the experience is fresh in Mia's mind.

> DOYLE: So I thought maybe you could teach your friends how to make gray.
> MIA: Gray.

Doyle puts out several photos that she has taken of the materials they used to make gray. "We need to tell them all the things you do. What would they need to get first?" Mia points to the photo of the cup and says, "First this one." Doyle asks Mia what is in the photograph and Mia replies:

> MIA: It is . . . is it . . . it is a cup and then they try to mix.
> DOYLE: First you get a cup . . . to mix?
> MIA: Yeah.
> DOYLE: What do they need to put in the cup?
> MIA: Paint.
> DOYLE: What color paint?

MIA: Get black in the cup.
DOYLE: How much black? A lot or a little?
MIA: Big. You need white.
DOYLE: How much?
MIA: Bigger (throwing her arms open wide).
MIA: You need this one (indicating the brush).
DOYLE: You need this *brush*.
MIA: You mix it.

Mia struggles with what she is trying to say next, and Doyle struggles to understand. Doyle suggests that they pause for a moment and go back to what Mia has told her so far, but this time Mia will enact the directions as she goes. Doyle reads, "First you get a cup to mix," and places one in front of Mia. "Then you put in a big amount of black." Doyle hands Mia the black paint bottle and Mia squeezes out as much as she can.

DOYLE: What's our next step?
MIA: Is it making it white?
DOYLE: So you need white? (Going back to Mia's dictation) You need bigger white.
Doyle squeezes white paint into the jar.
DOYLE: How's that?
MIA: Good!
DOYLE: Then you said, "You need this one." What is that?
MIA: It's a brush.
DOYLE: What do we do with that?
MIA: It's in the paint. You need to mix it.

Doyle holds the cup steady as Mia mixes. "What's happening?" Doyle asks. "It's turning more black," Mia replies, observing what is happening to the white paint at the top. After another minute or so of mixing, Mia gets a big smile on her face. Doyle asks her what color it is. "Gray!" Mia replies triumphantly, as Doyle writes it in Mia's book.

Later, Doyle and Tarzia watch the video of Doyle's session with Mia to assess how well their plan worked, what Mia seems to understand and not understand, and what Doyle's next steps might be. Just as the girls had gained insight into their communication with her when they watched the video of themselves giving instructions, Doyle gains insight into her communication with Mia She notices that, when she waited long enough for a response, Mia could answer open-ended questions without being given a binary choice. Perhaps she should try to find more opportunities to give Mia the response time she needs.

Tarzia points out that Mia's need for time in this case involved more than language. Following a procedure and then remembering the steps and retelling them in sequence is still a lot for Mia. "We could have made pictures with the key steps, like mixing, which we knew would be involved. And we could send those supports home with her so that she can tell her parents this story as steps."

You may have noticed how carefully Doyle structures projects and both individual and group lessons to build each child's cognitive, language, and literacy skills while offering appropriately challenging choices that allow them to shine as experts, helpful friends, and classroom citizens.[13] Because Doyle's class combines two grades (as classrooms designed to include children with special rights often do), Doyle gets to stay with the children for two years, getting to know them and their parents well.[14] The range of ages and abilities highlights developmental progressions, looking backward into toddlerhood and forward through kindergarten and beyond.[15]

A New Interest Emerges

While the color mixing and observational painting project is still going strong, a new interest emerges in the dramatic play area, which is set up as a kitchen so that children can pretend to make colorful foods and "eat a rainbow." Camila has begun approaching children around the room with a clipboard, taking food orders and going back to the dramatic play area to prepare the food her friends requested. She repeatedly approaches Doyle for help. "How do you write 'hot dog'?" "How do you spell 'spaghetti'?" After several days of this, Doyle proposes that Camila make a menu to help children make their selections and support "waiters" in writing down orders. Camila enthusiastically agrees. Doyle brings in some cookbooks and magazines and leads the class in brainstorming items for the menu. The dramatic play area soon becomes a bustling restaurant kitchen. After taking orders in the art studio, the reading area, or the school secretary's office next door, the children hurry back to fill them.

MICHAEL: I need pizza.
JACOB: I need those carrots. They're for my customer.

The kitchen/restaurant rapidly becomes the core of the classroom. Children participate even when they aren't directly involved in dramatic play. The readers in the library order and sip on tea. The artists in the studio have a picnic on the rug when their lunch is delivered. David makes a twenty-dollar bill in the writing area and runs over to Amalya, who is in the kitchen wearing a chef's hat and apron, and asks the price of what she is cooking. "A dollar," she says, taking David's twenty and counting out his change—a ten, a five, and four ones.

As new restaurant needs are identified, they are produced by children working in other centers. In the writing center, children—many of whom typically avoided that center—create additional menus with text and pictures and meticulously form numbers on and cut out dollar bills and coins. Children paint pictures of food and make signs in the art studio. The children are clearly interested in making their restaurant as real as possible, so having only plastic food to serve becomes increasingly frustrating for them. Sensing this, as well as the great opportunity for learning that the children's burgeoning passion has created, Doyle asks the children, "Do you want to make a real restaurant?" The answer is a resounding, "Yes!"

And so a second project begins, one that will involve the whole class and their families. The children do research as they play restaurant. Doyle takes them on neighborhood walks during recess, so they can peer into the windows of the neighborhood's many eateries. When Doyle realizes that some of the children have never been inside a sit-down restaurant, she arranges a class trip to a pizzeria. Eventually, Doyle, Breen, and the children decide to create a real restaurant: The Colorful Café. Of course, it needs paintings, along with signs that say "Open" and "Closed," a credit card machine, tablecloths, menus, flowers, cups, plates, trays, tables, chefs, customers, and servers. As they create the paintings—and work together on a giant Colorful Café sign—the children consult the how-to books (including Mia's) to make the colors they need.

After talking with the principal and polling parents to set a date, the children prepare for opening night. Doyle makes it clear that everyone will serve a very important role. They will all be waiters who perform four tasks: taking orders; placing the orders in the kitchen; helping prep the food; and delivering the food to their customers. The children begin practicing. With Tarzia's help, they all learn to take orders like pros.

The children generate a list of foods to serve on opening night and, with Doyle's help, narrow it down to four choices that are both affordable and feasible for a large crowd. Parents donate all of the food. Children make some dishes from scratch, with the help of two fathers who come to the school during the week leading up to the opening. The children's eagerness to share their creation with their families is contagious. Everyone grows more and more excited as opening day approaches.

When the big day finally arrives, the children play their waitstaff roles like professionals. When all the guests have been served, the children sit beside their families in a celebration of learning and community.

Clearly, the children in Doyle's class have been learning about more than colors, observational painting, and restaurants. For preschoolers, they have mastered some impressive math skills and concepts, such as making change for $20, counting off days to an event, and grasping the idea of mixing colors in a particular proportion to get the exact shade they want. They've practiced thinking like scientists: making predictions, formulating and testing hypotheses, and recording their procedures and results for others to replicate. They've learned a lot about reading and writing—some of them can read, sound out, and write familiar words independently. They've also learned a tremendous amount about working together and learning from each other.[16]

Close to home, in the intimate space of their neighborhood classroom, the children have experienced belonging to a small community, many for the first time outside of their families. They have been asking questions, being curious and motivated, and investing in real problems that affect their daily lives and the lives of their classmates. As their teacher has repeatedly asked for their opinions and listened carefully, sometimes writing their ideas on paper, they've experienced that their voices matter. And, most likely for the first time, they have experienced a shared sense of purpose with their peers, bound to processes of shared inquiry that come with real responsibilities. Not only have they learned about their community (both in and beyond their classroom), they have participated together in making democratic decisions and meaningful contributions. Although they may not have learned the word, they have acted as engaged citizens of both their class and their wider community.[17]

An appreciative father shared his response to the Colorful Café that his two daughters and their classmates created—and all of the learning that led up to it:

> What surprised me this most, I think, was the children's ability to bring together all of the parents and the community around a table. I know that from growing up in a different country that food does that. But the kids did that in an amazing way. The experience of preparing for an activity that has several steps in terms of complexity and having to relate to different kinds of individuals and adults and to have to be at their best. The kind of professionalism that I saw in four- and five-year-olds was quite amazing.

For school principal Traci Walker Griffith, what stood out most was the way that the teachers—and the curriculum—nurtured ideas that the children developed, teaching reading, writing, and math and engaging empathy and imagination by helping children pursue their interests together:

> It's inspiring that one seed can lead to such amazing, powerful learning. We can't continue to not recognize when students have interests. We need to continue to plant those seeds and help them to water them.
>
> They wanted to make a menu so that when they went into the office for Miss Anne [the school secretary], they had a menu from which she could choose. That involved students with and without disabilities, boys and girls, writing, and thinking about "How much does a hamburger cost?" You could order anything from the menu, which I thought was very important. They could dream anything and it could be on the menu. We

have a scripted curriculum, but here we're not stifling children's imagination. We're asking them to get engaged.

In the next chapter, we'll look more closely at literacy and math curricula, and see how play, instruction, and projects work together to build both basic academic skills and twenty-first-century competencies.[18]

Chapter Three

Building the BPS Early Childhood Program

Over the past twelve years, the BPS Department of Early Childhood (DEC) has opened nearly one hundred new preschool classrooms. They don't all look like Jodi Doyle's combined K0/K1 classroom, but each manifests the core principles that animate the DEC's work. Each bears the imprint of the collaborative work of administrators, coaches, teachers, families, data collectors, outside funders and evaluators, curriculum writers, consultants, and a host of other players. And although few meet all of the DEC's aspirations, a 2015 study of a representative sample of classrooms found that nearly 90 percent hit the "good" benchmarks on observed measures of classroom organization and emotional supports, and the vast majority demonstrated "Adequate" or better levels of instructional support and of literacy and math learning environments and activities.[1] Collectively, these classrooms provide a diversity of learning experiences of high-enough quality to support promising outcomes for children.[2]

In the first decade of its work, the DEC has adopted and continued to revise curricula for four-year-olds (K1) and kindergarteners (K2), and has begun transforming the first and second grades. The department has led hundreds of professional development (PD) sessions for teachers, paraprofessionals, and principals in the district and local community and across the state, and engaged in one-on-one coaching with hundreds of teachers.

How did this happen in a large, urban district rife with competing agendas, changing leadership, and its share of stifling challenges? This chapter tells the story of how the Department of Early Childhood came to be, and of its early struggles and accomplishments.

Dr. Jason Sachs, director of the department, was the DEC's first hire. "One of the best things I've done," says Sachs, "is to stay." In a district riddled with frequent leadership turnover, Sachs has stood at the helm of the department for more than ten years. In this time, he has led the DEC's expansion from a three-person team with jurisdiction only over prekindergarten programs, to its current status as a preK–2 office staffed by more than twenty-four coaches, curriculum writers, and project leaders. He hired staff who share his belief that public investments in early childhood should seek to create options for low-income families that are not only comparable to those available to upper-income families, but better.[3]

The DEC staff are a diverse team. They are teachers, coaches, data experts, and visionaries. They hail from public and private schools and represent Haitian, Latino/a, African American, Italian, Anglo, Pacific Islander, Cambodian, and Japanese backgrounds. What ties then together is a deep commitment to the children, families, and teachers of Boston—and to each other.

The team considers its diversity key to its success. Differences in background, role, and expertise offer different vantage points, allowing team members to see different needs, priorities, and possibilities. Their differing perspectives and passions inform their strategic thinking as they explore and advocate solutions and new initiatives in response to what they see on the ground and what they wish could be.

At times, the diversity of the DEC staff, and their attempts to both mirror and respond to the diversity of their city, complicates their work—even as they acknowledge that it makes them stronger and more effective as a department. They share a vision of young children as *curious, active, empathetic learners, capable of perspective-taking, reasoning, and reflection* (core principle 2). They also subscribe to a shared vision of high-quality teaching. Yet it often takes hours of respectful conversation to accommodate different perspectives on issues such as the balance of academic and social-emotional learning; the amount of time that should be spent on phonics or pretend play; approaches to working with teachers, principals, and families whose views are different from theirs; and how to ensure that their innovative curricula and pedagogical frameworks respect the cultural backgrounds and beliefs of the families who rely on their programs.

Boston is a "gateway city" for immigrants. The nearly 57,000 students in its public preK–12 schools collectively come from 138 different countries and speak more than 71 languages.[4] Although immigration and gentrification are rapidly altering historic ethnic and racial enclaves, residential segregation persists. Many middle- and upper-income families opt out of the public schools. Along with the goal of closing persistent achievement gaps, bringing more of these families into the public schools is an underlying rationale for offering programs for four-year-olds.

Speaking for his team, Sachs says:

> If you think this will be a straightforward story of progress, you're in for a surprise. Our journey has been anything but linear, although it's important to understand that story we are about to tell has always been guided by a strategic plan for improving quality and expanding access to early childhood programs in Boston. Our aim has been, and continues to be, to address social justice issues in the city and to ensure that all children experience a successful and joyful start to their school careers . . . This journey has been filled with challenges, some of which took us by surprise. We share our learning in solidarity with others who may be embarking on a similar quest.

Getting Started

In January 2005, Boston's four-term mayor Tom Menino announced a new initiative: the introduction of full-day slots for four-year-olds in the city's school system. The decision was a response to an ongoing local and national conversation about public responsibility for the education and care of young children and about how best to promote school readiness. Menino joined with the United Way in calling for a comprehensive approach, engaging with hospitals, museums, libraries, community-based nonprofits, universities, families, early educators, state and city agencies, and the private sector to ensure that all of Boston's children would have the early experiences needed to continue to succeed in school.

This comprehensive "Thrive in Five" initiative would not begin until 2008, when a diverse group of stakeholders would coalesce around a birth–five agenda of family engagement, universal screening, high-quality early education and care, and responsive communities and systems. But Menino was convinced by his aide Laurie Sherman, who had helped found the city's Countdown to Kindergarten program, which supports families in enrolling their children in BPS and easing their transition, to open prekindergarten classrooms immediately.[5] Tom Payzant, his longtime superintendent of schools, concurred.

Menino and Payzant were not starting from scratch. The city had opened three Early Education Centers in 1998, and had recently added three more. These centers now enrolled about 350 three- to five-year-olds of diverse background, most from low-income families. Boston also offered half-day programs for four-year-olds in a few of its elementary schools, serving about 400 children, though these were mostly used by middle-class families who could manage the transportation and childcare coverage challenges. Union contracts assured that teachers were paid well ($50,000–$70,000 per year), class size did not exceed twenty-two students with two adults, and teachers had common planning time with grade-level colleagues to plan curriculum and review student work.

Perhaps more important, Boston had taken steps to assure that its early learning programs were grounded in the science of how young children learn.[6] For example, in their expectations for both what and how children learned, the BPS Citywide Learning Standards: Kindergarten aligned with Early Childhood Program Standards of the National Association for the Education of Young Children (NAEYC), including social-emotional, language, cognitive, and physical development, along with approaches to learning like curiosity and persistence. To support children in becoming engaged and independent learners, the BPS standards advocated a "workshop approach" of hands-on learning and task-related conversations among students, as well as between student and teacher. And, like the NAEYC standards, they recognized the power of play. Each of the six Early Learning Centers was directed by a principal with a strong early childhood background.

The state had also taken steps to encourage early learning providers to follow the NAEYC standards. The head of Early Learning Services at the Massachusetts Department of Education (DOE), Dr. Elisabeth Schaefer, had made earning accreditation within three years and maintaining it thereafter a requirement of the state's preschool program for low-income families, Community Partnerships for Children (CPC). As a result, Massachusetts held the record for number of NAEYC-accredited programs during her tenure.[7] In addition, to encourage all school districts to offer full-day kindergarten, the DOE offered Kindergarten Development Grants, which, among other things, paid for a paraprofessional in each classroom. Seeking NAEYC accreditation, though not strictly mandated, was a priority grant activity. BPS received a $2 million grant in 2000 and in subsequent years.

When BPS became the fiscal agent for Boston's CPC grant, it hired Karen Silver as quality director. Silver, an experienced NAEYC accreditation coach who had worked in both school- and community-based settings, would oversee grant compliance and support accreditation—both NAEYC and NAFCC (National Association for Family Child Care)—and other quality improvement initiatives.

Fortunate Timing

In 2005, Schaefer's tenure at DOE ended with the inauguration of a new governor, and the CPC program became part of the new Department Early Education and Care. For Boston, the timing was perfect; Jason Sachs, who had been working under Schaefer in the Division of Early Learning Services, was available for hire. His résumé was a perfect fit for Mayor Menino's goal of closing learning opportunity gaps.

Before joining the DOE, Sachs had worked with community-based organizations that offered both early education and wraparound services, often fund raising and building partnerships to get families and children facing adversities the supports they needed and to build teachers' skills and their access to appropriate learning materials. His doctoral dissertation had focused on inequities in early childhood education.

At the DOE, Sachs supported communities to gather data that would help them determine supply and demand and invest in quality. He and his colleagues commissioned studies that looked at quality in community-based organizations, preschools, Head Start programs, public-school classrooms for three- and/or four-year-olds (most serving special education students in substantially separate or inclusive classrooms), and licensed family childcare homes.

Through this work, Sachs had learned where the early childhood programs in the state were strong, and where they needed help. He saw how well-intentioned but underfunded policies to support both families and the early childhood workforce could compromise quality and reinforce inequity, as policy makers grappled with competing demands from multiple stakeholders and made compromises on issues such as access and affordability versus quality and hiring or requiring teachers with relevant degrees versus recruiting and maintaining a diverse workforce with much-needed cultural and linguistic competencies. He became expert in gathering, analyzing, and presenting the data needed to make a case for enhanced funding and policy guidelines and to drive ongoing program improvement. After only one interview, Tom Payzant hired Sachs to direct Boston's new initiative.

The DEC's Journey Begins

One of Sachs's first acts as DEC leader was to bring Karen Silver into the department and to leverage the Kindergarten Development Grant to move more schools toward accreditation. BPS had also partnered with the University of Massachusetts to seek an Early Reading First grant to coach teachers as it implemented a new preschool literacy curriculum in the Early Learning Centers. Michelle High-McKinnon, a former BPS teacher and coach, was tapped to direct the effort. Sachs recruited Silver and High-McKinnon to join him as his first leadership team.

Their task was daunting. As a thorough needs assessment study conducted by researchers at the Centers for Women at Wellesley College would soon demonstrate, Boston was a long way from offering preK and kindergarten programs that met the quality standards, and a long way from offering most of its families access to free, or even affordable, early learning programs.

Should such programs be placed within the public schools? If the goal was to prevent later achievement gaps between children of different racial, linguistic, or income backgrounds, would it be more or less efficient, effective, and equitable to strengthen community-based offerings? Should the city try to do both?

Through his statewide work, Sachs had become familiar with Boston neighborhoods that were in particular need of more and better programs for their young children. And he saw what a difference it made when programs used rich, engaging, research-grounded curriculum as a backbone for teaching. He also observed some especially effective teachers, including Marina Boni, whom he would soon hire. Boni was a veteran teacher who had spent twenty years at a community preschool in Cambridge that served a diverse and mostly low-income group of children and families. She had studied the Reggio Emilio approach and had worked with Project Zero, a research group at the Harvard Graduate School of Education, on the Making Learning Visible initiative, a collaboration with Reggio Emilia educators. Her child-focused approach to teaching, and to collaborating with families and colleagues, would help Sachs shape the social-justice focused, children-as-citizens vision that he was beginning to articulate for Boston's programs.

Focused on equity and on meaningful, as well as measurable, outcomes, Sachs took a long view. He knew that change would be disruptive in the short term, but that sustainable progress would require systemic efforts that could make change at scale. He supported the emerging plan to situate high-quality early education programs within the public schools. His DOE work had convinced him that "a kaleidoscope of programs doesn't add up—the structure of the public schools potentially gives you an opportunity to make meaningful and deep changes."

Sachs recalls an especially pivotal meeting with Mayor Menino and Michael Contompasis, the chief operating officer in the district who later became superintendent:

> Mike was a very powerful figure . . . hence you had to make sure you knew what you were doing but once you could convince him, things moved

swiftly. . . . I asked them if the new preschool programs should be offered by community-based providers or if BPS should deliver the all the K1s. Menino . . . said that BPS should do it, because childcare providers could not afford to do it well. And in that five-minute meeting, sitting with two of the most powerful players in the city, a "disruptive influence" was concretized. BPS with its own resources was going to provide the first universal program for four-year-olds funded and run solely by the city. No finance schemes needed, no legislature, no initiative. Just a mayor telling a superintendent to get it done.

So, with a mandate to build early childhood programs of high enough quality to narrow achievement gaps and with the authority to seek outside help and objective assessments as well as private funding, Sachs got to work.

Expanding Quantity: Funding and Locating More K1 Programs

Sachs asked a lot of questions during his first few weeks on the job: How were children being placed in the existing K1 programs? Where were programs available, and were these in the parts of the district with the greatest need? He learned that space was the main deciding factor in where the district's current six Early Education Centers had been placed. But with goals to expand the scope of the programs dramatically, Sachs began drawing on data to figure out where the district's four-year-old population was in need of K1 classrooms. He created a data matrix, showing the number of children in need of a preK classroom by neighborhood and the number of existing programs in that neighborhood. Not surprisingly, he found the highest need in historically underserved neighborhoods like Dorchester, Roxbury, and East Boston.

But that was just the beginning. Classrooms needed to be located in schools. To meet NAEYC guidelines, they could only be on first or second floors and no more than forty feet from a bathroom. Ideally, there would be more than one K1 classroom in the school so that teachers would have colleagues to reflect, plan, and learn with. There had to be as least as many kindergarten (K2) as prekindergarten (K1) classrooms so that children would not need to change schools at the end of the year, and the school leadership needed to be willing to take on the extra grade. Working in partnership with a cross-functional team of leaders from operations, transportation, facilities, special education, academics, community partnerships, and enrollment, Sachs coordinated an intentional and responsive approach to expanding the city's preK programs.

And the expansion of preK programs would need funding. Despite Mayor Menino's strong support, the project could not be financed with district money alone. Sachs began working with the Barr Foundation, a Boston-based funder with a mission "to invest in human, natural, and creative potential, serving as thoughtful stewards and catalysts."[8] The foundation had been working to improve early education throughout Massachusetts. Kimberly Haskins, senior program officer for the foundation's education portfolio, was leading its early learning efforts. Haskins's vision, like Sachs's, was systemic. She was interested in quality as well as equitable access and knowledgeable both about the science of early childhood development and about early education policy. And she was familiar with the hurdles that Boston's low- and moderate-income families faced in obtaining care for their children that would prepare them for ongoing school success.

Barr agreed to give the DEC $3 million over a period of three years to open more classrooms, purchase curricula, and pay for coaches to mentor teachers in the new classrooms—provided that the district matched their investment. Haskins's long-term vision would help to ensure that both the K1 classrooms and the ongoing PD would sustain their quality across inevitable changes in school district leadership. At her urging, the Barr Foundation built in a provision the district would assume the costs of the programs and keep them running when the grant ended.

These commitments held. From 38 classrooms serving 750 children in 2005, the next five years would see a rapid increase to 110 classrooms in 2010 serving over 2,000 children (see figure 3.1).[9]

Expanding so quickly brought challenges: finding appropriate spaces; recruiting and hiring teachers with master's degrees (or who could get them within three years, as the district required) from an early childhood workforce where BAs were not yet the norm; hiring teaching assistants who could grow into their roles; and recruiting families—as well as having to turn many families away when there weren't enough slots.

Schools also faced logistical challenges in accommodating the new programs. Cafeteria, active play, and bathroom spaces had to be shared with

FIGURE 3.1 Expansion of BPS K1 slots 2005–2010

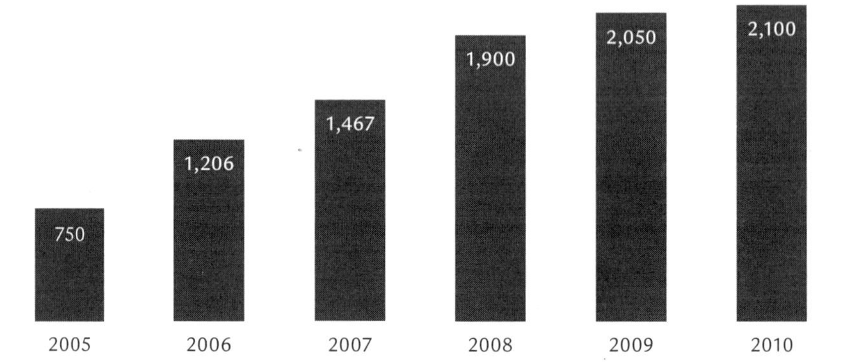

2005	2006	2007	2008	2009	2010
750	1,206	1,467	1,900	2,050	2,100

older children. Resulting lunch, recess, and specialists' schedules could chop a young child's day into awkward segments. In some schools, children ate lunch at 10:30, when they might have preferred a morning snack, and spent much of their day lining up to go from place to place.

Some of the roadblocks were physical. Many of Boston's school buildings were old, and hadn't been built for kindergarteners, let alone four-year-olds. Playgrounds had also been designed for older children, and some were unfenced. At one school, the playground was frequently littered with broken glass. The coach who was working with the K1 teachers called Sachs in frustration. "These children need to play outdoors, and they can't be playing where it isn't safe. I can't work with teachers on the new curriculum if I'm spending all my time picking up glass!" Sachs helped pick up the glass that day, then spoke with the principal to help find a more permanent solution. (He kept a shard of glass in the door of his car for months as a reminder of all the work still to be done.)

Broken glass could be cleaned up by daily patrolling, but staffing frustrations were more difficult to resolve. Sachs handpicked coaches and other members of his department, vetting not only their early childhood expertise and their commitment to Boston's young children and their families but also their commitment to systemic change that could guarantee Boston's children equitable opportunities for joyful and productive learning. But the teachers themselves were hired by the Boston Public Schools and chosen by individual school principals, many of whom had never studied early childhood and did not share the DEC's core beliefs. Teachers with tenure were protected by union contracts; they couldn't be fired, but they could be involuntarily transferred both within and between schools. The DEC soon discovered that many of the K1 teachers had been transferred from higher grades and lacked both early childhood training and experience with young learners. Coaches sometimes felt they were starting at the beginning—explaining basics like what young children learned from sand and water play and why dramatic play areas and pretend play materials were so important.

Still, working within a public school system brought some major advantages, including the ability to hire degreed teachers and pay teachers of four-year-olds at the same rate as teachers of five-year-olds instead of half as much. This better-educated and better-compensated workforce was therefore stable enough to make investments in ongoing PD worthwhile.

Building Quality: K1 Curriculum, Professional Development, and Coaching

Simply expanding the number of available K1 programs without deep consideration of their content and quality was never the DEC's aim. The department knew that quality could not be imposed; it would need to grow organically through the ongoing work of teachers, families, and administrators who had the knowledge and supports needed to be effective. The DEC could succeed only when teachers understood and embraced the underlying mission of engaging all children as curious, active, empathetic learners who deserved the best that their communities and developmental science could provide. And, in a public school system with an existing teaching staff, that vision could only come about if teachers were consistently treated as professionals and offered opportunities for ongoing learning.

To this end, Sachs and his team asked questions about classroom, curriculum, and teaching quality and decided to launch a pilot project to see what difference they could make by using the NAEYC accreditation process as a driver of change.[10] They chose fifteen schools, varying in size, neighborhood, and school structure (early learning center, preK–5, or preK–8). They included kindergarten and special education classrooms along with K1, hoping that the NAEYC accreditation process could serve as a lever to get into all early childhood classrooms. Initially, the DEC hired outside "mentors" who had helped community-based programs to achieve NAEYC accreditation. It soon became apparent that some seemed to be using the accreditation criteria as a checklist, rather than seeing the process as an opportunity to transform practice and drive quality. The DEC's solution was not to fire its new coaching partners, but rather to pair them with DEC coaches and to hold monthly meetings of all the coaches to monitor their mentees' progress. Over time, the DEC developed a NAEYC coaching methodology that enabled it to move the process to a deeper and more reflective level.

Baseline Quality Assessment

In 2006, Sachs used some of the Barr funding to hire a team of experts from the Wellesley Centers for Women to conduct a needs assessment study that would provide an early read on DEC efforts and a baseline to guide future quality improvement. Led by senior research scientist Nancy Marshall, the Wellesley researchers observed forty-three K1 classrooms (leaving out classrooms with fewer than ten children and substantially separate classrooms for children with special needs) and eighty-five randomly selected K2 classrooms. They used state-of-the-art observation tools to measure the environmental and teaching quality and supports for early language, literacy, and math.[11] They also surveyed teachers and principals on PD and classroom resource needs and conducted family needs assessments.

The results indicated large gaps between the quality of classrooms and teaching and both the BPS and NAEYC program standards.[12] As intended, the needs assessment revealed the scope of the challenge and pointed to specific improvement strategies. But shortly after the DEC received the report, the *Boston Globe* picked up the story. The front-page article announced that 70 percent of BPS preschool teachers were not teaching at a high enough level of quality. The article also flagged unsafe playgrounds and compromised health and safety practices at some locations.[13]

The Wellesley report, of course, was much more nuanced than the *Globe*'s summary. It pointed out health and safety concerns that the DEC had already been trying to fix, such as unfenced playgrounds near busy streets and lack of proximity to bathrooms or stand-alone sinks. Some of the low ratings were due to lack of equipment and materials that are standard in preschool settings, such as equipment for active play. Others stemmed from observations that play materials (such as blocks, puppets and dress-up clothes) were available for children to use for only brief parts of the day or not sufficiently integrated into classroom interest areas to provide strong supports for play-based learning. Most classrooms lacked a full-time paraprofessional or assistant teacher, and many exceeded NAEYC's recommended child/adult ratios as a result.

The majority of classrooms were rated "Adequate" on curriculum, instructional supports, literacy supports, and social-emotional supports; fewer than a third reached the "Good" benchmark in any of these areas.[14] The researchers recognized, however, that many of the K1 classrooms were using a brand-new curriculum and that, although the teachers had some PD, they may not have had adequate opportunities to learn the recommended strategies and incorporate them into their practice at the time of the observations.

In the area of instructional supports, more than a quarter of the classrooms were hitting a very demanding benchmark—receiving top ratings for their use of teacher-led instruction and learning routines; offering of engaging activities; promotion of reasoning and creativity in problem solving; and provision of verbal feedback that helped children express and develop their ideas. Most teachers were doing most of these things to some extent, but not consistently or skillfully enough to rise above the "Adequate" benchmark. The researchers recommended that they get more support from master teachers—the reflective coaching that the DEC was just beginning to implement.

Supports for literacy were especially weak in the K1 classrooms, not only in the availability and use of a variety of storybooks (including nonfiction), but in supports for oral language like carrying on extended conversations with children, using rich vocabulary, building on children's ideas, encouraging children's conversations with each other, and reading books aloud in engaging ways that invited conversation. Although teachers in K2 classrooms were doing more to direct children's attention to print and build both alphabet knowledge and phonemic awareness, teachers in both K1 and K2 classrooms were spending too much time directing children and not enough time engaging with them in genuinely interesting language-building conversations. Although 60 percent of the K1 teachers had received training on OWL, a developmental literacy-based curriculum with a strong focus on purposeful play, most were not yet implementing it as intended. They were missing opportunities to capitalize on what would prove to be the program's greatest strength—helping all children build a strong oral language foundation for literacy.

Teachers in both grades scored better overall on providing social-emotional supports—but only slightly. Although only 2 percent were rated "Inadequate" in this area, only 18 percent reached the aspirational "Good" benchmark. About half of the teachers scored high marks for their sensitivity, establishment of a warm relational climate, and management of children's behavior, but many fell down on items related to encouraging children's independence, collaborative work, and friendships. Many also were not consistent in responding to children—answering their questions; noticing when they needed help, encouragement, reassurance, or acknowledgement of their efforts and accomplishments; and addressing their questions and concerns effectively.

The DEC had hoped to place the needs assessment findings in the context of mitigating factors before the report was made public. The benchmarks used were demanding; Sachs knew from his DOE work that few early childhood programs in the state could meet them all. The department had just begun to roll out and adequately support the K1 curriculum and to make needed facilities improvements. Staffing was incomplete—especially the provision of qualified assistant teachers. The study had been done to assess needs, not to evaluate a nascent program. And the DEC had barely begun to bring kindergartens in line with the new BPS Program Standards and NAEYC's definitions of developmentally appropriate practice. But news of the report's results—and especially of the *Globe*'s critical summary—spread quickly. Now, it seemed, the whole city was questioning not only the quality of their programs but the value and viability of offering prekindergarten in the public schools. The City Council demanded that Sachs appear at its next meeting to explain what had gone wrong and justify continued funding.

Worried that the DEC program might be scrapped before it had really begun, Sachs turned to Michael Contompasis. He vividly recalls their conversation and subsequent City Council appearance.

> I went up to Mike's office . . . and I thought, "Well, this is the end of me," and I said I was truly sorry. He said, "Why?" He spoke with the mayor, and [the mayor's] only issue was that he was not given a heads up that the article was coming out. Later that week, Mike and I presented to the City Council, and he said, "Here we are, warts and all." The City Council said they had never been so proud of BPS, as we were willing to examine and fix ourselves in such an intentional way.

Shrewdly, Sachs had used the opportunity to explain to the City Council what high-quality early education programs looked like, the level of quality that research studies showed was likely to narrow or close achievement gaps, and what his department most needed in order to bring its programs up to that level. Protected by its champions, who understood the challenge of creating a quality program on as a large scale and as rapidly as the DEC was asked to do, the new department weathered its first storm.

The lessons in trust, transparency, and collaboration with those who would be most affected by their decisions that the DEC learned from this experience would become even more important in the years ahead. The respected yet somewhat marginalized position that it held within the school administration protected them this time, but it would take political skill and savvy, along with hard data, to stay true to its vision in the face of changes in leadership and shifting priorities.

Still, the disappointing data required the DEC to take an honest and unflinching look at its early efforts. Believing in collaborative data analysis with teachers, Sachs shared the needs assessment data with over two hundred teachers in a facilitated session at their annual Kindergarten Conference, to listen to their understanding of why they had received such low scores on instructional quality.[15] Their answers were instructive; some teachers said that they knew about good practice, but their administrators wouldn't let them teach in developmentally appropriate ways. Others pointed out that curriculum their school used was weak and would not enable them to reach their potential, or that their principals were pushing them to spend too much time on whole group literacy work. Still others shared that there was just not enough time in the day, and that they were spending too much time on assessments and not enough time on teaching.

Once the DEC team understood the challenges teachers were facing, the solutions became clearer. Members knew that they needed to help principals understand the unique learning needs of young children, ensure that teachers had the necessary learning materials and equipment, and support teachers in implementing developmentally appropriate practices. Although the DEC believed that teachers should follow children's interests, staff recognized that they were not doing an effective job of promoting quality with that model. They knew that they also needed to make sure that all classrooms were using a strong, integrated, comprehensive curriculum—one that would leverage time and leave space for authentic assessments. To ensure that all of the classrooms were meeting their basic expectations, they would need to roll out a consistent curriculum across the district, going against the grain of the district's semi-autonomous school policy.

Curriculum Rollout

Sachs had already turned his attention to curriculum; 60 percent of the K1 classrooms observed by the Wellesley researchers were using the literacy-based curriculum he had chosen, and 40 percent were piloting a new developmentally grounded math curriculum. That work had begun before Sachs came on board, when the Early Education Centers had agreed to pilot OWL. One of its authors, Professor Judith Schickedanz, an early literacy expert who was teaching at Boston University, would provide PD for the Boston teachers, including some classroom observation and coaching.

Taking a developmental rather than a narrowly skills-based approach, OWL is organized around a small number of thematic units allowing for in-depth investigation, interdisciplinary connections, and time for thinking, discussion, and reflection.[16] A rich collection of fiction and nonfiction storybooks, along with related songs and poems, underpins each thematic exploration. Daily routines assure attention to all developmental and learning domains, as children work in activity "Centers" (for art, reading, writing, sensory exploration, science, math, construction, and dramatic play) or gather for group activities and discussions.[17]

Literacy skills are embedded into the life of the classroom in ways that research demonstrates have lasting impact.[18] OWL's strong focus on oral language and vocabulary aligns with research that shows a high correlation between vocabulary at kindergarten entry and tenth-grade reading comprehension scores.[19] As they explore compelling science and social studies content and well-written trade books, children hear and have opportunities to master concept words, interesting words, and academic words related to each theme.

Systematic and sequential literacy instruction occurs daily, in short lessons tailored to students' individual levels of mastery. Songs, finger plays, action rhymes, and games build alphabet and phonological knowledge in playful, child-friendly ways. And, of course, children are immersed in storybooks and poems, which are read (and reread) aloud by the teacher or assistant; perused by children themselves as they "do research," recite the words from memory, or pretend to read; or shared in small group participatory readings, with a teacher or child pointing to words as they are read.[20] In addition, each unit contains a social-emotional skills component that includes a focus on emotion-related vocabulary.

As implemented in Boston, OWL was taught through daily routines of Circle Time (morning greeting and group bonding), Centers or Choice Time (when children could choose areas like dramatic play or the library and pursue self-chosen activities or group projects), Read Aloud, and small group lessons (brief skill-focused lessons, followed by hands-on activities set up in different classroom stations). Outdoor play was an intentional part of daily learning. With two teachers (a professional and a paraprofessional partner) in the classroom, one could work with an individual or small group while the other "floated" to support children engaged in various play and hands-on learning activities. When the lead teacher worked with the whole class, her partner could help a child who needed extra support to participate. Over time, the DEC phased in other routines, such as Thinking and Feedback.

Boston's initial implementation of the OWL relied heavily on teacher-supported socio-dramatic play to build early literacy skill. Children learned and practiced new vocabulary as they reenacted stories, played out scenarios, and incorporated new information into their shared fantasy play. As we saw in the Colorful Café (chapter 2), young children take their play seriously: "I need those carrots. They're for my customer." As they take on roles, assuming appropriate voices and personas, their language becomes more fluent and sophisticated, eliciting appropriately sophisticated responses from their play partners.[21] When teachers provide the time, structure, materials, inspiration, and supports that enable children to play at a mature level, children strengthen their oral language and storytelling skills, content knowledge, and content-specific vocabulary.[22] These capacities provide enduring foundations for ongoing reading success.[23] Children also build critical cooperative and executive function skills as they plan their play, gather and create materials, wait their turns, and take their partners' perspectives and ideas into account.[24]

Pretend play often provides motivation to write—especially with teacher encouragement and an accessible, well-stocked writing center. With or without adult help, children create labels, signs, menus, maps, and other needed props—often working out letter-sound correspondences as they attempt to write the words they need. This, too, is likely to impact later literacy achievements.[25]

Thanks to the financial support of the Barr foundation, Sachs was able to hire a few coaches in the early days to help roll out the OWL curriculum to all K1 classrooms and bring teachers up to speed on its literacy promotion techniques. Informing schools about the newly adopted curriculum was easy—the DEC simply wrote a letter to all principals housing a K1 classroom in their school and explained that OWL would be district-mandated, and that all teachers would receive training and ongoing coaching in the model over time. "That got us going," says Sachs, but the DEC recognized that embedding the curriculum in every classroom and coaching teachers as they worked with it was a long-term commitment.

The federal Early Reading First grant provided coaching to Early Learning Centers through a contract with HILL for Literacy, while the Barr-funded DEC coaches addressed the needs of the teachers in school-based K1 classrooms. The DEC deployed its resources carefully, recognizing that it would be more effective in the long run to offer strong coaching support to fewer classrooms at a time than to try to give everyone an equal share that didn't allow time for mutual trust and curiosity to develop. Unless coaches could be mentors, not judges or managers, the coaching would fail.

Strengthening Math

In the midst of the OWL rollout, Sachs was offered an opportunity to pilot *Building Blocks*, a new preschool math curriculum, in twenty programs in the district. The curriculum, developed by Douglas Clements and Julie Sarama with a grant from the National Science Foundation, was grounded in research on children's learning trajectories as they developed spatial and geometric concepts and competencies and numerical and quantitative understandings. Its pedagogy was based on "finding the mathematics in, and developing mathematics from, children's activity."[26] As children pursued activities of interest, they would be encouraged to represent and model the underlying mathematics, create original designs, make up their own problems, and explain their mathematical reasoning. The focus on deep understanding of young children's development and learning processes, hands-on and child-driven activity, and making learning and ideas visible to both children and their teachers fit with the DEC core principles.[27]

Building Blocks had the added advantage of aligning with TERC *Investigations in Number, Data, and Space* ("*Investigations*"), Boston's K–5 math curriculum. Designed by a Cambridge-based team of mathematics educators and curriculum developers and supported by two National Science Foundation grants, *Investigations* was designed to support a range of learners in mathematical reasoning, computation, and conceptual understanding. Its first goal was: "Support students to make sense of mathematics and learn that they can be mathematical thinkers."[28]

Dissatisfied with the math content of the OWL (which has subsequently changed to include more math), the DEC agreed to pilot *Building Blocks*. If the pilot was successful, they team would figure out how to roll it out across all of their programs. Marina Boni worked closely with two dedicated retired teachers, Mary Mazzota and Meg Daly, who conducted PD sessions and coached teachers in the new curriculum. The district's investment for the twenty-classroom pilot was only $150,000, but the results would be dramatic.

Significant Strides and Next Steps

By the beginning of the 2007–2008 school year, the DEC was reporting smoother sailing. It opened its October report to the Barr Foundation with:

> Year two of the three-year Boston Public Schools Kindergarten initiative funded by the Barr Foundation is producing tremendous energy and positive change throughout the district. The hiring of the coaches, who bring expertise, focus and passion combined with the Wellesley College needs assessment have become foundation for the Boston Public Schools (BPS) Department of Early Childhood. The Department has accomplished much for the children of BPS and it is safe to say that the success is largely due to the resources provided through this generous grant.[29]

The report went on to detail DEC's achievement of the grant's agreed-upon goals. OWL coaches, hired for both diversity and early childhood expertise, were helping teachers to improve their curriculum offerings, instruction, and assessment and the overall environment of their classrooms. Teachers were collaborating with their coaches and with each other. The Marshall School, described as having had "limited direction and expertise in early childhood" before the Barr-funded coaching, was held up as a model of transformation. Departmentwide PD had been redesigned, with an added focus on relationship building. *Building Blocks* was being rolled out across the district; only five classrooms had not yet received PD in how to implement the curriculum and integrate it with OWL. And twenty-three new classrooms had been opened.

Child outcome data from the Early Reading First study of OWL implementation and literacy coaching in the Early Education Centers was extremely promising. Children showed marked gains in vocabulary scores from fall to spring. Furthermore, English speakers scored at or above national norms regardless of background, essentially eliminating the achievement gap. English language learners also made strong strides as a group, with a mean score jump from 80 (moderately low) to 90 (within the average range) on the widely used

Peabody Picture Vocabulary Test.[30] The DEC hoped to replicate these results in all K1 classrooms.

Although the Early Reading First grant was ending, its evaluation team at the UMASS Donahue Center had agreed to work with Sachs to design districtwide data collection and evaluation studies. The DEC had sought and received funding for an evaluation of the coaching that would help them determine the most effective intensity and frequency. The Wellesley team had been contracted to conduct a follow-up quality study that would assess each school's implementation of the NAEYC program standards and readiness to begin the NAEYC accreditation process. The DEC felt confident that the results would not only validate the work they and the teachers had been doing, but point the way forward.

Christina Weiland had received a Rappaport Fellowship from Harvard's Kennedy School of Government to work with the DEC on designing data collection systems and evaluating the impacts of their programs. Sachs pointed out that results would need to be interpreted with caution, as it would be hard to control for factors such as parent choice, which could create selection bias in favor of BPS programs, and the quality of preschool experiences for children in comparison groups. Nevertheless, he felt that further studies would continue to inform the department's progress toward the excellent and equitable programming that would prevent achievement gaps.

In the following year (2008–2009), *Building Blocks* was added to all K1 classrooms in the district. DEC staff worked hard to integrate the OWL and *Building Blocks* curricula. They made it easy for teachers to see alignment of concepts and content, and to keep track of small group, whole group, and Center components, by creating "clipboard directions" (a reminder of an activity's purpose, with brief instruction suggestions) and other helpful tools. In addition to teaching guides and tools, the DEC was providing thirteen days of PD across the summer and school year, along with biweekly coaching visits. Some struggles still arose, of course. For example, an experiment with having teachers alternate between math and literacy small groups, depending on the day, backfired. As Marina Boni recalls, "That was not a good idea because it got people to think they should not be doing math every day."

So they tried again, and in time, the *Building Blocks* and OWL curricula together proved to be a winning combination. Boni explained the new approach:

> It's really hands-on, and that, when teachers are facilitating it well, it really challenges the children to think about mathematical concepts they are learning and really encourages them to articulate their understandings.[31] Now we're trying to mathematize the day, so it's not just during this distinct time that teachers and children are involved in math conversations. We're trying to point out where there are opportunities during centers so teachers can make reference to mathematical contexts.

As they worked to build an integrated curriculum that would free up teacher time, the DEC team also worked to strengthen teachers' observation skills and authentic assessment practices.[32] Knowing where children were developmentally, what they cared about, and how they learned would enable teachers to be more responsive to and supportive of individual needs and to tailor both curriculum and instruction to what children would be eager and ready to learn.[33]

By 2009, the pieces were falling into place. The DEC's vision of early childhood classrooms that provoke and engage children to be strong, motivated learners was becoming a reality in more and more of the K1 classrooms. Now 70 percent of them scored above the quality thresholds, as documented by the Wellesley Centers for Women team that had conducted the needs assessment.[34] The DEC made plans for the next challenge: kindergarten.

Chapter Four

Pathways to Excellence

Even as a small department—just three members in the beginning—the DEC team had a grand vision. They saw their mandate not only as building a universal prekindergarten program strong enough to close the achievement gap, but also as producing self-motivated learners who would be able to read, write, and communicate effectively by third grade and eager as well as able to take on new challenges. They knew that achieving these ends would require years of capacity-building work and more than schools alone could deliver. Indeed, some of the work would have to begin long before children were old enough to enter their K1 programs.

Three years into the project, the DEC had made important progress. Its 108 K1 classrooms were serving just over two thousand children. With strong curricula, supported by regular PD and reflective coaching, both teaching and learning in K1 classrooms were becoming rich and compelling experiences. Kindergarten teachers were reporting that they could tell the difference between children who had had the K1 experience and those who had not. K1 graduates were showing outcomes in number sense and mathematical reasoning that exceeded even those that *Building Blocks* authors Doug Clements and Julie Sarama found when they piloted their curriculum in Buffalo.[1] They were also excelling in vocabulary, letter recognition, and preliteracy and on measures of executive function, including working memory, deliberate attention shifting, and impulse control.[2]

But the DEC faced the inevitable challenges of competing school and departmental agendas and school reform efforts and state-mandated policies that might coincide or clash with its scientifically grounded view of high-quality early education. Developmentally appropriate practice, as defined by NAEYC and reflected in the ten program standards of its accreditation system, would need to become the norm in both K1 and K2 classrooms. And that would require administrative support.

Principals would need to understand young children's learning needs, protect them and their teachers from inappropriate and time-consuming assessments, and make sure that the physical environment, equipment, and learning materials were not only safe and appropriate for young children but also appropriately engaging. Teachers would need to treat children as curious, active learners, and engage both their empathy and their higher-level thinking (core principle 2).[3]

Working with Margaret Angell, a recent graduate of Harvard's Kennedy School of Government Masters in Public Administration program whose residency with the Boston Public Schools was supported by the Broad Foundation, the department crafted a comprehensive strategic plan. To ensure all children the high-quality early education experience it envisioned, the DEC would need to focus work on five drivers: improved classroom quality, improved school environments, supports for family engagement, enhanced BPS capacity, and program evaluation and the use of data to shape decisions. Figure 4.1 outlines the strategic plan.

Improving Classroom Instruction and School Environments

A closer look at the strategies behind just two of the drivers, "Improve School Instruction" and "Improve School Environment," reveals the complexity of the undertaking.

Improving school instruction, for example, would require more than excellent curricula. Teachers would need additional supports, including assessment tools and procedures that would give them relevant information in real time; these would enable them to track each child's learning and provide appropriate supports and challenges. These assessments would have to fit naturally into

FIGURE 4.1 DEC strategic plan

OUR MISSION: To ensure that principals, teachers, paraprofessionals, and school support staff have the knowledge, skills, and resources they need to provide a high-quality early education experience for all students. Our expectation is that all children will become internally driven and self-motivated learners and will be able to read, write, and communicate effectively by third grade.

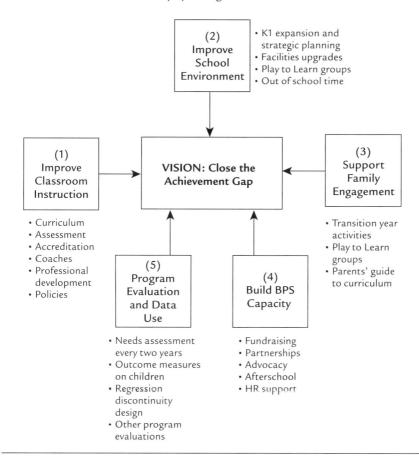

daily activities, not take the teacher's time and focus away from teaching and learning. To use the curriculum and assessments appropriately, teachers would need PD experiences, which could be offered in group settings, and personal coaching as they applied and adapted what they had learned.[4] Departmental policies on group size, child–adult ratios, staff assignment and qualifications, curriculum, and PD would need to support high-quality, developmentally-appropriate teaching in learning environments that would meet NAEYC's professional standards. And school-based policies on scheduling, use of space, and family and community engagement would have to support those same ends.

Initially, the team had thought that curriculum would be the key. Mandated PD would introduce it; coaches would provide follow-up support as teachers learned it and mastered its implicit pedagogy. In the process, teachers would begin to use authentic, embedded assessments that would enable them to meet children where they were and engage them in compelling learning experiences that would provide the right level of challenge. The play-based, comprehensive, and language-rich curricula would offer children connected, high-quality learning experiences that supported all areas of their development.

The DEC soon realized that curriculum-related PD and coaching would not be enough. Rather than using the curriculum as the primary path to excellent teaching, it first needed to build understanding of how young children learn, and of the developmentally appropriate practices that support that learning, not just among the teachers, but also among the parents, paraprofessionals, and school administrators.

The results emerging from the NAEYC accreditation pilot were encouraging. The 2010 needs assessments conducted by Nancy Marshall and her team at the Wellesley Centers for Women would show a strong association between schools that had achieved or were seeking NAEYC accreditation and the quality of their early childhood classrooms.[5] As the accreditation data emerged, it influenced the DEC's decisions and direction.[6]

Agreeing that NAEYC accreditation would be a step toward its larger vision, the DEC team wrote into their strategic plan the goal that all BPS programs would earn and maintain accreditation. The department began by seeking grants for the schools in Boston's "Circle of Promise" (Roxbury, North Dorchester, and high-need areas of the South End and Jamaica Plain) and in the diverse but geographically isolated neighborhood of East Boston.[7] It hoped to accredit all BPS schools with early learning programs within ten years. With only four of sixty-eight schools accredited and eleven in process when the 2008–2009 school year began, it was an ambitious plan, and an unusual step for a school system.[8]

Several members of the DEC were currently involved in coaching for NAEYC accreditation, and some had gone through the process themselves, as teachers, parents, or school leaders. They knew that coaching could be both supportive and transformative, and that coaching in a meaningful way is a time-intensive process that requires a commitment of financial resources. The DEC budgeted $75,000 per school ($6,000 per classroom per year), extending, on average, over a three-year period. Jason Sachs convinced the BPS Budget Department to set aside funds for the purchase of some required classroom materials. Convinced by the accreditation pilot data and the results they had seen in the statewide Community Partnerships for Children sites, the Barr Foundation committed $2 million to the effort.

Earning NAEYC accreditation is a rigorous process that can take several years to complete. It involves not only teachers and principals or center directors, but teaching assistants, other staff, and families. There are ten standards: Relationships, Curriculum, Teaching, Assessment of Child Progress, Health, Teachers, Families, Community Relationships, Physical Environment, and Leadership and Management. Each includes several criteria—forty-one in all. These are observable indicators that the standard is consistently met. NAEYC accreditation correlates with widely used measures of program quality and, along with those measures, correlates with improved outcomes for children.[9] Many states have adopted it as the gold standard in their Quality Rating Improvement Systems.

Like the DEC's core principles, the NAEYC standards define quality as beginning with warm relationships among all children and adults that support each child's sense of self-worth, belonging, and ability to contribute to the community. It is shaped and sustained by a curriculum that supports children's social, emotional, physical, cognitive, and language development and reflects the school's philosophy. Curriculum goals are realized through teaching that is developmentally, culturally, and linguistically appropriate for the children in the group. Systematic assessment informs teaching, decisions regarding individual children, and program improvement. It includes both formal and informal assessments that are linguistically and culturally appropriate and family involvement in interpreting results and thinking through implications. Health is critical; it includes nutrition and hygiene as well as prevention of and response to injuries and illness for children and adults.

In programs that meet NAEYC's quality standards, teachers have specific preparation in early childhood, usually at least a Child Development Associate (CDA) credential or BA degree. They also receive ongoing in-service training. Families are seen as important partners, and encouraged to participate in all aspects of the program. To achieve its goals, the program uses community resources and maintains relationships with community agencies and organizations that support children and their families. The physical environment is safe and well maintained and facilitates development and learning. Finally, strong leadership and management support high-quality experiences for children, families, and staff. The director or principal is educated in early childhood development. Policies on group size, child/adult ratios, discipline, health and safety procedures, and curriculum support program goals and are shared with families.

To earn NAEYC accreditation, a school first undertakes a self-study process to determine whether to pursue it. The process brings in stakeholders to assess the alignment of NAEYC's performance standards with their own goals and, if they decide to go forward, to create a plan and timeline. The school then submits an application to NAEYC and begins a self-study process to identify program standards and criteria in which it is strong and areas where it needs to improve.

The school then creates an application portfolio in preparation for classroom visits. The director or principal must be involved, and families must be included. The process prompts school leaders to reflect, examining school climate, interactions with and between teachers, policies related to family engagement, even the safety of the playground and the possibilities it offers for supporting active and imaginative play, social-emotional development, and academic learning. It requires them to integrate the perspectives of teachers, families, and children as the school collects relevant evidence through program and classroom portfolios, family and teaching staff surveys, and photographs or other documentation of observable criteria.

When the school can document that it meets at least 80 percent of the standards, along with licensing and staff educational qualification requirements, it submits its candidacy application to NAEYC and arranges a site visit. Using the self-study documentation as a guide, the visitor collects confirming data to assess whether the criteria have been met. A board of experts scores the results and, if the program meets the standards, awards accreditation.

Accreditation is meant to spark an ongoing process of self-reflection and continuous improvement for all involved. Programs submit annual reports, and can renew their accreditation every five years.

For the DEC, NAEYC accreditation would continue to be an entry point into schools and classrooms, including K2 classrooms and both substantially separate and inclusion classrooms for children with special rights. It also opened one path for collaborating with principals to improve school environments, engage families, and provide ongoing supports for developmentally appropriate instructional practices. For those who lacked early childhood backgrounds, it offered an opportunity to showcase high-quality classrooms and explain how well-supported early educators build relationships, engage children, ask thought-provoking questions, and support all areas of child development through intentional and productive play-based learning.

Recognizing that successful early education programs require more—and more varied—equipment and materials than principals might be used to seeing for higher grades, the DEC team created a detailed budget for a NAEYC-ready classroom. They worked with the BPS Budget Office to assure that principals who chose to pursue NAEYC accreditation could access the needed start-up funds. They also developed lists of consumable materials that principals would need to replace from their own budgets in subsequent years.

To supplement their own work with principals, the DEC contracted with the CAYL Institute in Cambridge to offer fellowships to principals who were willing to make the commitment.[10] The principals attended a summer "boot camp" in early childhood education and leadership run by the institute's director, Valora Washington, a nationally respected early childhood leader and author who, like Jason Sachs, had served on NAEYC's governing board. During the summer, the principals examined play-based learning, developmentally appropriate teaching and assessment, preK–3 curriculum alignment, family and community engagement, and related topics. They received coaching during the following year as they brought the lessons to their schools and worked to align their leadership with NAEYC accreditation requirements. Principals who had participated in the fellowships became a driving force for the kinds of changes that the DEC was trying to foster. With informed leadership and teacher coaching, the DEC felt confident that schools would be able to achieve and maintain the accreditation standards and continue to embody the DEC's core principles.

Coaching for Accreditation: A Portrait of Practice

Like all meaningful coaching (and all powerful learning), the DEC's coaching for accreditation begins with relationship building.[11] Teachers and others involved in the process need to see the coach as an ally and sounding board, not as an intruder with an agenda or a monitor who grades their performance. Coaches take the time to explain the process to principals and families and help them understand the roles they can play. Principals may also be connected with PD opportunities. But most of the work involves one-to-one collaboration with teachers.

Nicole St. Victor, a program director at the DEC, spends most of her time coaching for NAEYC accreditation. Born in Haiti, where she began her early childhood career, St. Victor completed a law degree in France, raised a family, and completed her master's degree in early childhood education at Wheelock College. She began as a volunteer at the Haitian Multiservice Center in Boston, and became the director of its early education programs. As director, St. Victor shepherded the school through the NAEYC accreditation process, enabling it to qualify as a Massachusetts Department of Education Community Partnerships for Children (CPC) site. She collaborated with Jason Sachs, Karen Silver, and other CPC members to improve the quality of Boston's early education programs. St. Victor joined the DEC in 2008, working first on OWL and Building Blocks coaching and then joining Silver, Michelle High-McKinnon, and Marina Boni to offer coaching to BPS schools seeking NAEYC accreditation.

St. Victor begins each coaching cycle by engaging teachers in a reflective conference session to identify areas of strength and areas where improvement is needed. Her goal is to create a space for teachers to become mindful of their practices and be conscious of their own learning needs. Achievable and consensual goals are set at the end of each feedback session. Guided by the teachers' goals, St. Victor plans her observation schedule. She often observes a routine or lesson selected by a teacher, taking notes as she completes their agreed-upon checklist.

Teachers choose the times for reflective discussion in advance. St. Victor tries to schedule them to accommodate each teacher's preferences: while children are resting or working with specialists, over lunch, or during planning time. St. Victor begins the sessions by asking the teacher to talk about her rationale or intent: "What were you working on with the child or group? What did you hope they would learn?" "Why did you choose that particular activity, approach, or strategy?"

She then shares what she sees as working well, and asks the teacher to elaborate: "What did you think about how Circle Time went?" "Tell me a little more about the learning goals of the art activity." "How do you think your questions changed the child's thinking or direction?"

In these discussions, St. Victor encourages the teacher's questions. She repeatedly challenges the teacher to look at his practice or choice through the child's eyes. "How do you think the child felt?" "How did your teaching strategy sustain the child's interest and engagement? "At the end of each feedback session, St. Victor and the teacher set their next goal together.

As an example, St. Victor recalls working with a teacher on the first set of NAEYC standards, which focuses on warm relationships among adults and children. The teacher saw her role as an academic instructor; she wasn't sure that building relationships with children should be a priority, and wondered why NAEYC considered it so important. The teacher, who was quite tall, often stood as she talked to seated children. St. Victor began with a brief conversation about why eye contact matters. "What do you think a child sees when he looks at you?" she asked. She meant the question literally. The teacher soon realized that the children were looking at her waist rather than her face. She was looming over them, a big and perhaps even scary presence, making it difficult to connect with children in a way that encouraged their engagement. "Is that why NAEYC expects us to sit?" she asked.

"Let's try an experiment," St. Victor suggested. "Sit down at some times when you would usually stand. Then at our next session we can talk about what you notice, and whether it feels any different." Two weeks later, the teacher had something to share. "When I sit with you, I can hear your voice better. I can see your face. I can be more responsive to the children, and they can be more responsive to me."

After several weeks, St. Victor noticed a dramatic change. The teacher was sitting on a cushion for Circle Time, with the children gathered around her. She was even lying on the floor to read or play with children, and they were all moving a lot more: dancing, gesturing, acting things out. The teacher was pleased with the changes. "This is way better," she said. "There is so much more joy."

With K2 teachers, St. Victor often faces an additional challenge. Many of them have early childhood backgrounds and perspectives but report a "disconnect" between what they believe is good for children and what happens in school. Even in Boston, the pressure to get every student to achieve the district's benchmarks in reading, writing, and math is already strong in kindergarten. Teachers fear that they will be evaluated on whether or not children hit those benchmarks, with little consideration for children's backgrounds, prior experiences, or preferred modes of learning and of demonstrating their knowledge.

St. Victor helps K2 teachers to see that the developmentally appropriate practices they espouse, which are embedded in the NAEYC criteria, are not opposed to skills-focused learning but can effectively facilitate it. Keeping the focus on what matters to children, teachers can set up and seize opportunities to support skills during free play, as Jodi Doyle did when she helped her four- and five-year-olds write labels for their paint colors and make replicas of money.

Teachers can present brief lessons with enthusiasm and help children see how they can apply what they are learning to projects and activities they choose. A math lesson that focuses on counting groups greater than five, for example, might be followed by opportunities to make drawings based on family visits to the supermarket or to "shop" in the dramatic play area "bodega" or "farmer's market." A storybook-related vocabulary lesson can help children delight in the power of words as they make word collections and dictionaries for their classmates to consult or use their new words to make a story that they can share with their family.[12] As teachers tap children's passions and creativity—and their own—learning becomes richer and more memorable.

St. Victor describes receiving a thank-you note from a kindergarten teacher who she had been working with for two years:

We were revisiting a sub-area of NAEYC's teaching standard, Using Instruction to Deepen Children's Understanding and Build Their Skills and Knowledge.[13] We had been talking about conceptual development, how children not only learn basic ideas but learn to apply them more broadly and grasp them at deeper levels. We had been discussing how each child comes with a history and knowledge base, and how differences in background experiences shaped the insights of children in her class. The teacher noted that imposing knowledge without consideration of where children were coming from and what they wanted to learn seemed to be less effective than first drawing out their ideas. In her note, she thanked me for helping her build new routines into her practice. Now she asks: "What do you think?" "Does anyone else have an idea?" She really listens to children as she writes down their ideas. She shared an example from the Animals and Habitats unit. Early in the unit, she asked children what animals they had seen in their neighborhoods and what they had observed about their habitats. She was then able to engage children in close observation, taking "field notes" (including words and drawings), research (in the classroom library and on Google images), and construction of homes and habitats for real and pretend animals.

The teacher's insights reveal her ownership and integration of several of the DEC's core principles.[14] She builds relationships with her students, and sees them as active learners capable of deep thought, focused observation, and original ideas. She recognizes that each one brings different experiences, knowledge, and interests, and takes the time to assess these so that she can align future learning opportunities with what the children already bring. For that teacher, as for many of those who St. Victor has coached, the curriculum and outcome goals may not have changed—but learning and teaching feel freer, more joyful, and more authentic because they are driven by what matters to children.

Occasionally, St. Victor encounters teachers or principals who strongly disagree with the NAEYC approach. In these cases, coaching is premature or inappropriate. More often, though, she finds teachers who take curriculum mandates too literally. They follow activities to the letter, or teach to the test. St. Victor tries to help them to step back—to ask themselves what really matters to children, try out new perspectives and strategies, and articulate their rationale for a particular activity, classroom arrangement, or instructional approach.

Over the years, St. Victor and her fellow coaches have found that coaching for good early childhood practice can be more difficult than coaching for curriculum implementation, but good early childhood practice is fundamental to implementing the curriculum as intended. The PD courses and seminars that the DEC offers emphasize good practice—getting teachers to try new techniques, materials, and approaches, and let the children's responses guide their next steps. As teachers seek to engage each child's interests and foster her strengths, they reflect with colleagues, specialists, a supportive principal, and parents. A schoolwide push for NAEYC accreditation, like a monthly visit from a coach or work with an outside partner such as Melissa Rivard from the Making Learning Visible project, affirms and enhances already excellent practice. For teachers who are truly resistant, a transfer out of the early grades or out of BPS entirely may be the best course. But most teachers can grow through every-other-week coaching sessions with clear, focused, and co-constructed agendas.

Building Capacity, Supporting Family Engagement, and Evaluating Programs

As Nicole St. Victor's examples illustrate and subsequent events would confirm, building NAEYC accreditation into the DEC's strategic plan turned out to be a powerful decision. The obvious stumbling blocks—inappropriate facilities and lack of essential equipment and materials—could often be overcome fairly quickly. The DEC had convinced BPS to budget for these expenses.

Other issues, though, required strong buy-in from teachers, assistant teachers, principals, and families, as well as administrative support from departments whose missions overlapped with the DEC's, including Special Education, Math, English Language Arts, Science, and Social Studies. For some teachers, especially those teaching kindergarten, meeting the NAEYC standards required different approaches to room arrangement, scheduling, student work, and teaching roles than they were currently using. The shift was especially challenging—and transformative—for teachers whose training and expertise had focused on older children.

As the DEC added new classrooms, rolled out the K1 curricula, educated and supported principals, encouraged schools to work toward NAEYC accreditation, brought in experts and partners to offer inspirational and aligned professional development, and offered intensive and supportive coaching, it was also reaching out to families. It partnered with organizations such as the Boston Children's Museum and Boston Public Library and joined initiatives such as Countdown to Kindergarten and Thrive in Five.

Within these partnerships, the DEC offered Play to Learn groups, where parents could bring their toddlers and three-year-olds for a fun-filled session of language and social-emotional skill-building activities. They helped families to navigate the K1/K2 choice, application, and enrollment process and, together with their partners, offered school-year and summer activities and resources that could help families prepare their children for the transition into K1 or K2.

The DEC continued to collect data to assess its own performance. By 2010, it had strong evidence that it was on course. The Wellesley research team had found, for example, that whereas only 42 percent of K1 classrooms had met the "Good" benchmark for Language and Reasoning supports on the Early Childhood Environmental Rating Scale (ECERS-R) in 2006, 60 percent did in 2008 and 77 percent did in 2010—even as more classrooms were steadily added. Although lags persisted in other areas, 85 percent of classrooms were now hitting the relatively demanding CLASS benchmark for Social and Emotional Supports—indicating positive relationships between children and adults that created a strong base for learning.[15]

The studies of child outcomes, conducted in partnership with Christina Weiland at Harvard, were also encouraging. Children were exceeding national norms in language, math, preliteracy, and critical executive function skills. Weiland's analysis also suggested that accreditation was making a difference. K1 classrooms seeking accreditation showed higher levels of observed quality on all subscales of the ECERS-R, and scored more than a point higher (on a seven-point scale) than classrooms that had not yet gone that route. As expected, seeking accreditation mattered even more for the kindergarten classrooms.

Looking at children's fall-to-spring vocabulary scores, Weiland found significantly greater gains for children in classrooms that were accredited or seeking accreditation. The relationship held when controlling for children's initial fall scores and when controlling for demographic factors, including race/ethnicity, eligibility for free or reduced-price lunch, home language, and whether or not the child had identified special needs. Even when controlling for observed classroom quality on the ECERS-R, children whose teachers were involved in an accreditation-seeking process were averaging higher vocabulary scores![16]

In an article published in NAEYC's *Young Children* journal, Jason Sachs and Christina Weiland speculated on the reasons for these results. It was possible that child outcomes had been affected by differences between schools that had sought accreditation and those that hadn't. They had found no differences in school size, percent of early childhood teachers with master's degrees, provision of before- and after-school care, third-grade test scores, or whether or not the principal had participated in the CAYL fellowship program, but couldn't rule out other factors. They speculated that it was the DEC's direct work with teachers that made the meaningful difference—enhancing both the quantity and quality of teacher-child conversation and thus building children's vocabularies, concept and content knowledge, and communication and literacy skills:

> Through coaching and by furnishing supplies and materials, the staff have helped teachers create more choice time for children and a higher likelihood that children will go deeper in their exploration of center activities. In turn, this promotes more in-depth and higher quality discussions between children and their teachers.[17]

A large body of research supports this contention. When most of the school day is spent in child-chosen learning-center-based activities, teacher-child conversation is more frequent, and likely to be both richer and more extended.[18] Children also have more opportunities to learn and practice new vocabulary in conversations with each other.[19] A ten-nation study by HighScope found that four-year-olds in such classrooms made greater gains in both language and cognitive development over the next three years than did those who mostly experienced large group instruction; that having more materials to explore predicted gains in cognitive development; and that in child-centered classrooms, children's language grew more when teachers talked more, although it grew more when teachers talked less in classrooms where teachers were doing most of the talking.[20] And a longitudinal study of Head Start students in Boston found that rich, extended conversations that went beyond the here and now (e.g., telling stories about past events, planning, speculating, predicting, imagining, and book-related conversation) were key to both vocabulary and literacy and that vocabulary at kindergarten entry strongly predicted tenth-grade reading comprehension.[21]

As they continued to gather data and discuss its implications, the DEC team realized that their whole was greater than the sum of its parts. OWL, *Building Blocks*, NAEYC accreditation and the PD and coaching that came with them were providing tools, inspiration, and opportunities for excellent teaching and engaged, effective learning. Teachers were picking up the tools and seizing the opportunities. And they were becoming adept at a critical component: observing their students at work and play, reflecting on their observations, and adjusting their planning, environment, and moment-to moment interactions to make sure that each child remained fully engaged in the demanding task of learning.[22]

The combined efforts of the DEC and its school-based and family partners were producing impressive gains in K1 classroom and teaching quality and in child outcomes, just as the DEC's logic model predicted. But, although accreditation and principal fellowships were making a difference in some kindergartens, what DEC coaches were seeing in most of the kindergarten classrooms they visited was no match for their K1 programs. The DEC knew that it was time for a new kindergarten (K2) curriculum—one that would meet both BPS and NAEYC standards, align with the K1 curriculum, and reflect the DEC's vision of children as citizens of their communities.

The team looked first for an existing, evidence-based program, and settled on Tools of the Mind. Like OWL, Tools of the Mind puts children at the center, supporting their growing capacities to manage their own behavior, pursue their own learning projects, and consider others' perspectives as they work and play together. Drawing on Lev Vygotsky's theories of social learning, co-construction of knowledge, scaffolding, and the zone of proximal development, Tools of the Mind is a language-rich program with strong outcomes in cognitive, social-emotional, and executive function skills.[23] Like OWL, it explores themes in depth and brings in a range of fiction and nonfiction books. The program is especially strong in its reliance on social pretend play and in its supports for children to play at a mature level—with planning, roles, props, dialog, and scenarios—and extended time to plan, play out, and elaborate on their stories.

After careful study, the DEC members concluded that, despite its strengths, Tools of the Mind would not work for their K2 programs. They needed a stand-alone, full-day curriculum, plus PD and coaching resources like those they had brought to the K1 curriculum rollouts. The DEC issued an RFP to developers, and selected Judith Schickedanz to create a follow-up to OWL. But OWL was now a leading preschool curriculum, owned and disseminated by Pearson, a major education publisher. Schickedanz would need Pearson's permission to create a similar program. Finding a kindergarten curriculum that aligned with what was working in K1 was proving to be a longer and more challenging process than the DEC had anticipated.

Trouble on the Horizon

As negotiations with Pearson were proceeding, a storm was brewing. BPS superintendent Carol Johnson had been a strong supporter of the DEC's efforts, but, like most urban superintendents, was under increasing pressure to demonstrate Adequate Yearly Progress in Boston's schools and to close achievement gaps. Her English language arts department had been searching for a new K–6 literacy curriculum. They chose Scott Foresman's *Reading Street*, a new program designed to align with the Common Core.[24] Its aim was to build on the most recent scientific research on learning to read and write. It sought to use technology innovatively and effectively to engage students, build content knowledge and vocabulary along with foundational decoding skills, and address the needs of different learners, including those learning English.[25]

But Sachs was not happy when he examined *Reading Street*'s kindergarten materials. Too many of the lessons called for lower levels of thinking and more superficial exploration of subject matter than what BPS students were already doing as four-year-olds. One particularly disheartening example was an activity sheet designed to teach the letter *V* and its associated sound. Children were given a worksheet with a picture of a vase containing two flower stems and asked to draw in the flowers. To Sachs, it seemed divorced from children's interests and play activity and offered little opportunity for creativity, investigation, problem solving, synthesizing of prior knowledge, or using reading and writing for one's own purposes. The activity offered no help for children who did not yet know which sound *V* indicates in English, or for those whose home language might not include the *v* sound or associate it with the letter *V*.

Sachs pushed back, hoping to convince the administration to choose a different course—at least for kindergarten. The DEC's K1 results in vocabulary, letter recognition, and executive function development were impressive, but BPS didn't collect data on these variables in higher grades. However, the school system did use the Dynamic Indicators of Basic Early Literacy Skills (DIBELS), beginning in the fall of the kindergarten year, to track children's progress in learning to read. Although the test focused on code-breaking skills, and paid less attention to the background knowledge, rich vocabulary, and higher-order thinking that figured more centrally in OWL and *Building Blocks*, K1 students averaged strong fall-to-spring gains on the Phonological Awareness Literacy Screening (PALS) and, at kindergarten entry, scored significantly higher on the DIBELS than BPS students who had not had the K1 experience.

Despite continued K1 gains on preliteracy measures, results from earlier classes suggested that the score gap between children who had attended K1 and those who hadn't would narrow as children moved through kindergarten and first grade. The DEC team and their outside partners were convinced that the problem was one of misalignment, not fadeout or starting too late to achieve lasting gains. They were measuring outcomes like vocabulary, number sense, and executive function that impact performance and well-being well beyond third grade. And if students encountered curricula in the early grades that were less demanding than what they had already mastered in K1, their learning of both basic literacy skills and more fundamental concepts and capacities could be slowed while they waited for their classmates to catch up. The team agreed that their data argued for a literacy program that could give children entering Boston's public schools in kindergarten the same boost that their K1 students were getting, and that could consolidate and build on those gains as children mastered reading basics and became fluent and critical readers.[26]

In addition, the push for NAEYC accreditation had been improving instruction in more and more kindergarten classrooms, and many kindergarten teachers had expressed interest in trying a curriculum that was similar to what they were seeing in the K1 classrooms next door. Judith Schickedanz had finally gotten her publisher and its legal department to recognize that her noncompete agreement applied only to prekindergarten programs, not to those for kindergarteners or older students. The DEC team was unanimous: it was time to focus on the K2 curriculum.

When Superintendent Johnson called him into her office to discuss the new reading program, Sachs had his arguments and supporting data ready. He explained why he felt the *Reading Street* curriculum was weak and the selection process flawed. Johnson listened, but stood firm. It was important, she argued, for the schools to have a cohesive approach to literacy that carried through the elementary grades. She told Sachs that he would be on her team supporting the district adoption of *Reading Street*. Although it was a severe blow to the DEC's efforts, he agreed to support the rollout.

The storm-tossed DEC decided to change direction. It put its dream for a kindergarten curriculum on hold and turned its attention elsewhere. NAEYC accreditation would become top priority. Rather than rolling out a new K2 curriculum and then helping classrooms they were working with meet accreditation standards, the DEC would focus its energies on NAEYC accreditation and use it as a path toward readiness to embrace a new curriculum and instructional approach in K2. The push for accreditation would also give the DEC entry into more early childhood special education classrooms.

The DEC would continue its focus on K1, working to make those classrooms more consistently excellent, more universally available, and more fully integrated into the elementary schools that hosted them and where the children would most likely be continuing their educations. At the same time, they would reach out to the community, strengthening their engagement with families, and families' engagement in preparing their children for school and supporting their ongoing learning. They would also look for ways to help strengthen community-based early education programs for four-year-olds, while continuing to open more K1 classrooms.

In chapter 5, our second classroom visit shows how much consistent excellence matters for children, especially for those who may be experiencing adversities. The curriculum—*Focus on K1*—maintains key elements of the integrated OWL/*Building Blocks* curriculum that the DEC had been mandating, but was recreated to align with the DEC's K2 vision.

Chapter Five

A House for a Dragon
A Visit with a K1 Child

with David Ramsey and Abby Morales

The following portrait is a composite of incidents that occurred in several of Boston's K1 classrooms, constructed by DEC program directors David Ramsey and Abby Morales. Although Jacoby, the child at the center, is a composite, along with his teacher and classmates, his story is based on true events. The incidents in this visit were intentionally selected and integrated to provide as authentic a view as possible of the current Focus on K1 *curriculum in action, while protecting the children's privacy.*

It's October, and the students in Ms. Gaynor's K1 classroom are deeply engrossed in the Family unit of the newly revised Focus on K1 *curriculum. If you watch and listen closely, you'll notice how smoothly math, literacy, rich language, factual information, art, collaborative problem solving, and physical activity integrate into children's imaginative play and storytelling as they move through a typical morning. You may also notice the children's excitement as they pull incidents and themes from the books they are reading and from recent learning experiences to weave into their play.*

Jacoby bursts through the door of his classroom with a grin on his face. "Ms. Gaynor! Can I do some more work on my cave today?"

"Yes, Jacoby, of course you can. Put your things away and come have some breakfast, and we'll get started in a few minutes."

Jacoby puts his backpack and his jacket in his cubby, washes his hands, and hurries to join his friends at the breakfast table. As he gulps down his milk and cereal, he leans over to his best friend Micah and whispers conspiratorially, "Micah, you gotta help me. I was thinking 'bout the biggest cave we can make. We gotta do it together. I'm gonna make the walls and stuff, and you can do the animals."

Jacoby has been thinking about caves and the animals that live in them almost nonstop for the past several days. Ms. Gaynor explains:

> Last week, we read a story called *The Seven Chinese Sisters*.[1] In the story, the youngest sister is kidnapped by a dragon that lives in a cave. As I was reading the story for the very first time to the children, I made sure to use a lot of enthusiasm and drama—I deliberately used different voices for the characters, and I used a lot of emotion to keep the children engaged and on the edge of their seats. I could tell they were excited because I didn't have to stop to redirect anybody while I was reading. You should have seen Jacoby! He was completely entranced."

Over the course of the week, Ms. Gaynor read *The Seven Chinese Sisters* three more times, as outlined in the curriculum, each time with a different strategy and purpose, but always emphasizing children's comprehension of the story as well as their understanding of its sophisticated vocabulary. She notes:

> When we read the story the last time, Jacoby couldn't wait. He was practically hopping off the floor, because he knew we were going to act the story out, like we always do in our fourth story read. He was the first one to raise his hand, because he wanted to be the dragon. By this time, he knew the story inside and out. In our second read, he remembered the plot sequence and understood why the characters acted as they did. When we read the story a third time, he was filling in bits of dialogue and chiming in, as is the goal of the third read. I've never seen him so alive as when he acted

out the dragon! He was funny and a little bit scary, and the other children loved his performance. He felt really proud of himself.

Jacoby's had a pretty rough time this year—he's actually living in a shelter right now. He's missed a lot of days because his mom has a hard time getting him here. Being in a shelter is an improvement from when he was living in a car with his mom and brothers for a few weeks in the summer. But the shelter is on the other side of the city, so his mom has to take him and his brothers on a bus, then the subway, and then two other buses in order to get him to school every day. A lot of the time it's too much for her to deal with, and he ends up staying at home, or going to his auntie's house instead of coming to school."

Listening to this teacher, you may have a new appreciation for time—a scarce commodity in too many settings. Ms. Gaynor has taken the time to get to know Jacoby well and to connect with his family. Even though Jacoby is often absent from school, he and Ms. Gaynor have built a solid, trusting relationship. She understands his current situation and appreciates his family's strengths and struggles. Her relationship with Jacoby helps her to see his strengths, capitalize on his interests, and offer him both powerful learning experiences and gentle guidance.[2]

You may have noticed, too, how Ms. Gaynor structures Jacoby's time, gently reminding him of morning routines, allowing him to continue activities and explorations over several days or weeks, and helping him recall past experiences and relate them to the present.[3]

Notice how the protocols and routines that the DEC has built into the flexible Focus on K1 *curriculum support Ms. Gaynor as she helps Jacoby and his classmates to incorporate research and new vocabulary into their play, appreciate each other's work, and collaborate on thinking through problems.*

"Ms. Gaynor, I finished my breakfast! I'm gonna go in the library. I want to see that book you got with the animals in the caves again. I gotta do more research so I can build my cave better at Centers."

After about ten minutes, Ms. Gaynor signals Clean Up. Jacoby places his book on the library shelf and joins his friends gathered on the carpet for Introduction to Centers. She starts:

Good morning, children. Today we're going to continue our centers from yesterday. Remember, we are working on caves inspired by *The Seven Chinese Sisters* yesterday. Here is a photograph of a cave that Jacoby and Micah built in Blocks. They researched caves in the library first, then they took what they learned about caves to construct their own in Blocks. You can see that they were using wooden unit blocks and different kinds of animals. Here's a drawing that Isabel made yesterday of a different kind of cave. She labeled her cave with words, like "dark," and "scary." You can also play in the water table, or you can paint at the easel, or you can play one of our math games.

The children disperse to different areas of the classroom, and Jacoby goes back to the library. His friend Micah follows him, saying, "Hey come on, we have to make our cave, we have to go in Blocks to make it bigger and bigger!"

Jacoby responds, "I'm coming! But I need this book. It's got a nice cave—I think it's better, and there's a good illustration that we need to look at. I got this one, you get the *Chinese Sisters* so we can see the dragon cave. Come on, let's go!"

The two boys take their books to the Block Center, where they see that Ms. Gaynor has posted the photograph of their cave from the previous day, along with photographs of caves that other children made. In addition, there are several photographs of real caves from both the Boston area and from other parts of the world.

When Ms. Gaynor sees that Jacoby and Micah are in Blocks, she comes to join them. She kneels down nearby and listens for several minutes as they begin constructing their cave. When they seem to be at a stopping point, she asks them how they knew how to build their cave.

"How do you know how to construct your cave? Did you make a plan?"

"We're looking here, we got research in these books, it shows us the right way to do it," Jacoby answers.

Ms. Gaynor is proud of the boys, and her face and voice show it. She glances at a piece of paper in a plastic sleeve that was posted on the wall in Blocks before continuing.

"I see that you and Micah are collaborating to create this habitat. What kind of creature will take shelter in this cave? In *Seven Chinese Sisters*, the dragon took shelter in the cave."

Center Language Support Sheets, like the one Ms. Gaynor referred to, are in all the centers. Teachers use them as reminders, to make sure they're having strong, intentional conversations with the children while they're playing. Ms. Gaynor explains:

> *We want them to really practice and learn vocabulary, so when I asked Jacoby about his cave, I looked at the sheet and decided to use the word "habitat," as well as the words "shelter" and "plan." I want Jacoby and Micah to hear those words repeated so they can practice them, too. Did you notice how Jacoby was talking about research when he came in this morning? That's one of the words that's on the Center Language Support Sheet in Library and Listening, and I use that word a lot with the children when they're over there.*

The boys continue their effort to make a perfect habitat for a dragon. "We need to make this cave sturdy! It's gotta be cozy and dry when the weather is cloudy," Micah says as he returns to Blocks from a quick trip to the art studio. He is holding several cotton balls and some pieces of felt. "These are for the bed. It's the dragon's bed. He wants us to make it comfy so he can get cozy and snuggle in there."

As Jacoby continues using unit blocks to construct the cave, Micah works on placing his materials inside. After a few minutes, Jacoby announces, "We did it! It's perfect!"

Micah looks at the cave and quickly realizes that something is missing. "Yeah! We did it! But we don't got a dragon! We only got horses and sheep and animals for the farm. We need a dragon like this one!" He opens *The Seven Chinese Sisters* and turns to the page with the dragon.

"Since we don't have a dragon in our classroom, what could you do if you need one?" Ms. Gaynor asks, as she hears their conversation.

"Ummm . . . I've got one at home. It's in our room. But we need one now. Come on, Micah! We gotta make a dragon!" Jacoby takes Micah's hand, then grabs *The Seven Chinese Sisters* as the boys walk to the art studio.

Jacoby and Micah spend the next twenty minutes in the art studio using a variety of materials and tools to create a dragon for their cave. Referring to the picture in the book, each boy draws a dragon with markers on a piece of paper, concentrating quietly for several minutes. Suddenly, Micah jumps up and retrieves some white glue from a nearby shelf. He races over to a shelf that holds several trays of fabric and other recycled materials, and returns with a tray of shiny red plastic circles.

"I'm gonna put these on the dragon. See, he's got these ones on him." Micah says, as he points to the illustration in the book.

"The dragon in the illustration has red scales, and they're curved like the pieces you are using, aren't they, Micah?" says Ms. Gaynor, who has come over to the art studio to observe the boys' progress.

As Jacoby and Micah continue their work in the art studio, Ms. Gaynor and her paraprofessional partner move through the classroom, sitting with children in the different centers as they play and work. In each center, the teachers make sure to look at the Center Language Supports posted on the walls as they converse with the children, and they also make references in their conversations to both *The Seven Chinese Sisters* and other books that have been read previously in the curriculum.

After about ten minutes, Ms. Gaynor hears Jacoby's raised voice coming from the art studio: "I can't! I don't know these letters! Micah! You gotta do it for me!"

She walks over and asks Jacoby why he appears to be upset.

"I'm trying to make the name for the dragon. He's got to have his name. But I was doing the letters and it's not the right way. Look!" Jacoby pointed to a piece of paper where he has drawn several lines.

"Sometimes if we need help doing something, we can collaborate with a friend and they can help us." Ms. Gaynor says gently.

"I know!" said Jacoby. "But I told Micah to do it, and he doesn't wanna. He's not helping me! "

"There might be somebody else who could help instead." Ms. Gaynor replies. "Can you think of another friend who could help you write the letters for the dragon's name? This morning during Introduction to Centers, I showed you and your friends a drawing that Isabel made. She wrote 'dark' and 'scary' on her picture. 'Dark' has the same sound like 'dragon' . . . *d* . . . *d*. 'Dark' and 'dragon' both start with a *d* sound. Maybe Isabel could help you make the *d* for 'dragon'."

"I'm gonna ask her to do it for me!" Jacoby says determinedly. He scans the classroom until he sees Isabel playing in the Discovery center. He walks over to her and quickly convinces her to come back to the art studio with him. He shows her his dragon and asks her to help him: "I need to put his name on, Isabel. But I don't know how to make *d . . . d . . . d . . . dragon.* Can you do it?"

Isabel nods and takes a marker. "It's *D*—you need a *D*. It's this one." She slowly draws a letter *D* as Jacoby watches. "I think there's an *r*, and a *g*. And then we have to do a *n*. Like that. Now it says *Dragon.*"

Jacoby grins and says thank you, then taps Micah on the elbow and shows him his labeled dragon. "Come on," he says, "we gotta go back to the cave! The dragon needs to sleep!"

The boys walk back to Blocks and place their dragons inside the cave. As they do, the roof of the cave collapses and the cave falls apart.

"Micah! Why did you do that?" Jacoby asks angrily.

"It wasn't me!" Micah replies. "Come on, let's fix it. We can do it together."

The boys work for the next ten minutes on their cave, but each time it looks as though they are almost finished, their enthusiasm gets in the way. A block wiggles, and the entire thing falls down.

"Ms. Gaynor! We can't make it! We did it before, but it keeps falling down! Now our cave is broken!" Micah calls out.

Ms. Gaynor comes over to the boys. "It's almost time to clean up," she says, "but maybe this is something you could bring to Thinking and Feedback. You could ask your friends if they have any ideas about how you could make your cave more stable. I'll take some pictures of your work so you can share after we clean up. Jacoby, you and Micah should take a minute and think about what you will want to say to your friends at Thinking and Feedback. How are you going to explain your problem to them?"

When Clean Up is finished, the children gather back on the carpet and face Ms. Gaynor, who announces that it is time for Thinking and Feedback. "Today for Thinking and Feedback, Jacoby and Micah are going to describe a problem that they were having in Blocks. They were doing work that was inspired by the book *The Seven Chinese Sisters*. Remember, the first step for Thinking and Feedback is looking. I'm going to show you some photographs of Micah and Jacoby's work in Blocks. Use your eyes and just look at the photographs."

"Next we are going to say what we noticed. You could say 'I notice that . . .' or 'I see . . .' Who can tell me what you noticed in the photographs? Angela? What did you notice?"

ANGELA: I noticed that the blocks were all messy. They were broken.

MS. GAYNOR: Jayden, what did you notice?

JAYDEN: I noticed that here, they had a dragon. I saw it on the paper. It's red.

MS. GAYNOR: Thank you, Jayden. Who else noticed something? Carlos?

CARLOS: I see there's those things, the white ones, it's soft. They put them on the bottom.

MS. GAYNOR: I think those might be cotton balls. Thank you for your noticing, Carlos. Now, we're going to listen while Jacoby and Micah tell us about their problem.

JACOBY: We made a big cave for the dragon. Like in the story, he's inside his cave. So we made the cave. It was really big, and we put soft parts inside for the dragon to sleep. But we didn't have the dragon, so we made him in the art studio. But when we put him in the cave, it knocked over. And we tried to fix it but it didn't work. It kept falling. We need some help.

Ms. Gaynor thanks Jacoby. The she says, "Now it's time to do some wondering. Who has a question for Micah or Jacoby? Is there something you want to know about their cave? Yes, Nene? We'll have Nene first, then Calvin, and then Josue."

NENE: Why does it got too many pieces?

CALVIN: Did you have a map?

MS. GAYNOR: Calvin, what would Jacoby and Micah have done with a map? How would that have helped them build their cave?

CALVIN: Cuz it's for showing how to make something. The map shows how you're going to do it.

MS. GAYNOR: Oh, a *plan*. That's true, they could have drawn or written a plan to help them with their work. Josue? Did you have a question?

JOSUE: Ummm . . . no.

MS. GAYNOR: All right, so now it's time to offer suggestions. If you have any ideas for Jacoby and Micah about how to fix their cave so it doesn't fall over, you can raise your hand. And remember, I'm going to write down your ideas so that we can try some of them tomorrow during Centers. Who wants to share first? Camron?

CAMRON: They gotta put the big ones down first. On the bottom. It's like when we did towers. We made it so the big ones are down first, so it doesn't tip over.

MS. GAYNOR: We did, Camron. When we were doing our Stability Challenge, we learned that it's important to have a strong base, a strong foundation. Who else has a suggestion? Arnel?

ARNEL: Maybe the dragon's too big. He doesn't fit. They gotta put a different animal in there.

MS. GAYNOR: Okay. Thank you, Arnel. So, I wrote down Arnel's and Camron's ideas, and tomorrow, Jacoby and Micah, I'll help you remember their ideas so you can try them out and see if you have more success with your cave. Right now, we're going to get ready for recess.

You likely noticed how Ms. Gaynor used the classroom routines to help Jacoby and Micah cope with a setback, taking time to figure out a good solution rather than rushing to solve the problem. You can see that the children are still learning important executive function skills such as impulse control, delaying gratification, coping with frustration, and holding multiple perspectives in mind—and that their teacher is able to give them just enough help to solve the problems they encounter for themselves. For a four-year-old, especially one who is coping with challenging life circumstances, Jacoby's resilience is impressive.

The children put on their jackets and their hats and line up at the classroom door. "On our way outside today, we're going to pretend to be like third sister in *The Seven Chinese Sisters*. Remember, she had to count so many trees, she counted them by twos!" Ms. Gaynor says as she moves to the head of the line. She opens the book and shows the children the illustration of third sister. "Remember, she was really good at counting. We're going to use our quiet voices and practice counting by twos as we walk out for recess. Ready? Here we go. Two, four, six . . .”

As the children disperse to begin their outdoor play, Ms. Gaynor explains how this playful transition activity furthers the literacy and math goals that her class has been working on with more focused instruction, while also supporting their developing executive function skills of memory, focus, and impulse control.[4]

> Counting by twos is a difficult idea for most four-year-olds.[5] I had two goals in having them practice counting this way as we walked out to recess. One, I wanted to help them make a connection back to the read-aloud book, *The Seven Chinese Sisters.* Two, I wanted them to think back to the Let's Find Out About It and small group lessons that we did yesterday, where I worked with children on counting small sets of objects by twos, so they could begin to understand the concept.
>
> In our Let's Find Out About It lesson, I demonstrated counting by twos; and in small groups, I worked with children so that they could practice this kind of counting themselves. Some of the students were able to count by twos to 4, and I had one girl who could do it to 6. Some of the students were not at a place where they could understand this concept, and so with them I focused more on practicing standard rote counting by ones, because that is where they are in their understanding of numeracy.

In the recess yard, some children are playing on a climbing structure that has a ladder, a slide, and a bridge, with different-sized platforms for walking or sitting. After a few minutes, Ms. Gaynor hears Erica and Camara talking to each other.

ERICA: I'm going to be Baby Sister. You gotta be the dragon and you chase me.

CAMARA: Okay, I'll be the dragon. Here's my bridge. This is the cave. You stay on that side of the bridge. I'm going to run on the bridge and snatch you. Here I come! I got you! Come on, Baby Sister, you gotta get in my cave!

Ms. Gaynor watches the children as their conversation continues.

ERICA: Help! Help! Where's my sisters? Sisters! Sisters! The dragon got me! Sisters!"

CAMARA: Yeah! Ha-ha! I got you! I'm gonna keep you in my cave cuz your sisters aren't here this time!"

As Ms. Gaynor watches, three girls run over to the climbing structure and shout up at Camara. "Hey dragon, let our sister go! Come on, let's rescue Baby Sister! You be the sister that runs fast, I'm gonna be the sister who made the soup. You gotta be the sister who jumps on the dragon."

As the children continue playing on the climbing structure, Jacoby runs up to Ms. Gaynor and tugs on her jacket. "Ms. Gaynor! Come on, I wanna show you somethin'. Me and Alex found it!"

Jacoby leads Ms. Gaynor to a corner of the playground where there is a pile of leaves. "This is what we need for the dragon!" he says. "It's gonna be a nest in his cave! So the dragon can sleep. We can make a nest with leaves."

Ms. Gaynor replies, "I remember this morning you made a soft bed in your dragon's cave with cotton balls and fabric. Do you want to bring some of these leaves inside our classroom so you can use them tomorrow during Centers? Maybe you could put some in this plastic bag."

Jacoby and Alex sit down next to the leaf pile. They've just begun to fill the bag when a sudden gust scatters the leaf pile. The boys jump up and chase after the leaves, spilling some out of the bag as they run around the yard. As Ms. Gaynor watches them, she hears Alex call out to Jacoby, "I'm Gilberto! That wind is mean! He's snatching up all my leaves! Wind, wind, stop blowing all my leaves!"

Ms. Gaynor explains:

Gilberto is a character from the book, *Gilberto and the Wind*, that appears later in the curriculum. I read the story to the class a few days ago, however, because they had come inside from recess on a particularly windy day and had been talking about how it was hard to play because the wind kept blowing dirt and leaves in their faces.

As the wind dies down, Alex and Jacoby continue filling their bag with leaves. Ms. Gaynor gives a five-minute warning, then leads the children back inside to get ready for a nap. She notices that Jacoby places his nap mat and blanket under one of the classroom tables. "Jacoby, that's not where you sleep. Your nap spot is over on the carpet next to Arnel."

"Yeah, but I'm in my cave." Jacoby replies. "I'm gonna sleep under here because I want to sleep like a dragon. I was gonna do it with my blocks but they fell down. So this is my cave now."

When the children are settled, Ms. Gaynor comments:

> Even though Jacoby was not in his proper nap space, I decided to let him sleep under the table, as this was another example of him making a connection to and demonstrating understanding of the plot and some key concepts from *The Seven Chinese Sisters*. Plus I know how important it is for him to feel safe and secure.

In their book, Powerful Interactions, *Amy Dombro, Judy Jablon, and Charlotte Stetson teach a three-step process: Be present. Make a connection. Extend the learning.[6] Although every interaction can't be powerful one, learning is maximized when a teacher gives a child full attention while being aware of what the child's play may mean to him, then uses her knowledge to connect with both the child and his play before introducing a new idea or, as Ms. Gaynor often does, reminding the child of a previous learning experience.*

As the description of Jacoby's day illustrates, Ms. Gaynor is able to use the Focus on K1 curriculum to make powerful connections for a little boy who had been dispossessed from his own home and is driven to build a safe and cozy new one for a pretend friend. At the same time, though, she uses Jacoby's passion to help him master both academic concepts and important social-emotional skills.

The ideas and skills introduced in the book Ms. Gaynor read aloud permeate Jacoby's classroom experiences as well as those of his classmates. Some of the connections are explicit and teacher-initiated; others are created by children as they play—as befits an integrated approach to building both basic literacies and twenty-first-century skills.[7] Ms. Gaynor's relationships with the children and her knowledge of developmental trajectories enable her to seize opportunities to propel children's thinking while engaging them more deeply with the story.[8]

Chapter Six

Redoubled Efforts
and New Directions

As the 2010 school year opened, the DEC continued its focus on accrediting classrooms and schools. Eleven schools had already earned NAEYC accreditation for their pre-K and kindergarten classrooms; four were well on their way, and seven were starting. Disappointed but undaunted by the blocking of its K2 curriculum plans, the DEC redoubled its efforts. Coaches and consulting mentors took on the work of leading schools and teachers through the process of learning and meeting criteria, with the belief that the process would yield enhanced quality in those classrooms and more comprehensive knowledge about the needs of young children for teachers and administrators in those schools. As new classrooms were opened, their teachers, schools, and families joined the cause.

At the same time, the DEC seized the opportunity to revisit its K1 curricula. Many of the coaches felt that teachers needed more options and tools for integrating OWL and *Building Blocks* more smoothly and for grounding both more firmly in the experiences of Boston's children and the hopes and dreams of their families. Some of what the team had envisioned for the new kindergarten curriculum would inform the updating of K1.

The DEC would have liked to open K1 classrooms faster, but quality was its top priority and the availability of suitable spaces and funding limited its options. The DEC team worried that the four-year-old children who needed them most were being squeezed out by families who were savvier about the application process and faced fewer transportation and childcare challenges.

Even so, complaints from community-based early education programs were growing as four-year-olds on whose tuition they depended entered the free K1 programs and more of their best-educated teachers (those with BA degrees) left for jobs in the public schools (BPS salaries were more than double what most community-based programs could afford to pay). Earlier efforts to locate K1 classrooms in community-based settings, as other states and localities had done, had created resentment when K1 teachers were paid twice as much as the teachers next door. Without a dramatic increase in public investment, there seemed to be no way around the dilemma.

The BPS school assignment policy compounded the problem. With a choice of public schools, families scrambled to get one of the "best." Some families chose based on convenience, proximity to their homes, cultural consonance, or personal, family, or neighborhood ties. Others based their choices on the schools' reputations or visited multiple schools before ranking their choices. But not all schools had K1 classrooms, and accepting a K1 slot in one school meant the child could continue there, but might have less chance of getting into a school that his or her parents might prefer for later grades. Families with better education and higher disposable income were better positioned to work the system.

Meanwhile, BPS data showed that four-year-olds from low-income families gained more in mixed-income classrooms than more homogenous ones.[1] This aligned with data emerging from universal prekindergarten programs in Oklahoma and elsewhere, as well as with research that demonstrated how much four- and five-year-olds learn from their peers.[2] With more than 70 percent of its students eligible for free or reduced-price food programs, Boston could take advantage of the Community Eligibility Option provision in the Healthy, Hunger-Free Kids Act of 2010 to offer free breakfast and lunch to all of its students.

But wealthier families were increasingly enrolling their children in the BPS K1 and K2 programs, just as Mayor Menino had hoped they would when he and Superintendent Payzant had launched the DEC. Kindergarten enroll-ment was up—and now included almost all of the age-eligible children who weren't in private or parochial schools. Families were beginning to figure out where the best programs were, and schools like Eliot Innovation School (the school you visited in "The Colorful Café") had long waiting lists. Many of the families who could afford to were enrolling their children in private or parochial schools just in case they didn't get one of their top choices, then forfeiting the deposit when they got their coveted K1or K2 slot.

Focusing on Families: Countdown to Kindergarten and Thrive in Five

Despite high-quality classrooms and impressive child outcomes, the DEC felt that its programs were falling short of their equity goals. Some of their out-side partners had moved on to bigger arenas, while the DEC team remained focused on Boston. And too many of the children who most needed the best that their city could offer were still not getting the learning opportunities and follow-up they deserved. BPS would have to do a better job of reaching and supporting their families, and the DEC would need to play a more active role.

Countdown to Kindergarten

Countdown to Kindergarten began in 1999 as a small initiative within the Boston Public Schools. It focused initially on helping families navigate the transition from preschool or Head Start to public school. Soon, Countdown to Kindergarten's data revealed a need for a ramped-up program.

Boston's school assignment process is complicated. Families choose schools within zones, ranking them in order of preference. In the year prior to enroll-ment, they can begin school visits as early as November, and can make their choices in January and February. Those in the know take advantage of this first round and receive their school assignments in late March. But Count-down to Kindergarten's early data showed that nearly three-quarters of the families with eligible children were registering later, by which time their top choices were often full—and since kindergarten is optional in Massachusetts, some weren't registering at all. Countdown to Kindergarten responded with community outreach, especially in Boston's poorest neighborhoods, sharing information on the benefits of kindergarten (and eventually K1 as well) and of early registration.

The group did not work alone. They partnered with community-based family facing organizations, including early education and care programs. They also worked with the Boston Children's Museum to reach out to the wider community. From the first year on, the Children's Museum has hosted an annual celebration for rising kindergarteners (whether or not they will be going to public school) and their whole families—with free admission, special activities, T-shirts and other giveaways, and information for parents on kindergarten expectations and a range of local resources. Its original purpose was to build a sense of community and a shared sense of excitement and pride around school entry, and it has succeeded in that effort. After a year of family outings, "Nursery Rhyme Flash Mobs" (outdoor neighborhood gatherings where young children and their families sing, dance, and enjoy word play) and mini-events throughout the city, more than fifteen hundred families crowd the museum each year for the big celebration, and more than a thousand others celebrate at smaller events in their neighborhoods.

In 2010, the Children's Museum opened a permanent Countdown to Kindergarten exhibit, where children could pack backpacks, ride in a pretend school bus, and play for as long as they liked in a realistic kindergarten classroom. By then Countdown to Kindergarten had worked with BPS to develop a calendar for parents and a set of materials, activities, and events. By 2011, 90 percent of kindergarten entrants were registering early, and only 4 percent of Boston's incoming first-graders had no kindergarten experience.

As part of the DEC, Countdown to Kindergarten gradually shifted from a focus on the registration and transition process to a broader definition of school readiness. This included Play to Learn groups for toddlers, three-year-olds, and their families, with an increasingly language-rich curriculum. More than five hundred families participate each year, engaging in gross motor, fine motor, dramatic play, and guided free play activities, often centered around an interactive read-aloud experience. Leaders model a variety of ways to engage children, and parents practice the techniques as they join in the fun As leaders get to know the families and children, they become trusted sources of information. As needs surface, group leaders refer families to other community resources and help facilitate connections.

With numerous city partners, Countdown to Kindergarten launched a public information campaign—"Talk, Read, Play"—to heighten families' awareness of the important roles they play in their children's learning from birth. Grounded in decades of child development research, its focus and messages are:

- **Why Talk?** Talking to your baby is one of the most important things you can do to help your child learn to talk and grow her/his vocabulary. Talk is also essential for learning to read and write.
- **Why Read?** Reading to your baby is one of the most important things you can do to help your child grow her vocabulary and develop a love of learning. Reading at home is also essential for learning to read and write once your child begins school.
- **Why Play?** Playing with your child and providing opportunities for him to play independently will help him develop his creativity, imagination, and social and emotional skills. Babies and children need stimulation and interaction to foster brain development. They learn how to interact with others and the world around them through play.[3]

With its partners, Countdown to Kindergarten emphasizes the importance and value of home language, and encourages adults to use the language that they are most comfortable with when speaking with their children. It explains the research findings, and offers suggestions and models for how to talk, read, and play in ways that prepare children to thrive in school. And it provides props, supports, experiences, and reminders to help parents, who are often pressed for time, build daily habits of talking, reading, and playing.

Thrive in Five

In contrast to Countdown to Kindergarten, which started small, Thrive in Five began as an all-inclusive school-readiness initiative, bringing initiatives like Countdown to Kindergarten under its tent, but also spawning new organizations and collaborative projects.

As noted in chapter 3, in 2006—the year the DEC first opened its universal preK programs—Mayor Menino had begun working with the United Way and the Barr Foundation to pull together funders, city agencies, universities, hospitals, early education providers, and community-based organizations in a coordinated initiative. Launched in 2008, Thrive in Five built on existing assets, such as Countdown to Kindergarten and Reach Out and Read, a national program to encourage reading aloud with babies and young children that had originated in Boston. Thrive in Five's original goal was "to catalyze a new citywide conversation, to inform how the City deployed its resources, and to spark new thinking in how services for families could be coordinated, so that all children enter school healthy and ready to succeed."[4] The DEC was an essential partner in that dialog, and Jason Sachs served on the leadership council.

Thrive in Five's driving logic model was an equation:

Ready Families + Ready Educators + Ready Systems + Ready City = Children Ready for Sustained School Success

In practice, "Ready Families" meant partnering with a hub agency in each neighborhood to connect families with community resources and parent-driven group activities that would support their children's development. Parents could participate at several levels. In addition to accessing resources and activities, they could join a Parents on School Readiness Roundtable to help plan, implement, and evaluate activities; receive a stipend to conduct outreach to other families; or even become activity leaders.

The Ready Families efforts also spawned a new nonprofit, Smart from the Start (Smart), a comprehensive prenatal through school-age readiness program in Boston's poorest neighborhoods. With an ever-growing group of partners, Smart reaches out to families, offering prenatal classes, baby showers, home visits, parenting and parent-child groups, parent leadership training and opportunities, family outings, parties, an "Address the Stress" summer camp, and play-to-learn spaces in local businesses. It arranges GED, ESL, and financial literacy classes; provides job referrals and help with college applications and attendance; and more. As part of the Smart "family," parents build a culture of talking, reading, and playing with young children; mutual support; and civic participation. Smart routinely tracks children's development by having parents complete the Ages and Stages Questionnaire (ASQ), a developmental assessment used throughout Massachusetts to measure school readiness.[5] Smart's graduates are well prepared for Boston's K1 and K2 programs.[6] And their parents have been primed to stay engaged.

"Ready Educators" referred to bringing community-based programs up to the level of quality exhibited by the BPS programs. It involved a two-pronged strategy: bringing the K1 curricula, professional development, and coaching to community-based programs, along with stipends for enhanced teacher salaries (Boston K1DS) and working with ten other centers and a family child-care system to assess program quality and child outcomes and use the data to guide capacity-building and quality improvement efforts (Project REQIP).

"Ready Systems" focused on child assessment. Using the ASQ, Thrive in Five launched "Screen to Succeed." This program was designed to improve the early identification of children whose developmental difficulties could be helped by early intervention. It was also designed to engage parents in tracking and supporting their children's development and to gather data that could shape program and policy decisions so that resources would be targeted more effectively. Countdown to Kindergarten became an essential partner in that effort.

"Ready City" was an affirmation of the commitment of so many of Boston's agencies, institutions, community-based organizations, funders, and residents to work together on behalf of their city's youngest citizens.

The efforts spawned by Thrive in Five piloted effective approaches and partnerships that continue to grow and to help prepare many more children for kindergarten. But getting children ready for kindergarten was only the first step. Kindergarten needed to be ready for them—and in 2011 the DEC felt that it offered too little.

A Dream Revived: Kindergarten Takes Center Stage

In 2012, the winds shifted. Carol Johnson announced her intent to retire at the end of the school year, to be replaced by an interim superintendent, Dr. John McDonough. While other departments had faced cuts and some schools had closed due to declining enrollments, the DEC's staff had expanded to fourteen as preK and kindergarten enrollment continued to climb. The department added coaches and curriculum writers; a Coordinated Family and Community Engagement (CFCE) grant manager to oversee state-funded partnerships with community-based agencies serving children birth-5 and their families; and a Manager of School Readiness who would oversee data-driven strategic planning, seek additional grants, and build a robust website.

McDonough continued to support the DEC. Longitudinal data showed that even their first year's efforts had paid off. Over 50 percent of the fifth-graders who had attended those early K1 classes scored proficient or advanced on the English language arts portion of the Massachusetts Comprehensive Assessment System (MCAS), compared with 38.4 percent of those who hadn't. All ethnic groups showed higher achievement scores and greater percentages of proficient and advanced scores for students who had attended K1, but African American students who had attended K1 showed a 44 percent achievement score advantage over those who hadn't.[7]

Reading Street had been required in all BPS elementary schools for three years, and the DEC coaches and administrators were not the only ones feeling frustrated. Kindergarten teachers were becoming increasingly exasperated. Many found the curriculum to be overly scripted, lacking in useful professional development supports, and at odds with what they knew about how young children learn. In many classrooms, children were working on drill and practice worksheets, seated at tables for too much of the day, and involved in more teacher-led direct instruction than either the teachers or their coaches felt was appropriate. Children were bored and fidgety.

Furthermore, *Reading Street* lacked alignment with the new Massachusetts Curriculum Framework for English Language Arts and Literacy, which incorporated the Common Core State Standards for preK–12. The first guiding principle of the document succinctly described the DEC's view: "An effective English language arts and literacy curriculum develops thinking and language together through interactive learning."[8] *Reading Street* placed too little emphasis on language and too often failed to engage either thinking or interactive learning.

Meanwhile, the national preK–3 movement was growing as researchers and school systems recognized both the benefits of high-quality prekindergarten (especially for children from low-income and linguistically isolated families) and the power of aligning approaches so that subsequent experiences would build on early learning gains. Convinced by this increasing body of research and reports from the field, the Foundation for Child Development had launched a "Pre-K to 3rd" initiative in 2009. Its opening "Policy to Action" brief laid out the case:

> Investments in excellent, research-based PreK programs are part of the answer to lifting student achievement nationwide—but only part. This "fade-out" has been reported for many kinds of programs, including both Head Start and state-funded PreK programs. The evidence is clear: By itself, PreK cannot inoculate children against academic failure.
>
> The good news is: We know how to sustain the gains. Decades of research have shown that high-quality PreK programs (for three- and four-year-olds) can boost later achievement if quality enhancements are carried forward. Moreover, when schools link PreK education with the elementary grades, creating a common organizational structure and coherent sets of academic and social goals, the gains that children make in high-quality PreK programs are more likely to persist.[9]

With a grant from the Massachusetts Department of Education, Boston had formed working groups that collaborated on observation and assessment, supports for English language learners and children with special needs, and curricular linkages, and were beginning to break down the siloes that separated the DEC from other departments.[10] The stars had finally aligned. It was time to "focus on K2"—the title the DEC would choose for its new kindergarten curriculum.

Focus on K2: A Kindergarten Curriculum for Boston and Beyond

Wanting to launch a collaborative process and elicit buy-in from as many K2 teachers as possible, Sachs called an open meeting and invited every kindergarten teacher from across the district to join the DEC in brainstorming ideas for a new, integrated K2 curriculum. Scores of teachers came to that meeting, and about a dozen volunteered their time to join working groups to begin developing the new curriculum. The DEC reached out to early childhood experts at local universities to join in co-constructing the program.

DEC members and coaches Beth Benoit, Mayra Cuevas, and Melissa To-nachel formed the core of the K2 advisory team that drafted most of the curriculum and steered the professional development effort. They were joined by university-based partners Ben Mardell and Megina Baker. Beth Benoit started the work, laid the framework for the units, and led the efforts to select read-aloud texts. When Benoit left the DEC, Mardell and Baker took the lead on curriculum writing. DEC coaches Cuevas, and later Tonachel, both of whom had had extensive teaching experience in BPS before joining the DEC, served as the DEC leads for the project.

Over the next fifteen months, nearly all of the DEC staff members would collaborate with their university partners and the teacher working groups to design the new curriculum. This homegrown effort was far more challenging than purchasing a boxed curriculum and hiring out-of-district PD coaches to train teachers on it. But the co-construction process meant that Boston could develop a kindergarten curriculum that aligned with the developmental and cultural values of the BPS community, and that it could continue to be a living, changing entity long after its launch in the district.

The resulting *Focus on K2* program has three defining characteristics: it promotes integrated learning through purposeful, guided play and deep exploration in interdisciplinary centers; it is organized through in-depth themes grounded in science topics; and it uses effective instructional practices through a combination of explicit instruction, small group work, and creative endeavors such as storytelling. In addition, strategies to engage and support diverse learners such as dual language learners (DLLs) and children with special rights are integrated throughout the curriculum. The following sections describe this living curriculum in its current form.

Focus on K2 Curriculum Design: Overview

Focus on K2 is a thematic, integrated, play-based curriculum, aligned with the DEC's core principles. As stated in the introduction to its guiding documents,

> *Focus on K2* was written for Boston's kindergarteners by Boston educators. It was written to help teachers promote children's creativity and their abilities to collaborate, communicate and think critically. It was written

to develop essential literacy and numeracy skills. It was written to connect children with their city. It was written to give our K2 students the adventure in learning they deserve.[11]

The DEC's first core principle—*Schools must promote our democratic society and support children's and teachers' sense of citizenship though multiple connections to families and community*—is at the curriculum's core.

The curriculum is also grounded in child development evidence and theory. From a socio-constructivist perspective, young children construct knowledge through interactions with other children and adults, and by hands-on exploration of materials and the environment. In this way, the child is viewed as a natural scientist, eagerly investigating, experimenting, and questioning topics that capture her interest.[12] Thus, when envisioning the flow of the year, the curriculum development team chose a few particularly rich science-based topics that offered children authentic opportunities to engage in hands-on, sustained inquiry.

Units are intentionally long—ranging from six to ten weeks—to invite deep exploration of concepts through long-term projects and provide time for children to formulate and test out "big ideas" and problem-solving strategies. Content and skills from across all discrete disciplines such as math, science, and literacy are interwoven into interdisciplinary center activities.[13]

Units of Study

Figure 6.1 provides an overview of the flow of the year in *Focus on K2*. The lens of community and the concept of citizenship permeate the year. In Our Community, children learn about each other and their school community. In Animals and Habitats, they learn that animals live in communities as well and begin to understand the concept of stewardship. In Construction, they collaborate to construct models together, and contribute ideas as citizens of Boston; and in Our Earth, they examine the collective impact that people have on the environment and collaborate in learning about and advocating for sustainable practices.

The following excerpts from the *Focus on K2* curriculum guide describe the focus and goals of each unit.[14]

FIGURE 6.1 *Focus on K2 flow of the year*

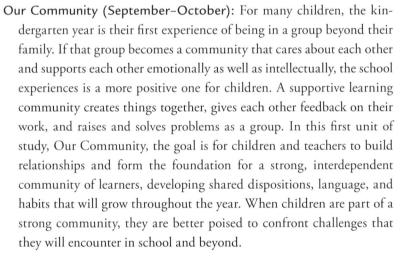

Our Community	Animals and Habitat	Construction	Our Earth
September–October	November–January	February–March	April–June
Social science, community, storytelling	Life science, stewardship	Physical science, civic engagement	Earth science, sustainable practices, advocacy

Children as citizens

Our Community (September–October): For many children, the kindergarten year is their first experience of being in a group beyond their family. If that group becomes a community that cares about each other and supports each other emotionally as well as intellectually, the school experiences is a more positive one for children. A supportive learning community creates things together, gives each other feedback on their work, and raises and solves problems as a group. In this first unit of study, Our Community, the goal is for children and teachers to build relationships and form the foundation for a strong, interdependent community of learners, developing shared dispositions, language, and habits that will grow throughout the year. When children are part of a strong community, they are better poised to confront challenges that they will encounter in school and beyond.

Fostering connections between home and school, and drawing upon the rich cultural and linguistic contexts from which children come, is a key goal in Our Community. Communities tell stories, weaving together the rich backgrounds of individual members. In Our Community, the practice of Storytelling/Story Acting is introduced. When children tell and act out each other's stories they share important interests and ideas, and form interpersonal connections. And through the Beautiful Stuff project, which also begins in this unit and continues throughout the year, home–school relationships are supported as children bring found objects into the classroom. Stories might be told about these objects as well, as children sort, label, and use the items to create artwork in the Art Studio.[15]

Animals and Habitats (November–January): Kindergarteners are naturally drawn to learning about animals. They tell and enjoy stories filled with animal characters and are curious to learn information about animals as well. They might have pets at home or see animals in their communities—a dog out for a walk, a squirrel in a tree, or ants on the sidewalk. In Animals and Habitats, this natural curiosity opens a door to deep learning about animals both familiar and unfamiliar to Boston kindergarteners. Studying some animals that live in the Boston vicinity (frogs, owls) teaches children more about their local environment, while learning about others found farther away (salmon, wolves) expands their horizons.

The unit is composed of three shorter studies: Fish and Tadpoles, Owls, and Wolves. In each study, children explore fiction and nonfiction books about the animals, learning to differentiate between factual and fictional information. They conduct STEM investigations that explore features of the animals' bodies, their needs for food, safety, and shelter, and how they live in communities with others of their kind. For example, in the Fish and Tadpoles study, STEM investigations invite children to observe live fish in their classrooms, and compare the structures of their own bodies to the structures of the fish's bodies. In Centers, they apply and deepen their learning by constructing habitats for salmon in the block area, writing science journals in the STEM center, and pretending to be the characters in *Lon Po Po* in the Dramatization center.[16] Comparing one type of animal to another, children gain a perspective about animals' physical characteristics and how these are adapted for their environments. They also learn about animals' life cycles, diet, and habitats.

Throughout the unit, teachers save artifacts of children's work from center projects, STEM investigations, and Writer's Workshop. In the last week of the unit, children and teachers collaborate to organize and display samples of work from across all three animal studies in a showcase of learning. These showcases allow children to reflect on their learning and provide teachers with authentic assessments of what children have learned. Families and members of the school community can be invited to the showcase to hear about and see what the children have learned.[17]

Construction (February–March): The Construction unit invites children to make physical science, engineering and technology connections through the building of structures, measurement and comparison, and experimentation with materials. It engages children in a construction process that involves envisioning (and being inspired), researching, planning, executing and revising. This process can support the construction of physical structures as well as the building of ideas and works of art.

In this unit, as children have grown more capable and confident and teachers know them as individuals and a group, the class is now better able to generate questions, solve problems and conduct inquiry. Thus, the Construction unit unfolds in unique ways in each classroom, as *Focus on K2* supports teachers to follow the responses and interests of their particular group of children. A discussion of *The Three Little Pigs* may lead to some children wanting to write their own versions of the story. Perhaps five devoted Celtics fans may decide they want to build the Boston Garden in the block area. Or, a visit to Dale Chihuly's glass sculpture, "Lime Green Icicle Tower," at the Museum of Fine Arts may inspire the construction of a very tall tower in the classroom. A carpenter who comes to visit may lead a small group to write a How-To book about how to build a house, birdhouse, or bookshelf. Teachers identify the path each class takes by documenting children's thinking (in their play, conversations and constructions), and discussing possibilities with colleagues. The Our Boston project is the culmination of the Construction unit, inviting children to share their ideas about how to make their city "a fairer and more interesting place for children" with the Mayor's office and with the public, and to display their constructions at City Hall.[18]

Our Earth (April–June): Today's kindergarteners will inherit a complex world where scientific, environmental, social, and moral issues intertwine. In order to meet the opportunities and challenges of the 21st century, children need an equally complex set of skills and abilities.

During the Our Earth unit, children will explore the natural world by investigating and researching the earth's properties, focusing on its surface and plant life. Responsibility, sustainability, and stewardship for the environment, as individuals and as members of a community, are explored in discussions and projects.

These are big concepts for kindergarteners. To help children engage with these ideas, the unit intentionally unfolds in three interconnected phases, drawing on skills and concepts learned in previous units. The unit begins with children's intellectual and emotional connections with nature, as explored in Animals and Habitats. Children use active investigations and background information to understand how plants grow. Building on an understanding of plants, the focus turns to trees and how they provide many things to other living organisms. Through the arts, children experience how the natural world can inspire new ideas and artistic representations. The second phase focuses on sustainable systems that reduce our impact on the earth. And the final phase engages children as citizens who can contribute to our earth. Drawing on the design process of Construction, children generate ideas for sustainable choices in their classrooms and school communities, then employ a variety of forms of expression to advocate for taking better care of the environment.[19]

Daily Routines: Key Activities and Instructional Components

Arrival Time. As they do throughout the Boston Public Schools, mornings in K2 begin with breakfast. Teachers meet their classes at the cafeteria, then go back to the classroom to begin their day together. Usually, there is a bit of a break before the whole group gathers, when children can read, draw, or do their classroom "jobs," while the teacher works with one child on an activity such as dictating a story for the Story Acting session that will occur later in the day.

Whole Group Time. Teachers and children begin their time together with a morning circle—a time to bond as a group. Rituals, songs, and games reinforce the sense of shared connection. As they engage children in conversations about who's here and who's missing, what happened yesterday or over the weekend, and what they will do today, teachers build relationships and reinforce social-emotional skills such as empathy, sharing feelings, and listening to each other. Whole group time ends with an introduction to Center Time activities, designed to send the children off with clear plans and a sense of excitement.

Center Time. Center activities are the heart of the K2 curriculum. As in K1, classrooms contain multiple centers for art, construction, dramatic play, research, writing, and STEM explorations. Children may engage in short-term projects or longer investigations. Teachers intentionally set up and introduce activities to intrigue children and push their thinking—leaving space for child choice and creativity.

Center activities are designed to enable children to develop competencies aligned with Common Core goals.[20] Children can choose from among centers and engage with materials. Teachers scaffold children's engagement in meaningful ways without coercion by gathering information about individual children's interests and skills and appealing to these as "entry points" for particular activities. True engagement with materials and ideas will lead children to take activities in different directions or to use materials in novel ways; teachers are encouraged and coached to be attentive to these possibilities and to discover how they can best extend children's learning.

Within this structure teachers embed learning opportunities across multiple academic domains. The act of deciding where to work and play is a process that cultivates higher-order executive functioning skills.[21] Children are grappling with mathematical concepts as they sort seeds by size and shape, then determine which category contains the most. Social learning is fostered through the collaboration and problem-solving that arises during play—especially during dramatic play and collaborative construction. Children work on literacy tasks in meaningful situations, for example by writing notes to themselves or others and creating labels and props to use in their play, as well as through engagement with books and printed materials throughout the centers. For children in the class who are learning English, the hands-on manipulation of materials and focus on collaborative work with peers fosters oral language development, builds vocabulary, and offers opportunities to practice conversational skills.

Thinking and Feedback. As we observed in chapter 2 ("The Colorful Café") and chapter 5 ("A House for a Dragon")—both visits to K1 classrooms that followed the K2 model—Center Time is followed by Thinking and Feedback. The whole group comes back together, and a child or small group shares a work product. As in K1, the discussion is guided by a protocol. In K2, the children move through the following steps:

1. *Observe* carefully and share what you notice about an artifact produced by classmates.
2. *Listen* to a child (or children) talk about their artifact.
3. Ask questions (*wonder*) about the artifact.
4. Provide *suggestions* to improve the artifact/work and note *inspirations* you take.

Artifacts that result from children's play processes can include drawings, paintings, clay models, constructions, video of dramatic play, and data sheets from science experiments. The conversation provides feedback to the presenters and possibilities to the rest of the class. It is an exercise in collective meaning making over something very engaging to kindergarteners: their own work and play.

Read Alouds. The benefits of reading aloud for young children's language, literacy and cognitive development are well documented.[22] *Focus on K2* includes a core set of texts for each of the four units of study. Informational and fictional texts across genres ensure literary variety and align with expectations in the Common Core State Standards. Multiple readings of each text provide opportunities for revisiting vocabulary, digging deep into concepts, and making connections with classroom activities.

In *Focus on K2*, Read Alouds are grounded in research-based approaches that encourage comprehension, vocabulary development, and critical thinking skills.[23] Strategies such as previewing, building on prior knowledge, and explicitly teaching vocabulary benefit all children, but are especially beneficial for young children who are learning a new language. These approaches are integral to the Read Aloud sessions.

Working on Words. Consistent with research supporting a balanced literacy approach, Working on Words (originally called Literacy Circles) explicitly introduces, teaches, and models foundational literacy skills (phonemic awareness,·

concepts of print, alphabet knowledge, letter-sound correspondence, reading strategies, writing) in playful, developmentally appropriate, and cognitively challenging ways that connect with what children have been talking, reading, playing, and thinking about.[24] Children work first as a whole group, then divide into smaller groups and circulate through activity stations for writing practice, word work (sound practice, segmenting and blending, recognizing high-use words), reading time (including perusing books, pretending to read, telling the story from memory or from the pictures, and reading the text independently or with a buddy), and discussion. One small group at a time works with the teacher on guided reading or writing practice. Poetry, songs, and games provide opportunities to practice the explicitly taught skills and strategies while building language.[25]

The activities and groupings enable teachers to differentiate instruction while facilitating all children's full participation in fun, engaging, and cognitively challenging activities that relate to their units of study and the ongoing life of the classroom.[26] One frequently offered writing activity, for example, involves "sharing the pen" to construct a piece of writing as a large group.[27] Guided by a teacher, children can contribute at their level of expertise while learning from each other.

Some schools elected to integrate other literacy skills curricula, such as *Fundations*, with the Working on Words component, to align with their first- and second-grade literacy program.[28]

Math Workshop. As they constructed *Focus on K2*, its developers realized that they didn't need to do everything. The district already used TERC *Investigations in Number, Data, and Space* (see chapter 3), which aligned with the DEC's hands-on, exploratory, language-rich, pedagogy.[29] Like the *Focus on K2* units, *Investigations* units extend over time, with only eight in the kindergarten year. They allow for interesting problem-solving and cognitively challenging conversation, as children count, compare, and measure objects in their environment, represent numerical relationships with symbols, make up and solve their own stories for mathematical expressions, create spatial patterns, and collect, represent, and use data. In consultation with the BPS Math Department, the DEC decided to leave the *Investigations* units and activities intact, while making explicit connections between math skills developed during the dedicated math time and Center Time activities. For example, the seed-sorting activity described above, which takes place during the Our Earth unit, draws on skills of categorization, one-to-one correspondence, and comparison that have previously been targeted during Math Workshop.

Writers' Workshop. Like Math Workshop, Writers' Workshop was an established practice in Boston's K2 classrooms. Schools had engaged with a variety of approaches and curricula, building continuity across the grades. In collaboration with the Writing Department, the *Focus on K2* team developed a set of writing rubrics and Writer's Workshop guidelines that are separate from, but connected to, *Focus on K2* units of study. They included guidelines for making connections between *Focus on K2* and any form of Writer's Workshop, allowing openness for schools to continue their respective styles and approaches. This strategy complicates the DEC's data collection and continuous improvement efforts, but it honors the diversity within the district.

Boston Listens: Hearing and Sharing Our Stories

Developed initially as a key element of *Focus on K2*, Boston Listens is a hallmark of the DEC's early childhood programming. Storytelling/Story Acting, a practice pioneered and honed by Vivian Paley, promotes young children's oral language and emergent literacy skills, while building on their love of story and of dramatic play.[30] In a 2013 article, Ben Mardell describes this practice as it lives in Boston Public Schools:

> At the heart of ST/SA is listening—teachers listening to children, children listening to classmates, and children listening to adults—all in the service of a better understanding of each other's ideas and enjoyment of each other's stories.[31]

Storytelling/Story Acting begins with stories that adults tell children. They may be fiction or nonfiction, remembered tales or accounts, or fantasies made up on the spot. They are chosen because the teller wants to share them with this particular audience. As adults tell stories and children listen, they build a culture of storytelling and of attentive listening.

Soon, children are encouraged to tell stories, even if they are only a few words long. As a child tells a story to the teacher, the teacher transcribes the words. The process is likely to include many teachable moments, as the child asks for an apt vocabulary word, or the teacher explains why an exclamation point was used. The idea is not to conduct a writing or phonics lesson, but rather to listen closely to the story and—when asked—help the child to share it.

Story Acting is the next step in the process. With a small group or the whole class as the cast and audience, the teacher reads the story aloud. The story's author chooses a character to enact. As characters (or inanimate objects that can be acted out) emerge in the story, other children are asked to play those parts. At times, the dramatization may be recorded or videotaped.

As with Read Alouds, the Story Acting session is followed by a conversation. Children may share what they liked about the story, or what it reminded them of. Teachers may introduce terms like "character," "plot," or "suspenseful" as they facilitate these conversations. The stories, and any recordings, live in the class library. Children may read them themselves or together, with or without adult help. They may even become inspirations for new stories to be told, dictated, written, illustrated, and/or dramatized. In the spring, many classes take advantage of the BPS partnership with the Boston Children's Museum. At a Friday evening event, the kindergarteners use the "Kids' Stage" to act out stories they have dictated for an audience of family members.

Using Storytelling/Story Acting well is an art. The developers of *Focus on K2* worked closely with Vivian Paley to incorporate it into their curriculum and its associated professional development courses. Paley gave an intensive two-day workshop at the DEC's 2012 Kindergarten Conference, an annual gathering of all K0, K1, and K2 teachers along with all of the DEC coaches. Afterward, the DEC stocked its Weebly, a growing online collection of resources for Boston's early childhood teachers (now available on the DEC's public website), with supporting Storytelling/Story Acting materials.[32]

Constructing the Curriculum: Challenges, Collaboration, and Compromise

As in any large urban district, the DEC is answerable to multiple stakeholders, with diverse cultural backgrounds, content foci, and perspectives on what children need. The department itself is intentionally diverse in background. Although all members are united around the DEC's core principles and the desire to do what is best for children, the process of creating a curriculum together brought out subtle differences in cultural perspective and educational philosophy. There were palpable tensions, on occasion, between knowledge of best practices for child development and pressures to satisfy teachers and administrators concerned that the curriculum might not prepare their children to perform well on standardized literacy assessments.

Working through such challenges led to a stronger curriculum. For example, a surprising disagreement occurred during the writing of the Animals and Habitats unit. The lead authors suggested that squirrels might be a good animal to study—almost all of the children would have seen them scampering and foraging in public parks and playgrounds or on sidewalks near their homes. They could build on their lived experience when connecting new knowledge gained through the curriculum. But several members of the DEC pushed back. "This is for Boston's children," a former BPS teacher who had been raised in Boston argued. "We want them to see beyond their everyday lives, to imagine something new." She continued to talk about the need for cultural understanding about what many families in Boston could want for their children. Those living in poverty imagine other futures. They hope that school experiences can broaden their children's horizons, not keep them tied to the same place.

After much discussion, the group found a way to honor both perspectives by writing three animal study cycles into the curriculum. "Frogs and Fish" would involve bringing live animals into the classroom that children could observe and touch to build real-life experiences. The remaining two cycles, "Owls" and "Wolves," would introduce animals native to New England but not to Boston.

As they delved into the units and began to write supporting materials for teachers, the team continued to talk about differences in cultural assumptions. Having chosen *The Great Kapok Tree* as a Read Aloud text for the Animals and Habitats unit, for example, they wrestled with how to be sensitive to different cultural and personal interpretations of *beauty*, a key vocabulary word both in that book and in related texts.[33] They then co-constructed a document that could guide teachers through their own classwide conversations on the topic. Here is an excerpt:

> The word "beauty" comes up many times in the literature for this unit, especially in the book *The Great Kapok Tree*. One's sense of beauty is both cultural and personal. Everyone has different ideas about what beauty means. Because beautiful things are engaging and young children have opinions about what is beautiful, discussions about beauty can foster critical thinking and creativity.[34]

The writing team agreed that their guidance around the use of the word *beauty* was imperfect, but also that it opened a space for teachers to reflect in their own ways on their use of language in the classroom. The team expects such conversations to continue throughout the life of *Focus on K2* implementations.

Rolling Out the New Curriculum

Not wanting to lose the moment of opportunity when the district was willing to hand over curricular control of K2, the DEC agreed to test the curriculum as a draft version with any schools interested in joining the pilot. Out of seventy-five schools with K2 programs, nearly fifty volunteered. The DEC piloted *Focus on K2* on a small scale during its summer program, then launched it in the "early adopter" schools in September 2014.

The speed and scope of the rollout promised a choppy ride. Only two of the four units had been written by the start of the school year—enough to get to through the winter vacation. The advisory team worked frantically to complete the last two units in time, while also supporting the pilot. Because many more schools than anticipated signed up to be early adopters, the team needed to run extra PD sessions to accommodate all the teachers. Not surprisingly, some of the teachers were not on board right away. They were involved only because their principals had signed them up, and were resistant to the new curriculum.

Getting curricular materials to teachers was often a last-minute rush. DEC members drove curriculum binders around the city to get them in teachers' hands on time. And the DEC was copying and distributing something designed as a draft—an unfinished work intended to be revised based on feedback from teachers, children, and coaches.

The initial feedback from both teachers and children was overwhelmingly positive, but, as expected, issues arose that sparked discussion, debate, and changes in policy. One that the writing team had wrestled with was the issue of child choice. Should children get to choose what centers they want to go to, or should teachers organize Center Time so that children participate in all the activities? What if children diverged from the suggested activity in a center? What if a child spent much time in some centers and ignored others?

In its pilot year, the curriculum suggested that teachers encourage children to visit a variety of centers, in part, by limiting children's visits to any one center to two per week. A tracking system was devised and deployed. Teachers and children found the system complex, confusing, and disruptive to the flow of long-term work. Some within the department felt the system went against the spirit of the curriculum and NAEYC's guidelines about child choice during play.

After extensive discussion, the suggestion was discarded. Instead, teachers were encouraged to allow children to choose centers and move freely between them. Guidance about how teachers should address deviations from suggested center activities was also discussed at length. A consensus was reached that teachers should look for entry points for children to engage in the suggested activity. If children veered significantly from the activity, the teacher should assess whether the enduring understanding was being addressed, and redirect only if necessary. Recognizing that true engagement with materials and ideas would lead children to take activities in different directions or to use materials in novel ways, teachers should be attentive to these possibilities and how they could extend children's learning.

These recommendations are based on a trust in children's abilities to direct their learning and a trust in teachers' abilities to guide children's learning. Fidelity of implementation of the curriculum involves listening and adapting to children's interests. The curriculum focuses on teaching children, not teaching a set of activities.

Over the next two years, the curriculum was completed, tested, and revised based on feedback from teachers and children. One major change was in the Literacy Circles routine. Coaches had noticed that, when pressured to show student progress on literacy measures, some teachers responded by cutting Center Time to make room for literacy instruction and worksheets. The DEC sought a middle ground that would target specific skills in focused but more developmentally appropriate ways. After many classroom visits and much teacher feedback, the authors modified the Literacy Circles to create Working on Words. Schools using *Fundations* could substitute it for the whole group instruction sessions. The compromise was successful enough that, in 2017, *Fundations* was adopted districtwide.

At the time of this writing *Focus on K2* is being revised again, in keeping with a program designed to be responsive to the changing needs of the school district and its teachers, families, and students. The curriculum is online, allowing collaborators to make changes when needed. Anyone who is interested can download its units, customizable lesson plans and calendars, recommended learning materials, classroom routines, and teaching and learning tools. Every teacher receives a laptop—to be used not only for lesson planning, but also for photo and video documentation of children's work products and learning processes; communication with coaches, families, and other teachers; and research. A family event introduces each unit, and Home Links in multiple languages offer families fun activities for supporting and extending children's learning related to each unit.

Teachers, parents, and visitors to BPS have commented on the coherence of the curriculum, and the authenticity and scope of its topics. Many express surprise that young children can, and do, grapple with concepts such as what it means to be an engaged citizen, make thoughtful choices about the activities they will pursue during Center Time, or give and receive feedback on each other's' work during Thinking and Feedback.

Eventually, *Focus on K2* received local awards and garnered the respect of the Massachusetts Department of Elementary and Secondary Education, which provided funding to train teachers and pilot the curriculum in interested districts across the state. In 2016, the DEC put on a full-day conference for administrators and teachers who wanted to learn about *Focus on K2*. As districts across the nation discover the program, the DEC has discovered a new revenue source to support its ongoing projects: consulting to other schools and districts that wish to try the approach, Still, its focus remains on Boston's young children and their families.

Chapter Seven

Tamara's Day
A Visit to a K2 Classroom

This chapter offers a look inside a K2 classroom, where we follow a kindergartener who is deeply engaged in her learning adventure. The classroom is typical except in one respect; as an integrated classroom where many of the children have special rights, it has two full-time teachers instead of a teacher and a half-time paraprofessional. Although the Thinking and Feedback dialogue is accurately transcribed, we have changed the teachers' and children's names and altered other details to protect their privacy. As you join "Tamara" for the day, we hope you'll notice how her experiences reveal many of the core principles that underlie Focus on K2 *(and all of the DEC's work): promoting democratic values and supporting children's sense of citizenship (core principle 1); seeing children as active learners and engaging their curiosity, empathy, and higher-order thinking (core principle 2); building positive relationships as a foundation for learning (core principle 3); supporting all developmental and learning domains (core principle 4) with a flexible, hands-on curriculum that aligns with prior experiences (core principle 5) and fosters mastery of basic literacies, knowledge, and twenty-first-century skills through pretend play, projects, instruction, and extended conversation (core principle 6); differentiating instruction to accommodate children's differing interests, learning styles, paces, and abilities (core principle 7); and using ongoing, authentic assessment to guide curricular and instructional decisions (core principle 9).*

It's late April, and as Tamara rides the bus to school from her family's apartment near Roxbury Crossing, she notices some spring flowers starting to bloom in the local park. When she arrives, she is greeted by the vice principal and joins her classmates for breakfast in the cafeteria, provided free to all children in the school community. Tamara's teacher, Ms. Martinez, meets the children and guides them to the classroom to begin their day together. Tamara seeks out a friend to walk with in line, hangs up her backpack and coat, and signs in at the attendance chart in the classroom meeting area. She checks the storyteller list while she's there, and sees that today is her turn to be a storyteller during Storytelling/Story Acting time. Eager to tell her story, Tamara rushes to find Ms. Martinez. Once the other children are starting to settle into their Arrival Centers (looking at books or drawing), they sit down together.

Ms. Martinez opens a notebook, and Tamara begins, "Once upon a time, there was a princess and unicorn." She pauses, allowing Ms. Martinez to copy down her words. Watching the writing carefully, Tamara resumes her dictation when Ms. Martinez pauses, telling how "an evil witch stole the unicorn." Sitting nearby, Liam asks with concern, "Does the witch hurt the unicorn?" Tamara reassures him all will end well, and the story concludes with the princess rescuing the unicorn.

Ms. Martinez reads the story back to Tamara and Liam, running her finger under the words as she reads, an evidence-based practice that she often uses during Read Alouds to cue the children to notice the print without interfering with their enjoyment of the story.[1] She circles the names of characters, and asks Tamara, "Who would you like to be?" Tamara points to the word "princess." Later in the day, Tamara knows, she and Liam will act out the story with other children as the teacher narrates.

As they watch Ms. Martinez transcribe the story, Tamara and Liam are learning how print works (e.g., in English, we read from left to right) and seeing how particular words and sounds are represented. They may also be hearing and using new or newly learned vocabulary and practicing elements of narrative structure.

You may have noticed, too, how Tamara responded to Liam's interruption by rec-
ognizing his concern and incorporating his perspective, as a professional storyteller
might do with an audience member.

Both the storytelling and story acting components of Storytelling/Story Acting
provide opportunities to strengthen listening skills. For children learning English
or with language delays, the acting component of the process provides an entry
point into the world of words. Tamara and her classmates are also learning to
collaborate as they tell their stories and act them out together together.[2] This is all
happening in the mode through which young children learn best: play. At the same
time, we can see how pretend play and focused instruction build upon each other.[3]

Soon, Tamara hears the good morning song playing on the sound system:
"Welcome everyone, good morning to you . . . " She hustles to find a seat on
the rug in the meeting area and joins in singing boisterously with her friends.
Ms. Martinez leads the class in familiar movements to the song—stretching
and bending and clapping—as the whole class gradually joins and settles on
the rug. When the song ends, she goes over the attendance chart. Noticing
that Cara is out sick today, she says, "I hope she feels better soon." Several
children murmur and nod.

Next, Ms. Martinez picks up a small whiteboard and starts writing the
letters NJ. "Today our Meeting Leader's name has these initials. Raise your
hand if you have an idea about who the Meeting Leader is today." Hands fly
up, and it is quickly determined that Carlo Jones will lead the greeting. It's
Carlo's job to choose a welcome game for the group, and he opts for a community favorite—Name Ball. Ms. Martinez asks him to get a small felt ball
from a basket beside her, and reminds the group about how to play, "When
you are holding the ball, you can say your name in any way you choose: a high
voice, a low voice, a spooky voice, a whisper . . . " Ms. Martinez models a few
options for her name, then Carlo begins with a spooky voice. Tamara giggles at
her friends' silly voices. Once the ball has made its way around the circle, Ms.
Martinez thanks Carlo for leading and reaches back into the basket at her side,
which is stocked with materials for demonstrating the morning's activities.

Today, although there will be more than eight different options open during the morning Center Time, Ms. Martinez focuses on two activities: a

dramatization area activity called "Growing and Preparing Food" and a new investigation with soil and worms in the Science area. The dramatization activity has already been underway for two weeks. Since the launch of the new "Our Earth" unit, children have been working to transform the dramatization area into a garden, pretending to plant seeds and harvest produce. Today, Ms. Martinez highlights some work that children did in the dramatization area the day before. She invites Justin and Marta to stand up and explain the seed labels they created. "So we know which seeds we planted," they explain, and show the labels, made on scraps of construction paper and fastened to the wall of the dramatization area with tape.

Ms. Martinez thanks Justin and Marta for sharing their idea, and encourages other children to continue making labels for the garden today. Next, she lifts a small container of soil and a live earthworm into her lap, and models how to hold the worm carefully in a flat palm to observe its movements. She also models using a note-taking sheet for sketching and labeling parts of the worm's body.

"This is a *live* worm. That means it can move and eat. So we need to handle it with *care* and place it gently into the *soil* when we are finished observing," she explains, embedding key vocabulary words from the Our Earth unit, using real soil to illustrate what that word means. Modeling the use of Unifix cubes as a measuring tool, she encourages children to figure out which worm is the longest.

As Meeting Time comes to a close, Ms. Martinez reminds the children of the other activities open this morning by holding up an artifact from each area and asking, for example, "If you'd like to start in the Art Studio and work on constructing imaginary trees today, raise your hand." Tamara's hand is up in a flash, and she heads over to the Art Studio to continue the tree she began working on the day before.

The warm, welcoming, and playful atmosphere of the morning whole group routines is an intentional part of the curriculum. You may have noticed how the community-building time with the Name Ball game honored each class member and how Ms. Martinez modeled empathy and caring by acknowledging a child who was absent. Beginning their days in this way strengthens relationships between the children and teachers and sets the tone for their ongoing learning.[4]

You may also have noticed how Ms. Martinez shared power with the children during the meeting. When a child acts as the meeting leader, the meeting is co-constructed, with Carlo deciding the game of the day. And when Justin and Marta share their work, their voices are heard and their classmates have a chance to be inspired by their ideas. The children are not just learning democratic citizenship; they are routinely acting as citizens.[5]

Specific academic skills are also woven into the experience. When Ms. Martinez provides a clue about the meeting leader, she sets up a motivating opportunity for letter recognition and phonemic awareness. Using children's work in the drama-tization area as a model, she also encourages writing for a purpose in the labeling of seeds. Using Unifix cubes to measure the worms embeds mathematical concepts of length, number, and comparison. Finally, modeling observational skills and careful handling of a live animal explicitly teaches several key science dispositions believed to be critical to developing an inquiry mind-set and included in the Next Generation Science Standards.[6] And by focusing on in-depth introductions to some of the morning's activities, the group builds shared excitement and awareness about the life of the classroom and curriculum.

Retrieving the imaginary tree she had begun to work on the previous day, Tamara sits down next to Sateen and Lily in the Art Studio. Tamara's tree is small—two pieces of wire twisted together with small pink and red pieces of paper taped to the sides. On the table are a variety of materials (paper, sticks, paper, and small Styrofoam balls), tools (tape, scissors, and markers) and the Dr. Seuss book *The Lorax*, one of the Read Alouds in the Our Earth unit.[7] Sateen reminds her friends that, "We have to make a lot of trees so we can have a forest."

The girls have just have started work when Anthony appears. Pointing to the Block area, he reminds Tamara, "You promised you'd help me make City Hall." Tamara gets up from her chair, prompting Lily to exclaim, "But you have to help make trees!" Tamara brings her tree back to the storage shelf, and Lily cries, "I'm not your friend."

Lily stomps off. A minute later, she returns with Ms. Martinez, announcing, "It's not fair. She has to help us." Looking unsure about what to do, Tamara begins to cry. Ms. Martinez asks each girl to explain her perspective about the problem to the other. A solution is reached where Tamara will build City Hall today and help create the imagination forest tomorrow. Ms. Martinez offers the girls a sticky note to write a reminder, and they write, using invented spelling, "RMbR FReST TOMARW" (Remember forest tomorrow).

Tamara's dilemma was a difficult one, especially for a five-year-old. It is also typical. Kindergarten-age children develop a strong sense of fairness, and are likely to insist that promises be kept. At the same time, they build strong friendships and often demand loyalty. "I am not your friend," is a common threat. Although it is not clear in this instance, Tamara may have been risking exclusion by violating a clique norm or the command of a demanding leader.[8] It's easy to empathize with her plight and want to step in.

Did you notice how Ms. Martinez resisted solving the problem for the girls, but instead helped then to resolve it themselves? In the process, they developed and practiced important academic and social-emotional skills: making a case, listening, taking another's perspective, and collaborating in problem solving to find a creative solution—integrating cognitive, language, and social-emotional learning.[9]

Although this was not a literacy lesson, you may have noticed the girls' use of invented spelling. As they attempt to write the sounds they hear, children often work out the alphabetic principle (that letters and letter combinations represent the sounds that make up words) for themselves. This is a key step in learning to read. Over time, children's attempts will increasingly approximate the conventional spellings that they see as they read.[10]

On the way to the Block area, Tamara and Anthony pass the library, where Riley, Will, and Erikson are previewing copies of Lynne Cherry's book *The Great Kapok Tree*, which Ms. Martinez will read aloud to the class later today.[11] In the dramatization area, Carly, Nick, and Alana have added a row of lettuce (green paper crumpled into balls) to their garden. And in the science center, children are sorting seeds according to size, shape, and color, recording information in their science notebooks about which collection contains the most seeds. Arriving at the Block area, Tamara and Anthony begin building Boston's City Hall, most likely inspired by yesterday's field trip to see their class's Our Boston model displayed there.

Ms. Martinez and her co-teacher, Ms. Jamison, are circulating among the centers, observing, taking notes, photographing the children, asking children questions about their work and play, and making mental notes of their assessments for future planning.[12] Ms. Martinez asks Tamara and Anthony to explain how they will make their structure stable. Anthony, points to a row of blocks at the base of the structure. "Oh, a *foundation*," Ms. Martinez responds.

Forty minutes into Center Time, Ms. Martinez asks four children to join her in the STEM Center for a conversation about compost. Over the next five weeks, the teachers will guide small groups investigating how worms begin to turn food scraps into soil.

At the very end of Center Time, Ms. Martinez consults with Ms. Jamison about which artifact should be brought to Thinking and Feedback. They quickly agree that Tamara and Anthony's block structure would spark a rich conversation. Ms. Martinez asks the pair if they would like to share their work, and they agree.

*You probably noticed that Anthony understood Ms. Martinez's request to explain how they would make their structure stable, but responded nonverbally. In her response, Ms. Martinez introduced what may have been a new word for Anthony—*foundation—*connecting it to his understanding of stability.*

Immediately after Center Time, the class gathers for a Thinking and Feedback session in the Block area. Tamara and Anthony are standing in front of the over-two-foot tall structure they constructed during Center Time. It is clearly influenced by what they saw during yesterday's class trip, with echoes of the atrium and the numerous people who populate the building during business hours, many of whom had stopped to admire the children's work. Tamara and Anthony stand behind their creation, while their twenty classmates sit in a horseshoe configuration, looking carefully at the structure.

Tamara begins the proceedings, confidently calling out, "Observe." After a few moments, children begin to raise their hands. Tamara looks over to Anthony to signal him to begin. He calls on Alea, who answers, "I notice there are lots of people on the ends." Anthony begins to explain, "Yeah, because there are," but Tamara taps him on the shoulder to remind him that presenters don't respond during the observing portion of the protocol. Anthony stops his explanation and Tamara calls on Morgan.

MORGAN: I notice there are, like, lots of blocks.

ANTHONY: Liam.

LIAM: What is that? Are those stairs or something?

ANTHONY (in a quiet voice): Yeah, they're stairs.

LIAM: OK.

TAMARA: Brandon.

BRANDON: Did you get inspired from where we. From City Hall or was it something else?

ANTHONY: City Hall.

ANTHONY: Jeremy.

JEREMY: I notice. Why is there a doctor on top?

ANTHONY: We wanted to put people who had different jobs.

JEREMY: Did you put those tiny babies?

ANTHONY: Yeah.

TAMARA: Babies don't have jobs.

JEREMY: Did you guys put babies? We could make a tower of a kids' museum and the babies could play there. Because City Hall doesn't have that. There could be two buildings. The kids' museum could be right there and you guys could finish the blocks with City Hall.

At this point, almost three minutes into the conversation, Ms. Martinez, who is filming the session, speaks for the first time. Referring to Jeremy's last comments, she notes, "That's a great suggestion" and reminds the children that suggestions come later in the protocol. She then prompts Tamara and Anthony to begin the "Listen" part of the conversation.

Tamara confirms the building's origins, stating, "We decided we got really inspired by City Hall. We decided to make it." She turns to Anthony who adds, "There are like a lot of people inside city hall and we wanted to make a lot of people." Tamara adds, "And we put in a lot of important people. Police."

Tamara moves the protocol on to the next phase, saying "Wonder." Many hands shoot up in the air. She looks around and calls on Marie, who answers,

"I wonder that . . . um . . . did you like? Um . . . did you guys?" While Sarah struggles to articulate her ideas, her classmates listen quietly.

MARIE: There is people (pointing to the figures on the top of the structure). And there is people down and people up.

MS. MARTINEZ: You're wondering how they got up?

MARIE: And, and. No. Like up and down.

ANTHONY: There wasn't a lot of space there (pointing inside the structure). So that's why we decided to put some of the people on the roof."

TAMARA: Allie.

MARTA: Why didn't you build more floors?

TAMARA: Because we didn't want City Hall to be really big, so we decided to make just two floors.

ANTHONY: Ms. Martinez!

MS. MARTINEZ: You guys said that you put important people. I'm wondering who are the important people.

ANTHONY: The police. Doctors. The mac-and-cheese cook. Painter.

TAMARA: Firefighter.

ANTHONY: Firefighter. Builder. Teacher. The farmer and . . .

TAMARA: The soldier. The police.

MS. MARTINEZ: So a lot of community workers.

TAMARA: Yes.

MS. MARTINEZ: One more wonder.

Tamara raises her hand to signal to her classmates she is ready to call on them and acknowledges Jenna.

CARLY: Does the doctor help people in there?

ANTHONY (nodding): The doctor is for people who are hurt. Sick. Have cuts.

TAMARA: Doctors aren't for cuts. It is if you have emergencies. Like if you're hurt.

Called on by Tamara, Nick notices that there are spaces between some of the figures. Anthony explains, "We wanted to make some spaces so all the people could be in different places and not be all squished." Tamara then signals a move to the "suggestions" part of the protocol. She calls on Ms. Martinez, who offers a suggestion: to make another floor between the bottom of the structure and the roof and offers to help in this effort. There are a few seconds of silence and then Tamara points at Anthony. He calls on Tamika.

> TAMIKA: My suggestion is, I want to add to Ms. Martinez's suggestion. Maybe another way to add more people. I mean—let me talk—I mean *floor*. The way you can put another floor is to use three big blocks and put them up and . . . Maybe you can add people when you make a new floor.
>
> MS. MARTINEZ: Great. So, once we add another floor, we can fit more people. Yeah. All the people who work in City Hall.

Ms. Martinez brings Thinking and Sharing to an end by having the class acknowledge and applaud Tamara and Anthony's work and facilitation. Nine minutes have elapsed. Tamara and Anthony have worked together seamlessly in facilitating the conversation, supporting each other with whispers, sidewise glances and taps on the shoulder. More than half their classmates have spoken. There have been forty-nine conversational turns. Forty-two have been by children.

As you can see, the children are learning skills needed to participate in conversations—taking turns, listening to one another, asking questions, clearly explaining their ideas. All are important Common Core State Standards (SL.K.1 through SL.K.6), and this group is demonstrating age-appropriate mastery.[13] But the learning goes far beyond this. Inspired by examples from the schools of Reggio Emilia and the work of the Expeditionary Learning Center for High Quality Student Work, Focus on K2 supports kindergarteners to become adept at reflecting, problem solving, discussing ongoing projects, respecting multiple points of view, giving and receiving constructive feedback, and supporting their peers.[14] As citizens of democratic classrooms, they are learning to learn from and with one another.[15]

It may not be obvious, but Anthony is a dual language learner; he speaks Haitian Creole at home. His verbal participation during the feedback session shows significant advances in his English language skills and communicative confidence since September, a testament to the curriculum's alignment with research-based practices for supporting children learning English at school. As early educator and language development researcher Patton Tabors explains in One Child, Two Languages, *a supportive curriculum for such young children includes predictable routines and classroom organization; a language- and literacy-rich classroom environment; modifications to the curriculum that help DLLs to feel "more comfortable, included, and competent," such as the use of concrete materials to facilitate dialogue and understanding in small groups, explicit yet contextual integration of vocabulary instruction within play, and facilitation of peer interactions through scaffolding of play and supporting monolingual peers to support DLLs.[16] The practice of Thinking and Feedback is one component of this kind of supportive curriculum that enables dual language learners to thrive. Focus on K2 teacher materials offer tips throughout for supporting individual learning strengths and needs and including all children as full participants in the classroom community.[17]*

When the children return from gym class, Ms. Martinez gathers them on the rug for Read Aloud. Energy levels are high on the heels of a rowdy walk down the hall from the gym, and it's clear that a redirection is needed if the story is going to be a success. Ms. Martinez launches a "match me" game, laughing and gradually moving from standing and jumping to sitting and clapping, regaining the children's attention along the way. Tamara continues chatting with her neighbor and is asked to change seats and sit closer to Ms. Martinez.

Careful not to wait too long and lose the group's focus again, Ms. Martinez holds up *The Great Kapok Tree*. She reminds the children about the books they have been reading about plants and trees: *From Seed to Plant* by Gail Gibbons and *The Gift of the Tree* by Alvin Tresselt.[18] "Those were nonfiction books with true information. Today, we are reading a story about a very big tree called *The Great Kapok Tree*. A kapok tree is a special kind of tree that grows in the rainforest. This is not a true story, but the author, Lynne Cherry, used real information about trees and rainforests when she wrote this story." Showing the map at the beginning of the book, Ms. Martinez sets the context and provides some background information about the rain forest.

As she reads, Ms. Martinez pauses to define key vocabulary and to make connections to children's prior experiences and other books the group has read. "*Depend* means that the living things need each other to live and be well. In a community, people or animals *depend* on each other, like we *depend* on each other to do our jobs in the classroom every day." When the story ends, she turns back to a specific page and poses a question to the group. "At the end of the story, the man stops cutting down the great kapok tree. Why do you think he decided to stop? Turn and talk to a partner." Familiar with the turn-and-talk routine, children quickly start to discuss, and Ms. Martinez asks a couple to share their ideas with the group, weaving the target vocabulary into the conversation again.

After lunch, the group returns to the book, this time for Working on Words, a whole group session that targets foundational literacy skills. "Let's build sentences about the animals in *The Great Kapok Tree*," Ms. Martinez says, then invites children to contribute ideas to a large easel paper. She shares the pen with the children, so Tamara and her classmates take turns forming letters and words to communicate a joint message together. Working on Words ends with a focus on words containing digraphs, using a matching game with words and associated images from the text. "Tomorrow, you can choose to play with the matching game again in the Word Work Center," Ms. Martinez tells the children, then gets the group ready for math workshop.

Noticing that the children may not have been ready to engage with the book, Ms. Martinez used humor and movement to bridge from a rowdy gym class to an activity requiring close and sustained attention. She introduced the book in a way that not only generated interest but activated prior knowledge, preparing children to expect a particular type of book and content-specific information. This context would make it easier for children to understand new words and follow the plot of the story. As they learn to read independently, these techniques will help them to infer the meaning of new words from context and to read with fluency and understanding.

You may have noticed how Ms. Martinez highlighted new vocabulary words as she read and offered child-friendly definitions, helping children to learn the words and understand the story. The Turn and Talk session engaged children's thinking—helping them to more fully understand the central character's motivation and the story's message about respecting and caring for the planet.

The subsequent Working on Words activities reinforce both decoding and comprehension skills within the meaningful context of a well written and highly engaging children's book. They offer children ongoing opportunities to practice a range of literacy skills as they deepen their understanding and appreciation of Our Earth and communicate their ideas about how to care for it.

The Focus on K2 *guiding documents and related materials on the DEC's website support teachers in implementing the curriculum with fidelity. But it is the professional development, coaching, and collegial support they receive that enables teachers like Ms. Martinez and Ms. Jamison to think deeply about their practice and continue to grow.*

Chapter Eight

A New Model of Professional Development

Professional development remains at the heart of the DEC's work. Today, it includes courses for teachers given by the DEC, daylong, multiday, and after-school sessions that bring teachers from different schools together, school-level workshops and regularly scheduled joint planning times, an annual Kindergarten Conference that early childhood teachers and paraprofessionals attend, and both curriculum-related and NAEYC accreditation–related coaching. All of the DEC staff members are involved in some of these activities, and most are involved in the one-to-one coaching.

DEC program director Melissa Tonachel explains the DEC's professional development practice of creating adult learning experiences that are grounded in respectful and supportive relationships, mirroring those that they encourage adults to build with children:

> As a department, we recognize that children will not be supported in classrooms unless their teachers are supported as professionals. Professional development (PD) must aim both to expand and strengthen teachers' repertoire of skills and to engage them intellectually and emotionally.

We don't deliver; we *facilitate*. We don't inform; we ask teachers to experience and then to try. We look more at artifacts of learning—artifacts from classrooms that tell something about the journey of getting to a finished product—than at decontextualized examples of student work. And we do this same work ourselves, honing our own practice as coaches and facilitators in order to best support teachers' development as professionals.[1]

Because the DEC sees PD as the key to teacher engagement as well as to equitable high quality, it offers a systemic PD program with the built-in flexibility to adapt to the needs of particular schools, teachers, principals, and paraprofessionals.

The program includes:

- **Curriculum-focused PD:** This is a key piece of each grade-level curriculum rollout. During days-long introductory sessions, teachers come together to explore the curriculum. They examine and discuss the knowledge, conceptual understanding, skills, habits, and dispositions that it is meant to engage, teach, and strengthen, and the underlying goals of prototypic activities. During the first year that a school implements a new or revised curriculum, teachers attend monthly seminars where they delve into particular practices and themes and have opportunities to share ideas and challenges with each other and with the DEC. Teachers new to a curriculum receive coaching that aligns with the curricular seminars but is tailored to their individual questions, passions, expertise, and challenges.

- **Practice-focused PD:** Practices such as Guided Reading, Storytelling/ Story Acting, Math Workshop, Thinking and Feedback, and Making Learning Visible are built into all of the curricula. In targeted PD sessions or series, teachers can delve deeply into the purposes of a practice and the techniques that make it effective. Extensive modeling, guidance through the steps of a process, sharing of successes and challenges, documentation of classroom experiences, and shared reflection enable them to implement the practice with confidence and integrity, adapting to the needs of their students.

- **Accreditation-focused PD:** Helping all of the schools to achieve NAEYC accreditation is a long-term DEC goal. Budgeting $6,000 per classroom per year, the DEC arranges for a coach to spend an average of three years shepherding each school through the process. The coach works with instructional leaders, offers sessions for parents and staff, and observes and coaches in individual classrooms.
- **Cross-cutting themes:** At times, the DEC offers PD sequences and coaching that go into depth on topics such as supporting children with special rights, dual language learning, or documentation. DEC members may also facilitate discussions during regularly scheduled common planning time.

Whether the focus is on curriculum, accreditation, a particular practice, or a more general theme, each PD or coaching session is designed to address four goals:

- To foster teachers' professionalism and sense of agency
- To support a high-quality, developmentally appropriate program for children, with a rich and engaging curriculum
- To create a community of intentional practice, whereby teachers participate in shared conversations across the district about teaching and learning
- To bolster strong practice in all teachers, grounded in a shared, sophisticated, and nuanced pedagogy

A Teacher's PD Journey

Maria Valarezo began her teaching career in 2012 as a Boston Public Schools K2 teacher in Roxbury after receiving her teaching license from the early childhood program at Boston University. That same year, she enrolled in her first DEC-sponsored PD course, "Boston Listens. This months-long course on supporting children's literacy, social-emotional, and executive functioning development is inspired by the work of Vivian Paley.[2] It focuses on the Storytelling /Story Acting described in chapter 6 and illustrated in chapter 7 ("Tamara's Day"). As the course emphasizes, the key to the technique is listening. Teachers learn to tell stories that have personal meaning for them in ways that will engage the children's active listening and questions. They learn to help children tell both actual and imagined stories that have meaning for them, and to become increasingly adept storytellers, even when they begin with stories that contain only one or a few words. Children learn to listen attentively to each other's stories, ask helpful clarifying questions, and act out the stories with respect. In the process, children learn and practice critical executive function skills of focused attention, impulse control, and working memory; social-emotional skills of listening, empathy, turn taking, and perspective taking; and critical literacy skills of storytelling and vocabulary.

As children dictate to their teacher, they see how written language represents what is spoken. Depending on their interest and the teacher's focus, they may sharpen concepts of print, phonemic and alphabet awareness, sight word recognition, and/or spelling skills.

New research suggests that Storytelling/Story Acting may be particularly powerful for African American boys. Telling stories that captivate an audience is a prized skill in many African American communities, especially for males.[3] Some children excel at it from an early age, but many do not. In a longitudinal study of African American children, most from families with low incomes, Nicole Gardner-Neblett and John Sedaris found that four-year-old boys who were better at creating a connected narrative to tell the story of a wordless picture book made faster progress in reading through the sixth grade than did those who had more trouble with this task. Girls in the same community tended to tell more connected and coherent narratives as four-year-olds. Their relative skill predicted strong reading achievement in the early grades, but was less predictive of how rapidly their reading scores increased over time. The researchers concluded:

> Fostering the early oral narrative skills of African-American boys may present a mechanism for supporting positive reading outcomes for a population of children deemed at risk of reading failure and poor academic outcomes.[4]

Valarezo was intrigued by the Boston Listens course but nervous about using the techniques with her students, a group she described as frequently exhibiting challenging behaviors. Nevertheless, she persevered, and soon began seeing the impacts of the Storytelling/Story Acting practice: "It was amazing," she recalls, "all the effects on the children's learning: vocabulary, their developing confidence, how it gave children a voice."

Valarezo credits the enthusiasm of DEC member and course instructor Marina Boni with keeping her going. "I am by no means an expert," Valarezo reports, "but I had my successes trusted and valued."

As you follow Valarezo's ongoing PD journey, you may notice the importance that trust and strong relationships continue to play in her willingness to take the risks that enable her to grow. What's true for children is also true for adults: relationships are central to powerful learning experiences.[5] In each PD experience, DEC members build relationships with Valarezo, and between Valarezo and her colleagues, through shared inquiry, empathy, and commitment to each other's success. You may also notice how DEC core principles of children at the center—as citizens, community members, and curious, active and capable learners—provide common ground for coaches' conversations with teachers and with each other.[6]

In Valarezo's second year as a kindergarten teacher, the DEC rolled out its new *Focus on K2* curriculum. Her school volunteered to be part of the first wave, and she attended a two-day summer workshop to get an overview of the curriculum and prepare for the coming year. As she began to implement the curriculum in her classroom, Valarezo joined other early adopters in monthly curriculum-focused seminars. She recalls her early engagement with the department:

> The thing that affects me most with the PD is the element of trust. You, the department, go above and beyond to make us feel safe. Seminars give me something to look forward to . . . You see teachers' strengths, value our ideas . . . You ask us, "What are your preferences? What do you think?" It is not top-down. And paraprofessionals are included. Their voices are honored.[7]

Valarezo was offered in-school coaching along with the seminars, and apprehensively agreed. Although the PD she received was helpful, her first year piloting the new curriculum had continued to feel challenging, as it is for many new teachers. She worried about how an observer would assesses her teaching, but soon discovered that the respect, encouragement, and patience she had appreciated in Boni's teaching was characteristic of the coaching as well. Her coach, Melissa Luc, made it clear from the beginning that she was there to help, not to judge, instruct, or demand compliance.

As they built their relationship, Luc did more listening than questioning or advising. Some things concerned her about the classroom, but she kept them to herself and let Valarezo set the agenda. Yet she could see that Valarezo, too, felt that some things just weren't working. Valarezo remembers the turning point:

> Sensing that I was upset, my coach said, "You know what? Let's start fresh. Let's change the whole classroom environment." I remember it was very late in the day, and Melissa was flexible enough to come then, after school. I was willing to try anything to motivate the children to engage more with the curriculum and to display more positive social behaviors.

The new classroom arrangement helped the children to focus and to engage in the *Focus on K2* activities in more thoughtful ways. As Valarezo recalls, "Children became more excited about their K2 experience." Luc agreed.

Valarezo's growing relationship with Luc and the changes she saw in the children gave her the confidence to take significant risks. Although she was still learning the curriculum, she signed on as a teacher leader in the first year of *Focus on K2*, learning facilitation skills to help her school-based colleagues work through dilemmas arising as they learned to teach the new curriculum while acting as a liaison to the *Focus on K2* team at the DEC.

Valarezo's PD journey did not stop with her successful implementation of *Focus on K2*. She enrolled in the Making Learning Visible course, an ongoing look at using observation and documentation to inform teaching. There, she encountered structures for reflective group discussions such as the Fishbowl (where participants in an outside circle observe and then discuss the conversation or activity in the center) and the See-Think-Wonder protocol.[8] As a teacher leader, Valarezo took the risk of engaging in the Fishbowl protocol, bringing samples of her students' work for the group to analyze. Sharing these artifacts with her colleagues as she applied what she had learned prompted her to think more deeply about what her students were learning, thinking, and imagining. The structured conversations also contributed to a strong collaborative relationship among the teachers, mirroring what they were attempting to create for their students.

Still, Valarezo felt that she was just beginning to grasp and apply the power of documentation. She had become fascinated with her students' stories, and wanted to analyze their growth more fully to support her implementation of what she had learned in the Boston Listens seminar. A colleague mentioned that she had taken the Making Learning Visible course twice; this possibility had not occurred to Valarezo, but she immediately embraced it.

In the second round, Valarezo had a much richer experience. Now she wasn't just learning about a practice that might be worth trying; she had an agenda. Focusing on Storytelling/Story Acting, she began to document children's work over time. She explored various elements of writing, such as voice, the use of dialogue, transition words, and use of more sophisticated vocabulary. As part of the course, she created a PowerPoint presentation that demonstrated the growth of the children's stories over time, analyzing both the stories themselves and her scaffolding conversations with the children, and including the children's thoughts about storytelling. The feedback her classmates and the instructor provided had a deep influence in how she modified her storytelling teaching techniques—and continued to learn from her students.

Valarezo continues to respond to nearly every invitation to participate in the work of the DEC, joining colleagues and DEC facilitators for conversations about teaching practice that are centered on children's work. She continues to come to every kindergarten seminar and to seize opportunities to collaborate, facilitate, and lead.

As a member of the work group setting out to design a new kindergarten report card, for example, Valarezo noted that the group functioned not only in an advisory capacity, but also as professional development:

> It gave me a better grasp of standards and of translating curriculum into standards; it also got me thinking about foundational pieces that make the curriculum so special. There was the collaboration—articulating a common belief system about how we want children to feel, thinking about families and how they would understand this.

Being invited is empowering, especially as a novice teacher. It reminds me that I am a stakeholder, that I do have an impact on children's learning and their experience. Not just the children in my class, but across the district.

Summing up her PD experiences, Valarezo adds: "Everything happened at the right moment."

For the DEC, PD is always a two-way street, and teachers are valued partners. They are often invited to join DEC staff in presenting at conferences and training sessions. They might join work groups on a special project. They are asked to review and offer feedback as curricula are undergoing revision. They may agree to be videotaped in their classrooms for use in other PD sessions or presentations and workshops outside of BPS. Recently, a group of early childhood teachers from several schools has coalesced as leaders of Early Childhood Leadership teams at their schools.

Guiding Principles for Professional Development

As in any teaching, tailoring PD experiences to the particular needs of specific learners and to the idiosyncrasies of a given group is essential. When the learning experiences occur "at the right moment," they are likely to be remembered, integrated, put to use, reflected on, and shared. For the DEC, creating powerful learning moments and learning sequences rests on four interlocking and intentional practices: building relationships, grounding discussions in content and practice, working with transparency, and sparking transformation.

Building Relationships

This step is critical, and can't be rushed. Relationships set the tone for successful and satisfying PD and coaching experiences; they also deepen and develop through these experiences.

DEC members spend a lot of time in classrooms. They make a point of getting to know the teachers as individuals, as well as trying to understand the particular school and community context in which each works. In a district as diverse as Boston, the process must include an appreciation for varying cultural values and experiences. It also includes respect for different teaching styles, school and family traditions, and curricular and programming decisions that may vary from one school to another.

DEC members also build relationships with principals, recognizing that they play vital roles in supporting teachers to create optimal contexts for children. The team works through PD and other channels to build multilayered communities, with connections between and among coaches, principals, and teachers. As they implement and extend ideas explored in PD sessions, teachers can continue to learn together, and to both support and challenge each other.

Many teachers are eager for PD and coaching; others initially come because it's mandated by their principal or by the DEC. Some are skeptical of the value of a particular offering or its fit for their classes, or are nervous about their ability to master and apply the material. Many are curious but need to be convinced. Melissa Tonachel describes the DEC's approach with teachers who are hesitant:

> Our first job is to bring them into a learning experience in which they can be successful and feel inspired. As with young children, we do this by recognizing who the teachers are, what they might contribute, and what questions they wish to entertain. We operate with the assumption that if we do this successfully, an authentic, ongoing, fruitful conversation about teaching and learning will ensue.

There is, as she reports, a natural tension between the DEC's genuine respect for diversity (and for building on its advantages) and their strong advocacy for particular curricula and practices. But with an approach that invites collaborative experimentation and mutual learning, the DEC members convey their respect for doubts and differences as well as for teachers' strengths and for the realities of their working lives. In turn, as Tonachel explains,

> teachers trust our intent and are ready to join with us and with each other in the experiments we propose . . . Rather than delivering PD so that everyone understands how to teach a particular series of lessons, we begin: "Think about your own experience with this topic. Talk with each other

about the way you might approach it with children . . . And then we'll share how we're thinking about it." The conversation goes two ways. We are constantly asking ourselves: to what extent do we give the teachers space to share their experience and expertise about what should happen in classrooms and to what extent do we articulate what we think should be happening? Teachers understand that our conversations with them are reciprocal; we are explicit about the ways their ideas benefit our own.

Grounding in Content and Practice

Whether focused on a grade-level curriculum, a particular practice such as documentation, an accreditation standard, or a cross-cutting theme or issue, PD sessions are always grounded in the content of the DEC's curricula, established effective early childhood practices, and the realities of the teachers' classrooms. Drawing "appreciatively and respectfully" from what coaches observe and from their conversations with teachers, DEC team members turn abstract ideas into practicable application—without shying away from dilemmas and ambiguities. Tonachel explains how tying the PD to concrete examples and dilemmas of practice builds solidarity and shared expertise among the teachers:

> A critical aspect of PD sessions is the time teachers have to peek into each other's classrooms through the windows of children's work, video, and discussion of teaching moves. This helps build the teachers' relationships with each other and with the curriculum.
>
> We might explore, for example, how Read Aloud texts can support rich conversation and interdisciplinary learning. A deep dive into a particular text that teachers are using during the current unit of study makes the conversation even more compelling: How are children enacting *this* story? What kinds of structures are they building in response to this illustration? What words from the text do you hear children using around the classroom? Now teachers can share their experiences with each other and develop common and directly applicable expertise. They leave the session with something they've contributed to, and something to go on.

Seeing PD and coaching sessions as learning opportunities for themselves as well as the teachers, the DEC strives to create respectful learning communities for adults that both connect with and mirror the inquiry-promoting environments they seek to create for children.[9] Tonachel elaborates:

> As we empower teachers to grab, realize, and enliven a practice in their own classroom we release that practice into the teacher's hands. We believe that if we value teachers' agency over fidelity to a curriculum, then they will participate in taking risks and trying new things. That requires in us a tolerance for teachers going off script, a trust that they will do so with informed intention, a willingness to see what comes of what they create. This is a a message to teachers that flexibility, trust, and openness affords space for wonderful things to happen. We hope that the same empowerment then extends to the children.

Transparency

Transparency is essential as DEC members negotiate differences in perspectives between principals, teachers, and themselves. Coaches keep principals abreast of their visits to individual classrooms while protecting the relationships they have established with teachers. Recognizing the differences in roles, expertise, mind-sets, and daily pressures between principals and teachers, DEC members sometimes play an intermediary role, as Tonachel notes:

> Teachers often ask us to convince, talk with, and explain to their principals about how young children learn best and what that might look like as principals observe and evaluate teaching. Critically, we play a role in disrupting the often-tense principal-teacher dynamic by establishing a shared understanding about children's learning.

One helpful technique is to offer "look for" guides to help principals see the learning and intentional teaching in what may seem at first like simply play—and also notice when the play is unproductive or the teaching is a mismatch with how young children learn best.

Still, the path to shared understanding of what is best for children is rarely clear-cut. Principals have agendas that may or may not align with the needs of young children or resonate with early childhood teachers. Teachers may have practices that collide with curriculum implementation. The DEC's pedagogy may differ from that of teachers or principals. The DEC coaches work to articulate and mediate these conflicting views and priorities in support of children's learning and teachers' development. One approach is to build pathways for teachers to become supported leaders within their schools who nurture inquisitive and productive communities among their colleagues. As Tonachel puts it:

> It is not a simple fix: in a profession where teachers and principals are pulled in too many directions and handed conflicting mandates, everyone is trying to make sense of how to fashion a cohesive practice. We assert that when we acknowledge these dilemmas, the teachers sense that we "get it" and the work can continue.

Transformation

PD sessions and coaching encounters do not simply affirm a teacher's practice. They are designed to push—to inspire, disrupt, extend, and transform. Even the strongest, most reflective teachers continue to deepen the questions they ask of themselves, their colleagues, and the children they teach. While some PD sessions are geared toward simply untangling the curriculum itself (perhaps preparing for an upcoming unit of study or practicing a component of instruction), the primary thrust is toward supporting teachers' growth. Tonachel explains their approach:

> Rather than assuming that all teachers will change in the same ways, we adopt the stance that all teachers are capable and thus capable of evolving: taking risks to adapt new practices, just as all children are competent and developing. This requires patience, of course, as transformation happens over time, in the context of one's own teaching environment, and with support.

The support comes from DEC coaches and facilitators and from colleagues who enter into discussions, ask seemingly risky questions, and share work from their classrooms. It also comes through mutual celebration of the work of teachers and children.

Of course, teachers are not the only ones for whom PD and coaching encounters are transformative. Coaches and facilitators expect to be changed as teachers pose challenging dilemmas, suggest different approaches, or encounter unexpected challenges or opportunities as they implement PD learnings. Pushing themselves in the same ways that they push teachers, the DEC staff try to approach each encounter as a learning experience, listening intently, reflecting alone and with each other, and remaining consciously open to transformation.

Nuts and Bolts of PD and Coaching—DEC Style

Teachers approach a published curriculum in various ways. Melissa Tonachel describes the range that she and other DEC coaches and PD providers have experienced:

> Some grab hold of the teacher's guide and read it as a set of instructions to be followed step by step, using exactly the materials and pace it suggests. Others take a look, get the gist, and toss it aside, letting it collect dust while they go about loosely interpreting curricular themes and relying on a combination of instinct, established teaching practice, and other curricula they have used. Most teachers fall somewhere in the middle. They read to understand the shape and intent of the curriculum, put most of the activities into action, and mix in additional activities as needed to meet school or district mandates, follow the interests of particular children or a group, and draw on their own passions, expertise, and favorite activities.

As the DEC team rolls out new curricula, they think carefully about how to support teachers in making these decisions, using the curriculum as a roadmap rather than simply following along in the teacher's guide. As Tonachel explains:

> In approaching the design of a PD offering or sequence, we rely on some familiar structures but we don't have a standard template. Instead, we ask ourselves questions that help us attune a particular experience or series of experiences to the topic at hand, to teachers' experience, to the particular curriculum and its demands, to the needs of schools and their administrators, to funding and scheduling opportunities and constraints. We must consider:

> - How do teachers learn? How do they extend, change, and adopt new practices?
> - What is the context that best supports this learning?
> - What tools do we use?

And we always go back to our guiding principles of establishing relationships, grounding our conversations in content and practice, working with transparency, and supporting transformation

Engaging Curiosity and Higher-Order Thinking Through Hands-on PD

The DEC believes that for learning to be truly transformational, it needs to be grounded in experience and adapted and mastered through reflective practice. The team is convinced that the ways in which teachers prefer to learn and learn best are similar to the ways in which young children learn—through active, playful experiences that engage their curiosity and creativity, and group and relational contexts that support inquiry, reflection, and collaboration. Tonachel describes the approach:

> In the initial training for all our curricula, we make sure that teachers have opportunities to experiment with the very materials that children will have in their own hands. We recreate a Centers activity time, explore the possibilities of Beautiful Stuff, consider inquiry questions of a STEM lesson through experimentation. Facilitators model and deconstruct Thinking and Feedback like a stop-action film: we play through a few moments, then stop to ask the group what they notice, what this makes them think and wonder about; to do this, we use authentic work from children.
>
> We dive into the curriculum together, reading aloud and stopping to consider questions the teachers will soon ask of children so that teachers can anticipate how it will really unfold in their classrooms. We act out the process of Storytelling and Story Acting so that teachers can see and hear and feel it. We ask teachers to think about and discuss some of the same questions that they will ask children. As we introduce the Our Boston project; for example, we ask teachers the question posed to kindergarteners by the mayor: "What suggestions do you have about construction in our city to make Boston fairer and a more interesting place for children?"
>
> Recognizing that teachers do not have enough time to plan and too rarely do it together, we make sure that teachers can plan together during PD. We provide both time and structures to address practical and intellectual dilemmas so that they can confidently go back to their classrooms,

even the very next day, and enact some piece of an idea they entertained with colleagues.

Fostering Collegial Relationships and Collaborative Learning

In seminars and courses, teachers have opportunities to share and plan around artifacts from their own classrooms. These include samples of individual and group work, transcribed or videotaped conversations, and photographs from an evolving exploration or project. Small group discussions, supported by protocols and framed around artifacts of learning contributed by the teachers from their own classrooms, result in explorations of specific curriculum elements and broader conversations about teaching and learning. Teachers' assumptions, habits, pedagogical stances, and practical inclinations are considered by colleagues and then addressed through helpful questions: What will you do next? How will that work? What challenges might you encounter? What kinds of resources will be helpful?

Even with large groups, the DEC finds ways to use the room arrangement to facilitate conversation and active involvement. In Tonachel's words:

> We need to allow for people to see each other in the whole group and to interact meaningfully in small groups. We want to make sure that people are physically comfortable. We want to facilitate a conversation but not be at the center of it, so that the work with children and the exchange among teachers is central. The size of any given group and the activities and conversations we've planned dictate how chairs and tables are arranged; these details matter a great deal. Just like we want teachers to consider their classroom environments as a powerful force for fostering learning, we consider the ways adults are in a room together.

But the context that supports transformational learning is, and must be, broader than a single session or even a two-day workshop. One of the keys to the DEC's success is its fostering of ongoing collaborative learning among teachers, intentionally forming what others refer to as *communities of practice*.[10] They continually ask themselves: How do we assure that teachers feel supported to take risks in their thinking and to try new things? How do we create a feeling of community in which each member feels valued for her or his perspective, experience, and ideas? Tonachel describes their aspirations:

> Explicitly or by modeling and facilitation, we share values for how adults interact in a learning environment. We want to be certain that differing kinds and degrees of participation are valued. We want to find ways to nurture the group of individuals who collect around a topic to become a true learning group in an environment where thinking expands and the group's members can envision doing things in new ways in a spirit of inquiry.
>
> It is not enough for teachers to show up to PD sessions (although it is important to document their attendance); we aspire to offer them membership in a critical group of colleagues who challenge, support, and inspire each other toward greater professionalism and more satisfying practice—with the belief that these qualities ultimately improve children's experience and learning.[11]

Kindergarten and first-grade teacher Lena Jar-Curran describes the experience:

> PD sessions are led by asking open-ended questions that allow us to be more introspective and analyze our teaching practice . . . When I am in PD sessions, I am able to be a teacher researcher and try new things out and share what I have tried. I listen to colleagues in different schools and their approaches to teaching. Often I get inspired by what I hear.

When teachers get together, they want to talk. They want to share their strategies, problems, and successes and hear about what their colleagues are trying. The DEC uses conversation protocols and playful activities to shape and focus these conversations, mirroring some of what they ask teachers to do with children. Tonachel elaborates:

> Conversational protocols are well defined and chosen to surface particular aspects of the work at hand. We want to make sure to achieve a balance of sharing successes and dilemmas, of expressing confidence and asking questions. We find that teachers often want to talk and hear from colleagues about what they have done that has gone well—"In my classroom we always . . . "—and it's trickier to convince them to consider letting go of established

practices in order to make way for new ways of doing things. Protocols that assure that everyone has a chance to speak and that focus everyone's talk on a shared theme make for more productive and satisfying exchanges.

The "Mocktail Party" is one such protocol. Based on the Micro Lab, a conversation protocol featured in *Making Thinking Visible: How to Promote Engagement, Understanding, and Independence for All Learners*, this protocol asks teachers to converse in trios.[12] Participants stand, real or imaginary drink in hand, and talk with less familiar colleagues, with tight time limits on each person's contribution. The DEC uses this protocol as a playful way to build cross-district relationships while also keeping conversations focused.

Other strategies and protocols call for more serious and probing reflections and feedback. For example, when instructors ask teachers to bring artifacts of children's learning to a seminar, they scaffold critical conversations about the work at hand, possible next steps, and implications for teachers' ongoing practice. The discussion protocol guides teachers through clarifying, appreciating, wondering about, suggesting, and reflecting/planning, giving each small group direction and purpose.

In the Storytelling/Story Acting course, for example, participants are encouraged to capture and share videos of the emerging practice in their classrooms. As they share, they can elicit the kind of focused attention and thoughtful feedback that they might get through a classroom visit. Using a See-Think-Wonder or Ladder of Feedback protocol allows both practitioner and observer to notice, articulate, and discuss small moves in the teaching/learning dance.[13] They may notice details of a child's approach or response that would be difficult to catch in the moment, or recognize micro teaching practices and habits that a teacher may not have even realized she was doing. This often leads to an appreciation of skill that inspires others, a rethinking of a stance or response pattern, or a new question to investigate.

At the end of almost every PD session, teachers are asked to reflect in writing. This gives the participants a moment to process what they've experienced, and it provides the instructors with feedback that shapes both next steps with the group and future sessions with others. Prompts for these reflections focus the comments:

"I used to think . . . Now I think . . ."

"I am inspired . . . I am perplexed . . . My next step is . . ."

"My main takeaway . . . My main question . . . Something that worked
     well/didn't work well today . . ."

Coaches as Allies

When is a good time to come to your classroom? That simple question begins the
coaching relationship that is key to the success of PD, especially for early childhood teachers.[14] The DEC begins each school year with a teacher-by-teacher
needs assessment process with teachers who are new to the grade and/or curriculum they are teaching. In an initial visit, DEC members go to classrooms
and observe, chat with teachers, and make assessments about the intensity
and focus of coaching and related PD from which each teacher might best
benefit. From there, they consider the capacity of their coaches, given their
ongoing commitments, and then coaching begins. A written contract between
the coach, teacher, and school principal codifies expectations and acts a tool
for evaluating the coaching collaboration over time.

DEC members enter classrooms in two roles—as coaches for new curriculum or as coaches/mentors in the process of NAEYC accreditation. They
are not always welcomed. Teachers being coached around curriculum often
worry that coaches are there to make sure they are "doing it right." The coaches
take time to explain that the curriculum is designed to be both a guide and
a springboard for building a healthy classroom environment—and that the
coach's job is to help each teacher learn to use it well.

Once a relationship is built, coaches can help teachers bridge the ideas they
explore in a PD group with the opportunities and challenges of their particular
classrooms. Their support might involve conversations, walkthroughs and
focused observations, testing of materials, role-playing between coach and
teacher, or modeling or co-teaching with the children and then debriefing
and planning next steps.

With accreditation, the trust-building process is a bit different. Schools
in this process are working toward a certification of excellence according to
specific criteria. Teachers as well as administrators need to complete checklists
and portfolios to document their compliance. It's hard for teachers not to feel

judged or graded when they know that whether or not their school succeeds in meeting an important goal depends in part on their performance—as rated by an outside observer when the school's application is ready.

Following their guiding principles of trust and transparency, DEC coaches and DEC-hired outside mentors situate themselves as allies of the teacher and the school. They help both principals and teachers to see the accreditation process as an opportunity for individual and collective reflection and one-to-one coaching, with each teacher and coach co-constructing their agenda, using the NAEYC criteria as a common language and guide.

The process often becomes an opportunity to build relationships between the DEC and teachers. Teachers who become interested in further involvement with DEC PD may seek out courses such as Boston Listens or Making Learning Visible. For the DEC, the door to initially resistant classrooms opens a little wider.

Whether it is meant to support curriculum implementation, school accreditation, or ongoing professional growth, coaching is a dynamic process. The following quotation from Bob and Megan Tschannen-Moran's *Evocative Coaching* captures the DEC's vision:

> We are not always taking the lead, and we are not always following. We are rather moving back and forth among these different steps, exploring stories, empathizing with feelings and needs, inquiring into strengths, or developing and prototyping designs, intuitively initiating and responding in ways that bring out the best in teachers. We want teachers to feel engaged, intrigued, open, willing, stimulated, supported, and challenged by the conversation. We do not want to be wandering around aimlessly or getting out of sync through the coaching process. We want to know where we are and where we are going. We want to know when it is time to circle back and when it is time to move forward.[15]

DEC coaches use a "coaching sequence" to achieve a productive, organically changing balance between teachers' goals and their own and to maintain forward momentum: Goal Setting; Observe/Model/Lesson Planning; Feedback/Reflect/Analyze; Plan; Implement; and then repeat the cycle.[16]

Goals are set collaboratively, initially involving the principal as well as the teacher and coach, and are attached to measurement tools and evaluation criteria.

The next step involves targeted classroom observations, debriefing sessions, and often modeling of strategies by the coach, followed by planning of next steps in the teaching sequence. Coaches sometimes facilitate common planning time sessions for their mentees and other teachers.

The third step, the heart of the coaching process, is feedback: actionable, specific, goal-oriented, and grounded in shared observation and reflection. This is followed by the teacher's creation of a specific implementation plan, including a plan for collecting information on the implementation and its results. As part of the implementation process, the coach and teacher reflect together on the results, and the coach provides a written summary of what has been accomplished. Together coach and teacher set their next goal.

Over time, and as funding and demand have allowed, the DEC has experimented with different coaching ratios—from a low of eight mentees per coach to a grade-level focus of 20:1. They've learned to differentiate both frequency and strategies, based on the teacher's knowledge level, goals and willingness to change; the supports for change provided by supervisors, specialists, and colleagues at the school; and their own focus and goals.

Growing Together

As essential as PD and collaboration with colleagues are for any professional, finding time for these activities is rarely easy. In BPS, PD hours are required and filled by school instructional leaders, and also monitored by the teachers' union. The DEC can claim a few slots, but rarely as many as it—or many of the teachers—would like. It is therefore challenging for teachers to take on a course of meaningful inquiry of the kind the DEC believes that thoughtful teaching requires without running over the contractual PD hours. Some instructional leaders are able to release teachers from some school-based PD sessions; many teachers simply forgo important family or other out-of-work time to participate.

Tonachel explains the DEC's compromise solution:

This dilemma compels the DEC to design PD sessions to allow for both learning about the curriculum components and figuring out, through experimentation and consultation with colleagues, how to put them into motion. This includes negotiating (*If I start doing this, I'll have to give up that*), strategizing (*I can help children to do this by using these visual supports*), repurposing (*If I move the furniture in this way, I can use this for . . .*), and talking and comparing with colleagues (*How did you do that?*). We insist that this process can be fruitful with a classroom-based coach but that learning together in a group of teachers from across the district enlivens and expands the possibilities for teacher practice. Thus, we design professional development seminars to be elongated conversations whose threads we pick up over the course of many months. We hope that the teachers who gather around these seminars attend consistently enough to form a cohort that can pick up where it left off from one session to the next, and we rely on our relationships developing over this long time to help build and hold the group's cohesiveness.

The DEC staff practice a nuanced, sophisticated, and ever-evolving PD and coaching methodology. It's the heart of what they do with teachers—and with each other. They always work in teams to plan, offer, and debrief PD and coaching sequences. They preserve time at staff meetings for mock coaching and debrief sessions and share coaching templates and other resources electronically as they create them. They develop shared vocabulary and understandings through discussion and electronically shared and edited documents.

At grade-level meetings and at department staff meetings, DEC members also consider coaching dilemmas. These conversations are often facilitated by a small group of DEC colleagues. These circles of support—coaching, offering feedback to each other as coaches and PD providers, learning more about coaching and PD, and calibrating approaches—are intentional and always available.

When asked to describe her PD experiences, K2 teacher Christy Nelson reflects on how the relationships they fostered built communities:

> Developing relationships with teachers is paramount in nurturing any kind of success . . . When community is developed, then teachers come together to have the same values and goals. I truly believe that we are moving past collaborating with one another to a true collegial group . . . supportive relationships, connectedness. It was clear to me that we had something

special when a new teacher came with me to her first early childhood PD and said, "How do you know all these other teachers? How do they know about your classroom? I have never seen that before."

Reflecting on her experience in monthly seminars, Nelson describes the transformations she observed:

> I saw teachers who have been teaching for twenty years, comfortable with the way things were. Yet with trust, I slowly witnessed teachers' conversations shift . . . from talking about when to find the time to pull guided reading groups to how are we going to build a culture of feedback. Teachers trusted our professional coaches, relied on fellow teachers for support, and took chances. Ultimately, I saw a shift in both mind-set and practice.

For the DEC, PD is not only necessary for the rollout of new curricula and enhancing and maintaining classroom quality. It is also a political act. It strengthens teachers' individual voices and builds their collective power. As Melissa Tonachel and her colleagues have repeatedly observed:

> PD is a platform by which we can encourage teachers-as-advocates to stand up for what young children need in educational settings. When teachers feel empowered, we suspect that it's more likely they are empowering children as well. They are giving children more choice in their learning, more engaging ways to grab onto a curriculum and pound it, like clay, into interesting shapes. Teachers can stand up for what is right for children as it is embodied in the curriculum content and in their teaching practices. They reimagine what school might be. In turn, they articulate children's needs to their school administrators, those who make decisions about children's schedules which can either support or interrupt children's important work. Beyond their own schools, teachers can lift their voices for district and national issues such as how much standardized testing young children are subjected to and the value of play.[17]

When early childhood teachers see themselves as professionals, they are more likely to seek out and ask for resources, learning opportunities, and time to plan together. They find the research that backs their practices and use it to advocate for vigorous and robust professional lives and school environments.

As a group that shares both knowledge and values, they may begin to feel powerful enough to agitate for changes that they know will benefit children.

Finally, teachers who are collectively empowered themselves often collectively empower others. Sharing their passions, convictions, and collective decision-making tools with students, parents, and colleagues, they promote democracy in their classrooms and schools. They are primed to both treat children as citizens and educate them in practicing citizenship.

Chapter 9 peels back another layer to look at how the DEC coaches and other staff collaborate to bring their PD programs, curricula, and other initiatives to life.

Chapter Nine

The DEC at Work

The DEC's offices are on the fourth floor of the Bolling building in Dudley Square, the historic heart of Boston's African American community. Completed in April 2015, the renovated building houses both an economic incubator and the Boston Public Schools offices. Compared with the DEC's former office space, improvised in the basement of an aging brick school building between a storage room and an unlit hallway (damp smells and mice included), this new space is impressive. It presents a welcoming face to the public and reflects how far the department has come. It is modern and bright, with comfortable conference rooms and desks for all members of the growing DEC staff. Yet, on a typical morning, most of the desks are empty. Where is everyone?

For DEC staff, desk time takes second place to active involvement, and they are often spread out across Boston and engaged in a variety of projects. For example, on a morning in October 2016, Melissa Tonachel was on her bicycle, headed to a school visit to coach teachers as they implement the DEC's newest curriculum pilot: *Focus on 1st*. Marina Boni was on the MBTA's Blue Line, headed to East Boston to work with K1 and K2 teachers in a school seeking NAEYC accreditation. David Ramsey was meeting with colleagues in the history department about the new revisions to the *Focus on K1* curriculum (showcased in chapter 5). Abby Morales was working with Anthony Valdez, who joined the department to work with community-based prekindergarten providers, to prepare for a PD session with their program directors later this week.

But every other Friday, the entire DEC team comes together for an all-staff meeting.

A Visit to a DEC Staff Meeting

This "visit" provides a glimpse of how the DEC team works together. As you eavesdrop, think again about the nine core principles. How do the DEC's views of children and teachers, learning and relationships, and citizenship, schooling, and social justice in a democratic society shape their conversations and priorities? How do their interactions with each other mirror those they seek to create with teachers and children?

The DEC staff has gathered in the large conference room for their bi-weekly meeting. Also attending is a six-person team from the Omaha, Nebraska, who are touring the DEC's programs. Today's three-hour meeting opens with an interactive "identity tree" presentation, in which a staff member talks about her background, family, and passions, and how these shape her work.

Staff members present before each meeting on a rotating basis. The DEC began this practice a few months ago, after Jeri Robinson, the Vice President for Early Learning Initiatives at the Boston Children's Museum and co-chair of the Thrive in Five effort who would soon be appointed to the Boston School Committee, spoke to the group about growing up black in residentially and educationally segregated Boston and building museum programs for young children and their parents amid the hatred and violence that marred the court-mandated desegregation of Boston's schools. The DEC team realized that sharing their own histories would help them to keep in mind the experiences and perspectives of the families who will be entrusting them to be partners in their children's education, and to deepen their relationships with each other, creating more fertile ground for collaborative learning.[1]

But the heart of this meeting is an extended discussion about coaching, a critical practice that everyone in the room engages with on a daily basis in one way or another. It's part of a series of conversations intended to ensure that the group shares a coherent, well-articulated vision of coaching. Marina Boni leads the group through a three-part protocol to dig into the new "Guiding Principles" document that she and several colleagues have written to make the coaching process more codified and transparent for coaches, teachers, and administrators across the district (summarized in chapter 8).

After giving everyone a few minutes to review the Guiding Principles, which include statements about "relationships," "transparency" and "transformation," Boni asks the staff to count off and form small mixed-grade groups, inviting the visiting team from Nebraska to join in. As she hands out a set of prompts, Boni asks the groups to try to structure their conversations to address each question and suggests that they choose one person to keep them on task.

Boni leads a group that includes Unicia Young, Chris Bucco, TeeAra Dias, Marie Enochty, Karen Silver, Mayra Cuevas, and Blaire Horner. Horner, one of the DEC's five managers, handles budgets and work plans. Silver, whose coaching for accreditation predates the DEC, is the senior NAEYC accreditation manager.[2] Dias is the project manager for the new Preschool Expansion Grant, a state-sponsored project to bring *Focus on K1*, coaching, financial resources, and other supports to community-based programs that provide full-day, full-year early education and comprehensive supports for families with low incomes. The others are program directors, with coaching as their central focus. As the group digs into the second prompt, "What questions do we have that beg for clarity?" they raise some tricky questions:

YOUNG: I have a teacher who doesn't want me in. I haven't met her, I've emailed her, but I can't even get in the door. I've never had this happen before. I'm hoping she will come to PD but she hasn't yet. So I'm going to take a step back. They want to have contact via email but to do that I need context.

BUCCO: I've found it helpful when we're able to meet with teachers in groups during team meetings or after school—that helps to build that trust. Because maybe one of the teachers there has had experience with one of us as a coach and can share that experience with other teachers. But definitely, with some teachers it can really take a while.

DIAS: Yeah. I have a community-based lens, so for me the coaching model is really about explaining to the teachers why you're there, and what's that going to look like or feel like. Because oftentimes, with the NAEYC observations, supervisor observations . . . they might think, "Oh, here's another person who's going to judge us." But I take a chance to explain to teachers who we are, why we are there . . . and to explain to directors what supervision might look like in the long term—building a relationship with teachers, coming up with solutions, a way to model for directors what supervision might look like.

HORNER: It's so time-intensive just to get to the point of building relationships.

DIAS: Oh yes. At one point, Abby had to have a meeting and pull all the directors in and explain what the coaching model looks like. And because of that, we now take a different approach. We get all the directors together in August and talk about what the coaching model will look like in specific programs.

HORNER: Do we share these kinds of detailed documents with the people we're coaching?

BUCCO: That's a good question. Yes—absolutely.[3]

Fifteen minutes have passed when Enochty, who is keeping time, gives a one-minute warning to signal the end of this part of the protocol. Boni, hearing that conversations are still in full swing, suggests adding five more minutes. When this part ends, she regroups everyone into project-oriented teams to continue their discussion. Unicia Young's concern about teachers resistant to coaching is revisited by the "new teachers" team, a group focused on supporting teachers new to the district:

ENOCHTY: Where is it appropriate to request that they need to come to PD? Some new teachers think that having a coach supersedes them having to go to seminars about the new curriculum. But where do we say, "You're a new teacher to this curriculum, you need to go to the seminars. We can support you in your room, but we are not a substitute for the PDs." I think there needs to be something around that piece in the agreement.

BONI (facilitating the small group, notices that Silver and Cuevas both want to speak): OK—Karen, then me, then Mayra.

SILVER: We know that PD and coaching is maximally effective. And the idea that we've been floating around, that if new teachers don't come to PD, that they don't get coaching . . . we could put that in the agreement.

BONI: I agree. Because two things are happening: one, folks new to teaching a grade level don't come to PD, or . . . they don't want us. So there is something that needs to happen in an agreement . . . that whatever level of coaching we offer . . . is bound by PD?

CUEVAS: But I'm going to push back on that conversation. Are these situations happening because we don't have the rapport with the teacher to begin the coaching? Because if we all think back about when we were teaching . . . As a new teacher, I remember not wanting anyone in my classroom because I knew my faults and I didn't want anyone watching. If I didn't trust where you were coming from, what happened? And if I did trust you, then what happened with my teaching? Because in these guiding principles, we have "dialogue" and "rapport." Are we taking enough time to build rapport?

To conclude this experience, each group shares a "headline," or big idea that surfaced in the conversation, supporting colleagues from different projects to connect with each other in this work. As Sachs wraps up, he reminds everyone that these conversations about coaching will be a recurring thread during staff meetings throughout the year.

The DEC at Work: A Culture of Collaboration

Reflecting on this snapshot of themselves at work, the DEC team describes the culture they have built within the department. Despite the fact that it has grown to more than twenty full-time members, it has not become bureaucratic. Meetings are structured as times when ideas and questions are raised; decisions are made by consensus after thorough discussion. "We are so early childhood here," Marie Enochty says, "that we are always trying to accommodate everyone." Yet DEC members are also respectful of each other's time, and their meetings are remarkably productive. As Marina Boni puts it, "We work hard to create spaces within our work as a department that mirror the kinds of learning experiences we want to create for young children in Boston, where we engage in democratic dialogue together about real problems and real goals."[4] The DEC also aims for transparency, which is why the team from Nebraska, one of many groups that visits each year to learn and to share their own experiences, was invited to join in the meeting. "Of course, we don't always achieve these goals," Boni reflects, "but we keep trying."

Over the past ten years, the department has worked hard to create norms, rituals, and other structures that support them in their work. They regularly revisit and revise these structures to enable meetings to be efficient, rewarding, and forward-moving. They rotate leadership and responsibility with the goal of engaging everyone's participation while respecting each other's different perspectives and learning styles. Structures and processes that they use include:

- **Interactive agendas:** Before team meetings, the leadership team puts together an interactive, online agenda with a clear order of business and how long the group should plan to spend on each agenda item. Any necessary supporting documents or resources are hyperlinked into that agenda so everyone can prepare in advance.
- **Norm setting:** Each fall, when the team revisits their work and sets goals for the year, they take time to establish norms for their conversations. These norms may change over time given the needs of the group. Figure 9.1 shows an example.
- **Facilitation:** The DEC staff rotates facilitation so that during the meeting, members take leadership of the components that they know best. In larger meetings, the DEC may assign a "friend of the facilitator" to track those who want to contribute to the conversation and call on people. There is always an assigned timekeeper to keep the conversations moving. As you saw in the opening vignette, timing is sometimes adjusted to extend a discussion, but this is a calculated and clearly voiced decision.
- **Identity trees:** The diversity of the DEC's staff is the result of intentional hiring. To ensure that they get to know each other deeply, staff begin each meeting by inviting one staff member each meeting to share their

FIGURE 9.1 Example of DEC meeting norms

Start and end on time

Commit to the agenda and follow up

Listen with the intention to understand

One person speaking at a time

Monitor your own airtime

Allow wait time

Be fully present and limit distractions
 · Attend respectfully to self-care
 · Silence electronics
 · Limit sidebar conversations
 · Use technology only as it relates to the purpose at hand (e.g., note taking or pulling up documents relating to the meeting)

Ask questions

Flag the facilitator

Take time to consider new ideas

Assume positive intent

Respectfully initiate and respectfully respond

Arrive at and communicate a unified message

Honor confidentiality

> Norms are subject to change based on the group's needs.
>
> These norms are for meetings. We may create additional norms for our work environment.

"identity tree," which includes personal, relational, cultural, and professional aspects of who that person is and what drives them to be a part of the work.

- **Protocols:** Using protocols to guide their conversations helps the DEC team form collective visions that they can all articulate and pursue together. The protocols are derived from the work of Project Zero and the School Reform Initiative, and include the Ladder of Feedback (to structure a feedback process when writing a new curriculum unit), See-Think-Wonder (to look, for example, at teacher documentation shared during a PD session and then consider next steps), and the School Reform Initiative's Consultancy Protocol (to tackle a difficult dilemma).[5] They create and adapt additional protocols as needed.

- **Debates:** To help refine public communications and department priorities, staff members set up a debate during their meeting by first dividing the group to represent two sides of an issue (for example, using the word "play" versus "exploration" in a document or whether to provide the coaching follow-up to a PD experience or work to have schools form their own supports). During the debate, each side argues and rebuts. Halfway through the process, half of the members from each team split off and become the "Yes/And" group. They then help to articulate a more synthesized view.
- **Online collaboration tools:** The DEC uses Google Docs and other online collaborative spaces to write curriculum together, organize documents, and give each other feedback on pieces they are writing. Everything is easily accessible to the team and can be shared with external partners as needed.

The DEC at Work: Strategic Planning, Ongoing Learning, and Priority Setting

Observation is central to the DEC's work at every level. As you have seen in the classroom visit chapters, children in BPS early childhood classrooms use the Thinking and Feedback protocol, which begins with "Observe," to guide their conversations about each other's work. Teachers (or students) ask, "What did you notice?" and "What questions do you have?" before taking or making suggestions. Coaches and teachers use similar protocols to guide their conversations about what activities or lessons the coach should observe and to reflect together on what each of them noticed and where to go next. Frequent, systematic, and systematically shared observations by coaches and Jason Sachs of what is going on in classrooms and schools between students and other students, students and teachers, teachers and family members or colleagues, and teachers and administrators provide fodder for ongoing conversations.

Every two years, the DEC hires an outside evaluator to assess classroom environments, relationships, and instructional practices with tools that include the ECERS, CLASS, ELLCO, and COEMET.[6] These observations lead the team to think more structurally: to identify the roots of ongoing problems and locate their cores. Is the issue focused at the teacher level, the school level, the district level, or some combination? Where is the best leverage point for resolving the issue in ways that will benefit all of its stakeholders, but primarily Boston's children.[7]

Every five years, the DEC refines its strategic plan. The department's original logic model still holds: Improve classroom instruction, improve school environment, support family engagement, build BPS capacity to do these things; and evaluate programs to drive change and sustain gains. These activities should lead to high-quality experiences for children and narrow gaps in learning opportunities and achievement. The DEC has just launched the version that will guide its work for 2017–2022. Its theory of action reflects how far the DEC has come in integrating its work with that of other BPS departments to build preK–3 alignment of curriculum and pedagogy and coherent learning trajectories for all children:

If we:

- Align our work to the BPS vision and implementation plan and APL [adult professional learning] instructional vision
- Expand the early childhood vision to grades 1 and 2
- Use data to constantly improve our own PD, coaching, and assessments
- Target PD and coaching to make specific changes in instructional practice
- Build capacity for quality preK in community-based organizations
- Expand out-of-school time programming to support working families
- Collaborate with teachers, instructional leaders, and other departments and
- Leverage partnerships to build our capacity and share our findings

then all children will become internally driven learners, able to read, write, and communicate effectively by third grade, and BPS will close the achievement gap.[8]

Based on the strategic plan, individual teams within the DEC create plans to guide their work over the life of a project, with benchmark goals and timelines along the way. The DEC uses team retreat time each year to write and revise work plans and to decide who feels most passionate about working on which project. Teams set their own budgets for their initiatives, in collaboration with Sachs, who manages the department's budget.

Each fall, the DEC brings together all the early childhood teachers from the district for a full-day professional development session known as the Kindergarten Conference. The team prepares for this well in advance, using the forum as an opportunity to launch new initiatives, build enthusiasm for ongoing work, and deepen understandings about a curriculum, approach, or topic. For example, a few years ago, Vivian Paley, a former University of Chicago Lab School kindergarten teacher and renowned author, conducted a workshop on her Storytelling/Story Acting methodology as a way to jump-start this new component of the K1 and K2 curricula. Other recent topics have included "Loose Parts" (playing and creating with recycled materials and other "beautiful stuff"), "Family Engagement," and "Powerful Practice for an Engaged Citizen."[9]

Sachs freely admits that the DEC always has too many initiatives under way, and people sometimes get stretched too thin working on multiple projects. It's an ongoing challenge, but it's also part of the team's strength. Sachs insists that coaches spend half of their time in classrooms, which keeps the whole group grounded in teaching practice that puts children at the center. He also encourages DEC members to spend up to 20 percent of their time working on projects that reflect their personal passions and aim to make change. Some of these projects become PD courses or Kindergarten Conference topics; some get incorporated into curricula and supporting documents, and some lead to new research studies, grants, and partnerships. Sachs works closely with the BPS Budget Department to find the funds for the DEC's many initiatives as well as its day-to-day work.

Much of the funding the DEC needs for its work comes from grants. In the beginning, the Barr Foundation funded its most important initiatives. Even before the DEC existed, though, BPS received state and federal funds for early childhood programs and partnership with university-based experts. The accreditation work that Karen Silver was doing, for example, was in partnership with the Massachusetts Department of Education. Michele High-McKinnon's work with the OWL pilot was supported by an Early Reading First grant, in partnership with the University of Massachusetts.

Today, grant writing is part of the DEC's routine operations, and one of school readiness manager Brian Gold's major responsibilities. It supports ongoing work and new initiatives and enables the DEC to partner with leaders in the field and bring in new ideas.

Over time, the DEC has entered into a variety of partnerships. Some partners have brought agendas that overlapped with the DEC's. Often, where the DEC maintained a focus on Boston children, a partner looked toward a national audience. In contrast, partners like Judy Shickedantz and Doug Clements, who piloted their OWL and *Building Blocks* curricula in Boston, Ben Mardell and Megina Baker (now at Project Zero), researchers and data analysts Chris Weiland and Nancy Marshall, and Kim Haskins at the Barr Foundation were fully invested in the success of the DEC. Boston's early education programs have become a research magnet, so the DEC chooses partners carefully to avoid overcommitment.

Ongoing Challenges

Tackling too many projects at once is just one of the DEC's ongoing challenges. Others revolve around relationships with partners within the school department. As the group's leader, Jason Sachs explains how the department has navigated these tricky cross-currents.

> Our office has long held both an elevated and marginalized space within the Boston Public Schools administration. With strong support from the mayor and superintendent, we have experienced unusual visibility; our activities and outcomes are regularly brought front and center to the School Committee and the City Council. This affords us a direct line to high-level leadership and has also provided additional access to external funding partners, like the Barr Foundation and United Way. But it can hinder collaboration and alignment with other BPS departments and initiatives, something we need in order to build coherent experiences and learning trajectories for children and their families.

Preschool is often seen as different from K–12, requiring a different content focus, different modes of instruction, and different administrative structures. For the DEC, it has been a slow and often arduous process to fit early childhood programs within traditional school structures. This challenge with integration is in part due to the fact that there have been separate departments and offices in BSP that oversee content areas related to K–12, special education, and practices and supports for English language learners. Because of this, the DEC often hears that preK and K–12 practices do not align (e.g. "That might be fine for the babies (preschool), but instruction needs to be more academic").[10]

A related challenge has been the shifting requirements, expectations, and priorities of a changing cast of district leaders. Sachs describes some of DEC's frustrations, strategies, and successes as it sought to maintain its core vision and strategic focus:

> A lot of our challenges result from leadership changes in the school department, which often lead to reorganization as well as new people, goals, and priorities. In Boston, higher-level leadership has been changing almost every two years. This destabilization in academic leadership has been an enormous challenge for us as well as for the schools we work with, as the changes usually come with new mandates and priorities that the DEC and its partners must accommodate.
>
> Aligning our work within the new framework and attention span/bandwidth of new leaders has been a real challenge. We have made it work, but I do think that a real challenge to successful urban education and perhaps most government is the lack of continuity. In order for anything to be done well it needs time and resources. When both are moving targets, it's a challenge. You need to find the right sweet spot of getting leadership to buy in but not make it completely theirs so that if they leave or change focus you are not left in the dust. If we think of our initiatives as branches on the school system's tree, our challenge has been to reach out as far as we can while staying close enough to the trunk to avoid being trimmed or broken off.

Much of the time, Sachs reflects, he and his team have felt like sailors on the high seas, trying to keep their course true in the face of unpredictable storms.

We've been navigating the district's shifting infrastructure throughout our journey, communicating both vertically with leadership above us and laterally with the various academic departments that have traditionally had a say in the academic content and pedagogical approaches of early childhood classrooms. Within this kind of organizational structure, with each content-driven department articulating specific approaches and suggestions, it has been a challenge for us to hold up our image of the child as a whole child, our image of curriculum as integrated and play-based, and our insistence on creating time for both children and their teachers to explore ideas in depth, through hands-on activities, close observation and reflection, and extended cognitively-challenging conversations.

The lessons in trust and transparency that the DEC learned in the beginning, when disappointing early results and bad publicity had threatened to end the project, have repeatedly proved their value. Sachs and his team proactively build relationships with counterparts in other departments. They share DEC's initiatives in their early stages, inviting experts from each content-area department to join them in co-construction of curricula and give feedback on learning goals and plans for learning experiences. They often invite members of content-area teams to join their team meetings in order to share their latest ideas and to hear about the DEC's ideas from team members.

As it navigates the BPS administration and collaborate with various departments, the DEC also nurtures its own relationships with schools. "Schools are their own systems," Sachs explains, "with their own stakeholders and processes. Even when they are open to our partnership and we embrace a common agenda, timing, priorities, and procedures may not align."

In the face of shifting priorities and competing agendas, the DEC tries to keep focused on the whole child and all the children of Boston, while respecting the perspectives of their partners within and outside BPS. But when the team has to choose, when they encounter misalignments with the central administration, schools, and partners, Sachs says, they tend to err on the side of working directly with teachers. As he puts it, "It is a means of cutting directly to those who most closely work with children and families."

Perhaps the hardest challenge for the team has been patience. Knowing how high the stakes for Boston's children are, they find it hard to wait for others to make decisions. Sachs articulates the frustrations they share:

> You need the time to explain the rationale for the project—often several times. New leaders come in with their own ideas, which may be only tangentially related to the work you want to do. Getting them to make complex decisions takes time for them to understand and then for them to make a bold or difficult decision, such as mandating a curriculum when some principals are resistant. We try to wait and not to always take things personally, even when we know that students' educational experience is not being maximized. This has been especially difficult with assessments. We've been able to use state of the art tools in K1, but, although we've been trying for eleven years, we have not yet been able to develop and implement a preK–3 assessment system that reflects both current scientific thinking and what we know is best for children and teachers. Still, through our collaborations with outside researchers and the BPS research department, we've been able to collect and analyze a lot of pertinent data—and use it to drive change [see the appendix for more detail].[11]

The next chapter brings the DEC's story up to the present, as its initiatives come to fruition.

Chapter Ten

Reaching In, Out, and Up

In 2013, Mayor Tom Menino decided not to run for reelection. He had served as Boston's mayor for a record twenty-one years, and had been a stalwart early childhood champion. The DEC team held its breath. Would a new mayor continue to champion its cause? Would he or she seek a superintendent to succeed acting superintendent John McDonough, who understood the importance and unique opportunities of the early childhood years?

Their fears were soon allayed. New mayor Marty Walsh didn't need convincing. He was part of a wave of city leaders who had already heard about brain development, early learning, and the importance of being able to read by third grade. He was committed to ensuring that every Boston child—and every Boston family—would have the opportunity to thrive. In his inaugural address on January 6, 2014, he spoke about this responsibility:

> Study after study has told us that universal early education and these other changes can be transformative. They give every child a more equal chance to thrive and succeed. Yes, these things cost money, but we must find a way.

Walsh also didn't need to be convinced to support the DEC's agenda. He was well aware of the DEC's growing local, statewide, and national reputation. Once reliant on the Barr Foundation, the DEC was now getting grants from an array of local and national funders, including the US Department of Education, the Foundation for Child Development, the Target Foundation, and the Jessie B. Cox Foundation. The new mayor selected Jeri Robinson, who had been on Menino's educational team for years and was working closely with the DEC on Countdown to Kindergarten and the Ready Schools component of Thrive in Five, to head his educational transition team and serve on the search committee for a new superintendent.

The DEC continued with its strategic plan: rolling out the *Focus on K2* curriculum with strong professional development and coaching, continuing to add K1 classrooms where it could, using data to drive continuous improvement, developing new tools for family engagement, and forging new partnerships. It never lost sight of its nine core principles of promoting democratic citizenship; engaging children as curious, active, thoughtful, empathetic, and capable learners; developing strong personal relationships as a foundation for powerful learning; addressing all learning domains; aligning learning experiences over time to build knowledge, basic literacies, and twenty-first-century skills; offering a balanced mix of learning opportunities involving play, projects, extended conversation, and thoughtful instruction; creating ongoing learning opportunities and environments for adults that mirror those they aim to offer children; and using a variety of documentation and assessments to "make learning visible" and drive change at both the classroom and district level.

The DEC also took the opportunity to revisit the K1 curriculum to strengthen its alignment with K2 and make it more "diversity wise" to better address children's individual strengths and challenges, affirm their cultural and linguistic backgrounds, and broaden their horizons. The team created a homegrown hybrid curriculum, integrating OWL and *Building Blocks*, bringing math concepts and conversations into Read Alouds, explorations, and play-based Center Time activities, and adding components such as Storytelling/Story Acting and Thinking and Feedback that teachers had begun to explore in the annual Kindergarten Conference and other professional development sessions.

As with *Focus on K2*, the curriculum and guiding documents were shaped by Universal Design for Learning (UDL) principles and Culturally Sustaining Pedagogy.[1] Texts and activities were chosen with an eye toward cultural and linguistic awareness and sustainability. Teachers were given specific guidance and coaching support on how to implement curriculum components in ways that would enable all children to fully participate, including English language learners and children with special rights.

Like *Focus on K2*, *Focus on K1* would have a small number of units that lent themselves to wide and deep exploration. These would include "Family," "Friends," "Wind and Water," "Shadows and Reflections," "World of Color," and "Things that Grow." The K1 classroom you observed in chapter 5 ("A House for a Dragon") was using the new *Focus on K1* curriculum.

At the same time, the DEC continued to focus on NAEYC accreditation. By the end of the 2013–2014 school year, 27 schools had earned accreditation, out of a total of 77 schools with at least one K2 classroom. Six had earned reaccreditation. In 2017, BPS would have 40 NAEYC-accredited schools serving children ages three through five, with and without identified special needs, 18 of which had been reaccredited.

Reaching In: Connecting with Families Within BPS

The DEC team and their partners also worked to deepen family engagement. Schools seeking NAEYC accreditation continued to include families in the process. With other BPS departments, DEC members participated in the development of Family Guides to Learning, to excite families about what children were expected to learn and deepen their engagement.

Following an idea proposed by their university partners, members of the DEC also developed the structure, family training sessions, professional development, and pilot for what has become Home Links, a set of family activities for each *Focus on K2* unit. Home Links is grounded in an extensive research literature that shows that worksheets and similar assignments have little or no benefit for young children, but that daily reading, playing board games and other math games, setting aside times and places for school work and related learning activities, doing science experiments and activities together, regular family dinner-table conversations, and strong connections between home and school measurably enhance learning, especially for children from low-income families.[2] Home Links activities are designed to be fun and engaging for all family members and to draw on each family's interests, heritage, values, and experiences. The DEC offers versions in Cape Verdean, Chinese, English, Haitian Creole, Portuguese, Spanish, and Vietnamese.

The BPS "Parent University" offers one-day sessions to help families of children preK–12 understand BPS programs, procedures, and curricula and support their ongoing learning. In workshops for K1 and K2 families, parents discuss the important roles they play in their children's learning, using strategies such as "turn and talk" that are similar to the routines their children use in their classrooms. They learn what the research says about the limitations of traditional homework and the value of family engagement, especially daily interactive reading. They learn about the content, skills, and methodologies featured in their children's curriculum, and talk about how they can extend the learning through conversations that engage their children in thinking more deeply about the world around them.

K2 families learn how the Home Links they will receive differ from traditional homework in their emphasis on twenty-first century skills of communication, critical thinking, collaboration, creativity, and problem solving. An introductory letter at the beginning of each unit, and a weekly Home Links activity sheet lay out their roles: they are expected to read with their children daily and to choose three Home Links activities to complete on their own timetable. In the workshop, family members move between activity centers, as their children do in classrooms, to try out different Home Links activities. They also practice read-aloud techniques, with a focus on using books as springboards for conversation.

The Home Links for *Focus on K2* have been well received by children, families, and teachers, and the DEC has plans to create them for all of its curricula. Those for *Focus on K1* are being piloted as this book goes to press, and the first- and second-grade equivalents are on the drawing board. But supporting teacher-family partnership remains a work in progress. The DEC is still working to sell teachers on the idea, while also seeking funds for send-home books and learning materials for families.

The DEC's strategic plan includes working with before- and afterschool care providers to strengthen children's out-of-school time learning opportunities and align them with what they are doing in school. But that has moved more slowly than hoped. With a mixed delivery system, a shortage of funds, and the DEC's already full curriculum development and coaching plate, forging meaningful and sustained partnerships with community-based organizations (beyond the Preschool Expansion Grant [PEG] sites) continues to be a challenge.

However, for several years, the DEC had been offering summer sessions for K1 graduates whose teachers and parents felt they needed a little extra help to be fully ready for kindergarten, though not enough to qualify for special education services. In 2013, the sessions included incoming K2 students who had had no prekindergarten experience, and the DEC made special efforts to reach out to families in high-poverty zip codes. Sited mostly in conveniently located community-based settings, these five-week, full-day Summer Early Focus programs are taught by BPS early childhood teachers, with two teachers for every class of no more than twenty students. Their size has waxed and waned based on the availability of funding and of appropriate spaces. Other grades have been added, sometimes even including children entering the third grade.

In 2014, Summer Early Focus initially provided an opportunity for the DEC to pilot parts of the *Focus on K2* curriculum that they would begin to roll out in September. Today, the program uses the same classroom routines as will be used in each child's new classroom, with units especially constructed for summer interest and neighborhood field trip possibilities. Entering kindergarteners explore local seashore and ocean animals; rising first-graders learn about insects and their habitats; children entering second grade study foods and restaurants from different cultures; and those entering third grade learn how bicycles work and create designs for bike-friendly communities.

A 2009 research study showed that an earlier incarnation of Summer Early Focus, Summer Learning Academy, fostered significant gains in preliteracy skills for entering kindergarten students, relative to children who applied but did not attend and to demographically similar children who had not applied. Gains were especially strong for English language learners, boys, and African American children.[3] Internal DEC data continue to show summer literacy gains for children who attend Summer Early Focus. Today there is an application process to select those most in need and a waiting list for all four grade levels. The programs continue to be pilot sites for new DEC ideas, but now the DEC partners with other departments to be sure that its summer programs align with English language learner and special education policies, priorities, and strategies.

In 2017, 45 percent of BPS students spoke a language other than English at home, and 31 percent were considered English language learners. It is likely that today the percentage is even higher, especially among the youngest children. Many of these children come to school already bilingual or trilingual, with the early advantages in perspective taking, cognitive flexibility, inhibitory control, and working memory that speaking more than one language brings.[4] Others need extra supports. Strategies for supporting dual language learners— including visual and peer supports, multicultural and multilingual storybooks, thematic and categorical contexts, vocabulary work, and conversation protocols—are built into all of the *Focus* curricula and professional development, following Universal Design for Learning and Culturally Sustaining principles.

Between 2003 and late 2017, Massachusetts law privileged English and requires English-only instruction for young children, despite a preponderance of research that demonstrates that early bilingual education has many benefits and no harmful effects.[5] But the state did grant waivers for two-way immersion programs, for which the research case is increasingly strong. Dual immersion programs report better school attendance, higher parent involvement, and fewer discipline problems than English-only programs. Their students seem happier in school and earn higher grades.[6]

After English, Spanish is the predominant language spoken by BPS families with young children, followed by Haitian Creole. BPS offers four elementary school Spanish-English dual immersion programs, all of which begin in K1. One uses the Pearson's Spanish-English version of the OWL for K1; the others use a published Spanish curriculum in addition to a self-designed program for K1 and K2. The DEC supports the teachers with PD and coaching.

In 2017, the DEC and the BPS Office of English Learners collaborated to open what is likely the nation's first Haitian Creole–English dual immersion program with twenty-five K1 students and plans for adding a grade each year. The program resides in a newly opened BPS elementary school. The bilingual and bicultural curriculum, delivered mostly (70 percent) in Haitian Creole, will be aligned with *Focus on K1.* Children will be encouraged to use both languages as they work and play together.

As with most of its innovations, the DEC is working with community and university as well as BPS partners as they develop and implement this new initiative. Families and community-based organizations have been involved in advocacy, planning, and student recruitment. Michel DeGraff of the MIT linguistics department is providing guidance on instruction in Haitian Creole language and literacy, and Nicole St. Victor, with a knowledge of both languages and both cultures, will be coaching.

Reaching Out: Community Partnerships

In January, 2013, the DEC began a pilot project with fourteen community-based preschool programs serving very-low-income families. Called Boston K1DS (K1 in Diverse Settings), this Thrive in Five partnership aimed to improve both classroom quality and child outcomes. It provided teachers of four-year-olds with:

- Instructional materials and support to implement the OWL and *Building Blocks* curricula
- Professional development alongside BPS early childhood teachers
- Monthly one-on-one curriculum-focused coaching
- Supplements to teachers' salaries and/or benefits, as requested by center directors in their applications

The pilot was funded for a two-and-a-half-year period. An evaluation completed in 2015 demonstrated notable successes despite multiple challenges.[7] The children came from families whose incomes tended to be lower than those of families who used the BPS K1 programs. In contrast to the BPS K1 classrooms, which served only four-year-olds (with a strict age cut-off), more than a third of the children in the community-based classrooms were only three at the beginning of each of the two school years. Lead teachers held BA degrees (a project requirement but an ongoing recruitment challenge), but BPS teachers who did not come in with MAs were required to obtain them. Most of the K1 teachers had earned their MAs at the time of the study.

In general, the Boston K1DS partnership worked smoothly. Teachers and directors reported satisfaction with the PD (though they had some suggestions for improvement) and particularly appreciated the coaching. Teachers successfully implemented the curricula, although not as fully or intensively as the DEC had hoped. Classroom quality improved, both in terms of relationships and instructional supports (as measured by the CLASS) and in the quality of the literacy environment (as measured by the ELLCO). There was some slippage in the second year (likely due in part to staff turnover), but quality scores remained above baseline levels in most areas, although still lower than BPS K1 classrooms.

Based on interviews with directors and teachers, as well as surveys, observations, and other data, the evaluators noted nine barriers to implementation:

- Insufficient planning; resulting in administrators being insufficiently versed in the new curricula to provide optimal feedback and support, and some teachers moving too quickly through units rather than following the pacing and planning guides used by BPS teachers
- Continued use in many of the classrooms of curriculum activities and sequences such as Creative Curriculum (which aligns with the state-mandated Teaching Strategies Gold assessment system) along with the new curricula
- Challenges in scheduling enough time for the new curricula due to children's staggered arrival and leaving times and the teacher shift changes needed to accommodate them
- A lack of common planning time for teachers implementing the curricula
- Finding and paying for predictable substitute coverage, including coverage for teachers not participating in the pilot, so that pilot teachers could consistently attend PD sessions and directors could schedule coaching sessions and classroom observations
- Administrators' lack of sufficient time, protocols, and systems for providing teachers with feedback and support regarding instructional practices
- Insufficient supports in some cases for dealing with challenging child behavior
- Mixed-age classrooms, including both three- and four-year-olds
- High rates of teacher turnover, coupled with challenges in recruiting and retaining teachers with BA degrees

Some of these barriers could be addressed with longer project planning time; provision of PD, support, and tools for directors and other instructional leaders; and different site-based decisions regarding curriculum, supervision, and staffing. Others are more endemic and harder to avoid, including shortage of and competition for qualified teachers and substitutes, teacher and director turnover, and a day that is long enough to require shift changes. Although mixed-age classrooms can be extremely successful (chapter 2 shows one such example), they also have drawbacks. The many benefits found in the research can be overshadowed when the curricula have been designed for four-year-olds and teachers lack needed planning time and supports.[8]

Despite the challenges, the pilot suggested a promising direction. The Massachusetts Department of Early Education and Care modeled its federal PEG proposal after Boston K1DS. Massachusetts received the maximum award in two grant cycles. The DEC also applied for a grant, to continue its work with some pilot classrooms and include some new ones. It identified nine sites, two of which included Head Start programs, and offered program directors and teachers of four-year-olds the same curriculum and related PD experiences (including coaching) that they did for BPS K1 programs.

The DEC also reached out further—to offer its K1 curriculum and its accompanying professional development and tools for teachers, directors, and coaches to other Massachusetts gateway cities that were pursuing PEG grants. In accordance with the grant's requirements, all sites agreed to pay the teachers enhanced salaries, require BA degrees, maintain 1:10 teacher-child ratios, offer full-day/full-year programming with a robust set of comprehensive services and family engagement activities, assess children's development, and work to earn NAEYC accreditation and/or a top-tier rating on the state's Quality Rating Improvement System (QRIS Level 4) within four years.

In Boston, participating sites capped the number of three-year-olds in PEG classrooms and took steps to reduce teacher turnover, such as paying teachers salaries comparable to what they could earn at BPS. They also required common planning time, along with PD and coaching. Some of the sites had already achieved NAEYC accreditation, along with more than half of Boston's early education and care centers.[9]

As coordinator of the PEG, TeeAra Dias, an early educator with more than twenty years' experience as a teacher, director, and PD provider in community-based nonprofit and for-profit settings, became one of the few DEC staff members to focus exclusively on one project. The PEG project is time-limited, so Dias and her DEC colleagues worked with their community-based partners from the outset to ensure its sustainability as well as its success.

Early reports are promising. A first-year evaluation by ABT associates found that, in the summer of 2016, PEG children statewide scored close to what would be expected for children entering kindergarten in understanding early math concepts, early literacy, and vocabulary comprehension.[10] And in Boston, the evaluators found that sites that faithfully implemented the *Focus on K1* curriculum earned high CLASS scores, including moderate or high ratings on instructional supports (an area in which preschool programs, including BPS K1's in the beginning, have tended to score low).

In her book, *The Most Important Year*, Suzanne Bouffard follows two Boston families as they begin the preK application process; one child enters K1 and the other enrolls in a Boston K1DS site. Bouffard offers portraits of both programs, contrasting them with high-achieving public programs in Elizabeth, NJ (an Abbott District), and Washington, DC. In both Boston settings, Bouffard captures high-quality, thought-engaging teaching; active, happy, empathetic, and curious children; and satisfied parents who are impressed with how much their children are learning.[11]

Mayor Walsh shares Bouffard's belief in the importance of preK, and is an advocate for increased state support. He is moving toward the expansion of Boston's preschool programs in both the public schools and community-based programs. To ensure equity in quality, Walsh designated a task force to oversee the design of a mixed delivery system. The DEC hopes to create a "connective" system between community-based organizations and BPS that will facilitate communication with families and information sharing between public school and community-based professionals as children move from one setting to another. There is also the possibility of school/CBO partnerships that create designated pathways for students, so that parents can choose a community-based program for their four-year-old (or younger) child without fearing that their child will miss out on the K1 experience or be less likely to get into the associated elementary school than children who had enrolled earlier. Following this thinking, CBOs and BPS schools might even become interdependent; for example, families could apply for BPS slots, and associated CBO's could recruit from the waitlist.

In contrast to Dias, NAEYC accreditation coach Marie Enochty, a former board member of the Massachusetts Association for the Education of Young Children, plays multiple roles. One is to manage the ever-increasing stream of visitors who want to see firsthand what Boston is doing. She coordinates their visits, offering site visits to schools, play-to-learn groups, and DEC meetings, as well as opportunities to meet with a range of DEC staff and to explore curriculum, PD materials, and student work.

For the DEC's first decade, most of the staff were supported by state, federal, and foundation grants. Today, more than half are fully supported by district funds. The state-funded PEG and a large federal research grant are the major sources of outside funding. But the DEC also has a new fee-for-service funding stream: consulting to school districts and nonprofit organizations that want to replicate or adapt their curricula and models.

Reaching Up: Adding First- and Second-Grade Programs

By 2015, it was time to reach up. The pressure had been growing. First- and second-grade teachers had been noticing what was happening in K1and K2, and were expressing interest in having their own versions. Parents of children in K1 and K2 classes wondered why their children couldn't continue the content-rich exploratory learning that had come to value. PreK–3 alignment was now a national buzzword, backed by evidence that it could make a difference in children's long-term success.[12] But why couldn't the alignment work from the bottom up instead of from the top down?

Although the DEC had formed relationships with the administrators in charge of the various academic departments, it had often felt that its early education programs and young children themselves were being siloed. The team had fought for their vision, which saw the child as a whole person, developing as a unique individual in multiple domains that could never be truly separated.[13] They continued to fight for an integrated curriculum that placed children at the center, as citizens who were entitled to stimulating and engaging experiences that built on their interests and expanded their horizons through in-depth exploration and play-based skills development.[14] They had also pushed for collaborative adult learning environments where curiosity and close observation generated rich discussions and a diversity of voices were engaged and valued.[15] And they had proved that these approaches worked.

The time had come to argue for a new administrative structure; one that would group preK–2 programming together and allow for bottom-up alignment. Aided by a site visit report from the Council of Great City Schools finding that BPS academic departments were "badly fractured, distrustful, and lacking a sense of teamwork or shared responsibility for the district's students," the DEC joined with others to fight for reorganization.[16] As Superintendent Tommy Chang came on board in March 2015, he implemented a new arrangement: as head of the DEC, Jason Sachs would now report to Buudoan Tran, Head of Adult Professional Learning. Curriculum decisions for preK–2 would come under Sach's purview. Countdown to Kindergarten would become part of a new Office of Engagement, along with Parent University and other family and student welcome, engagement, and support efforts, but would continue to collaborate with the DEC.

New Mandates and New Opportunities

Under a new superintendent and a new leadership structure, the DEC could truly be a Department of Early Childhood, from three-year-olds through second grade—no longer seen as "just for babies." It could now look holistically at the needs of children, families, and teachers; craft curricula that built on each other; and follow children's learning over time. It would be its responsibility to achieve early gains, and to keep them growing all the way up to the critical third-grade watershed. Although the whole child approach still engendered resistance from some BPS academic department leaders, the DEC program was gaining momentum.

When Superintendent Chang and his team moved, in Nicole St. Victor's words, "to tie everything to teacher evaluation," the DEC was prepared. It was already collaborating with teachers to assess their work in real time. It was walking principals through their curricula, helping them to know what to look for in each type of lesson, activity, or intentionally arranged environment and how to scaffold teachers' success and ongoing professional growth. It had successfully fended off state-mandated assessments in K1 in favor of more authentic and teacher-friendly evaluations. And more and more teachers were committing to the DEC's curricula and pedagogy. Despite their concern that children whose teachers were not yet on board might be shortchanged, the DEC team felt that they could be patient. They had learned through experience that trusting teachers and giving them time to learn was a surer path to the results it sought for children than mandates or high-stakes tests.

A 2012 K2–3 needs assessment conducted by the Wellesley researchers who had been tracking K1and K2 classroom quality since 2006 found, in a random sample, that the quality of BPS first-, second-, and third-grade classrooms was markedly lower than that of its K2 programs.[17] A majority of teachers failed to meet the quality benchmarks in key areas, despite strong educational backgrounds and experience.

Under its new mandate, the DEC began to tackle the BPS first- and second-grade curricula. In first grade, *Reading Street* would be replaced by National Geographic's *Reach for Reading*, a program more compatible with the DEC's philosophy and pedagogy.[18] The DEC would modify and consolidate it, featuring fewer themes for more in-depth study, and integrate it into a new curriculum—*Focus on First*—just as it had integrated OWL into *Focus on K1*. First- and second-graders would continue to use TERC's *Investigations* for math, but as in *Focus on K2*, the curriculum would be integrated into the larger program to provide opportunities for mathematization, quantitative reasoning, and problem solving throughout the day. *Focus on K2* would become the model not only for *Focus on K1*, but also for *Focus on First* and *Focus on Second*.

Focus on First—and Second

The six units of *Focus on First* are united by the theme of "Our Changing Global World," a fitting area of investigation for students growing up in an in increasingly interconnected world. The program begins with a two-week launch called "Learning Around the World" that introduces the learning routines the children will be using, while simultaneously engaging them in readings, conversation, and reflection on how they and children in other countries learn. Building on each other, the curriculum units move from people (Families, Communities, and Connections), to the things they use and how they are produced and distributed (Goods and Services), to the environment (Animal Distinctions and Adaptations; Understanding Weather). Students then look at how communication technologies and other inventions have changed the way we live (Technology's Inventions and Innovators), and conclude with a unit on Maps and Mapping. Conceptually rich texts serve as a platform for both content learning in the physical, biological, and social sciences and skill development in literacy, math, and the arts.

As they delve into these units, first-graders use many of the learning routines that characterize K1 and K2, such as Centers, Thinking and Feedback, Read Alouds, and Storytelling, along with dedicated times for math and literacy. But, as befits children's increased maturity and skill, routines have been renamed. "Centers" become "Studios," "Read Alouds" may be followed up with "Close Reading," and "Research" includes increasingly independent reading. Children also do culminating projects (as the kindergarteners do in "Our Boston" when they respond the Mayor's invitation with a class construction that integrates much of what they have been learning).

The connection between oral language (including vocabulary) and reading/writing remains a strong pedagogical theme. Teachers are encouraged to engage children in extended, cognitively challenging conversations and to give children opportunities to engage in such interchanges with each other. Repeated readings of Read Aloud texts spark conversation, writing, and extended projects. Studios offer opportunities for in-depth exploration and extended collaboration, often including specialized vocabulary.

In Learning Stations, students talk about what they read and write and write about what they discuss. They also work in targeted ways on building vocabulary and word knowledge, mastering phonics and spelling patterns, reading closely for accuracy and information, and the craft of writing. As students move between the literacy-focused Learning Stations each week, teachers have opportunities to differentiate skill-focused instruction.

The program is designed to be academically challenging. It is based on the Massachusetts version of the Common Core State Standards and covers quite sophisticated concepts and content. But it is also firmly grounded in early childhood pedagogy and developmentally appropriate practice.[19] Children remain at the center, making choices and decisions, asking questions, building an inclusive classroom community together, leading discussions, and learning in their own ways and at their own paces through hands-on exploration, active involvement, and play.[20] Social-emotional learning, creativity, and aesthetic and physical development are integrated throughout the curriculum and throughout the day. Teachers intentionally arrange environments to prompt inquiry, work with children in large and small groups and one-to-one, talk with children about what they are doing and thinking, and scaffold children's increasing independence and mastery.

To ensure a successful rollout, the DEC invited teachers to apply to be part of the pilot, just as they had when they rolled out *Focus on K2*. Pilot teachers committed to implementing the curriculum, with appropriate PD and coaching, and also to provide feedback that would shape its future iterations. One of the application questions was, "How does this fit with what you are already doing?" For many of the teachers, the fit was clear. For others, though, the proposed program would be a welcome departure from a curriculum that they had found to be too prescriptive. It would allow them to teach and continue to learn in ways that they believed were right for children.

The DEC was surprised by the applications. It had expected push-back from first-grade teachers and their principals to be stronger than it had been for kindergarten, since the teachers were less likely to have had early childhood training and faced greater pressure from parents as well as administrators to focus on skill-building. Yet it had enough early applicants to choose thirty classrooms to support for the initial 2016–2017 school year. It added more the following year, bringing the total to nearly seventy, and expects to support sixty additional first grade classrooms in 2018–2019.

Focus on Second is under construction as this book goes to press. It will be entirely homegrown, using trade books and other texts rather than starting with a packaged curriculum. Seventy second-grade classrooms in twenty-six schools have applied to implement the new curriculum. It is being piloted now, and will be ready for a formal rollout in 2018–2019.

The changes in first- and second-grade programs go deeper than curricula with aligned content. The format of instruction is also changing to reflect the DEC's core principles. Students will spend substantial portions of their time in Studios, actively learning through explorations, projects, collaborative creation, and play. Instruction will take place primarily in small groups, and student work will focus on active and deep engagement with materials and ideas. Much of this activity will be directed by students themselves, with teacher support. Teachers will have more opportunity to tailor their instruction and scaffolding to individual needs, including those of children who have not experienced *Focus on K1*. And perhaps most important, first- and second-grade teachers will get the curriculum-focused PD and the coaching and peer learning opportunities that have been so important for K1 and K2 teachers.

Initial feedback has been very positive. The developers continue to tweak the program to incorporate what they learn from classroom observations, coaching sessions, and teacher and administrator feedback. To strengthen all of the curricula, the DEC has added a new staff member whose core responsibility is analyzing and assuring alignment through the grades.

What Really Matters for PreK–3

When they began their first- and second-grade work, the DEC reached out to Dr. Nonie Lesaux, a Harvard Graduate School of Education professor. Lesaux was the lead author of *Turning the Page*, the report that formed the basis of An Act Relative to Third Grade Reading Proficiency. This Massachusetts law established an Early Literacy Expert Panel to guide the state's early, K–12, and higher education departments on the alignment, coordination, and implementation of curricula, instructional practices, professional development, assessment, and family partnership strategies that would implement the report's recommendations for birth through third grade language and literacy building efforts. Lesaux served as co-chair of the panel.

As they crafted *Focus on First* and planned *Focus on Second* to align with *Focus on K1* and *Focus on K2*, the DEC team had data and research on their side. In literacy, DIBELS scores continued to show that teachers using the *Focus* curricula were successfully teaching letter naming and letter-sound correspondences, "constrained" (discrete, finite, and easily measured) skills that are relatively easy to teach. In a review of studies of early literacy skills and instructional practices that support their development, the 2009 report of the National Early Literacy Panel (NELP) had highlighted the importance of these decoding skills for learning to read.[21]

In a widely circulated article, however, reading expert Susan Neuman had put the NELP findings in context. Looking at a broader range of studies and a longer span of development, Neuman argued that content knowledge, including concepts and vocabulary, is more important for skilled reading than mastery of isolated decoding skills and comprehension strategies. Skilled readers understand and learn less from novel texts when they know little about the content area than do poorer readers who bring strong background knowledge. What really matters for literacy, Neuman argued, are "content-rich settings in which skills are learned through meaningful activity" and that build the deeper, twenty-first-century skills of thoughtful reading and writing.[22] That is exactly what the Focus curricula, implemented in NAEYC-accredited settings, aim to deliver.

The eleven guiding principles of the 2017 Massachusetts English Language Arts and Literacy Curriculum Framework begin with explicit instruction in skills, cited as especially important for narrowing achievement gaps. But they move through developing vocabulary and background knowledge; promoting a love of reading; engagement with well-crafted texts in a variety of genres; writing for a variety of audiences and purposes; and family engagement to a focus on social-emotional strengths (self-awareness, self-management, social awareness, and relationship skills) and the broader, twenty-first-century goals of empathy and perspective-taking, vigorous critical thinking, communication with diverse audiences, creativity, and citizenship.[23] The Framework explicitly states that "the standards define what all students are expected to know and be able to do, not how teachers should teach."[24] But its thrust and teaching examples align with the DEC's balanced approach of building oral language, academic and specialized vocabulary, and both basic and higher order skills through pretend play, projects, extended conversation, and thoughtful instruction.[25]

In math, too, the DEC's approach aligns with current research in terms of both short-term gains and those that grow over time. Doug Clements and Julie Sarama's studies, for example, have found that *Building Blocks* leads to large effects (more than a standard deviation in a randomized control design study conducted in Boston and Buffalo), and that these effects occur regardless of low-income status and substantially narrow the achievement gap for African American children. They also found that when kindergarten and first-grade teachers receive PD related to children's developmental trajectories in understanding math concepts and are encouraged to ask probing questions that engage children's reasoning, these effects are sustained over time.[26] Trusting in the *Investigations* curriculum and the STEM themes and activities built into the *Focus* curricula, the DEC doesn't write its own math curricula or provide math-focused curriculum coaching beyond K1. As the team spends more time in first and second grade classrooms, however, they plan to engage with teachers in a research study that explores children's math learning trajectories.

The *Focus* curricula are designed to build basic literacies and twenty-first-century skills over time, with knowledge and skills building upon each other and honed through ever more challenging practice.[27] Like all good designs, the curricula need to be implemented, adapted by users, evaluated, and improved in an ongoing cycle.

As the DEC reached down to better align its K1 program with *Focus on K2* and reached up to build *Focus on First* and then *Focus on Second*, it won a five-year grant from the US Department of Education's Institute of Education Sciences (IES) to take a hard look at its model and its implementation, following children's school and out-of-school experiences and learning trajectories as they advance through the grades. JoAnn Hsueh, Christina Weiland, and Catherine Snow work with Jason Sachs as co-principal investigators.

In collaboration with research teams at Harvard Graduate School of Education, the University of Michigan, and MDRC (an education and social policy research organization), Sachs and his DEC team will explore the relationship over time between strong instruction, strong curricula that are fully and faithfully implemented, and student outcomes. The three-part project began in 2016, with a descriptive study of the DEC's curricula, policies, and teacher supports, and the state, district, and school-level policies and cultures that might foster or impede their full implementation. Together, DEC staff, researchers, and teachers have developed rubrics for assessing fidelity of implementation. With these in hand, they will be able to track where deviation from their model weakens or strengthens results and where it makes no difference. They will be able to hone their pedagogy, curricula, PD, and messaging to highlight essential components, and provide coaches, administrators, parents, and teachers themselves with authentic evaluation tools.

This ongoing work creates a context for a second study that begins with documentation of how teachers are using what is offered: where they implement the model with fidelity and where they adapt it; the balance in their classrooms between time spent on constrained versus unconstrained skills; their embrace of or resistance to the DEC's beliefs and values; their stress levels, morale, and support networks; and the quality of their relationships, classroom management, instructional supports, and literacy and math environments. This is paired with outcome measures to examine which potentially malleable features of observed implementation and teaching practice correlate with students' literacy and math success within each grade and support their development of social-emotional and executive function skills.

The third study, overlapping in time with the second, looks at children's experiences at home and during the summer as well as at school. It tracks children's development and learning across grades, and looks at how prior and cumulative skills and experiences affect third grade success.

Together, the three studies will enable the DEC and its research partners to "track features of classrooms and instructional practices that differentially support students' gains on both unconstrained and constrained skills that are central to high achievement in both literacy and math domains. In doing so, we aim to inform which aspects of children's classroom experiences could be enhanced to better promote children's longer-term academic success."[28]

Preliminary observational results are promising. CLASS scores are strong in the randomly sampled K1 classrooms, although there is some inconsistency, especially in the critical area of instructional supports (Concept Development, Quality of Feedback, and Language Modeling). But the highest instructional support scores—and the most and longest conversations that engaged children's thinking—were recorded during the Centers Time STEM-based activities that are the heart of the interdisciplinary *Focus* curricula, as we saw in chapters 2 and 5 (our K1 classroom visits).[29]

This ambitious investigation is situated within a set of studies by a consortium of research groups who have received IES grants. All will follow similar models, including:

- A descriptive study of systems-level policies and practices that support early learning
- A classroom observation study to identify teaching practices and other classroom-level malleable factors associated with children's school readiness and achievement in preschool and early elementary school
- A longitudinal study to identify malleable factors associated with early learning and school achievement over time from preschool through the early elementary school grades (e.g., kindergarten through third grade) for preschool attenders and non-attenders[30]

Along with BPS, collaborating districts include Fairfax County (Virginia) Public Schools, twelve urban and rural school districts in Nebraska, four rural counties in North Carolina, and the State of Ohio. Together, these studies promise new insights into what really matters for preK–3 and long-term success.

The link with MDRC on the IES study has brought an opportunity for a parallel longitudinal study of the impacts of Boston's K1 programs, when followed by aligned curriculum through the second grade. Called ExCell P–3, the study will take advantage of the fact that, despite its best efforts, the DEC has only been able to open enough K1 classrooms for 55 percent of Boston's four-year-olds. The natural experiment provided by Boston's K1 lottery allows for a randomized controlled trial—the research gold standard—that compares the trajectories of children who enter at K1 with those who enter at K2 and asks what makes the difference not only for achieving positive outcomes with public school–based prekindergarten, but for sustaining them. Like the IES study, ExCell P–3 is part of a network of studies with national educational policy significance.

But for the DEC, it is still about the children of Boston. The team is already thinking about next steps. Where are the inequities and how can they mitigate them? How can they use what they learn to improve learning experiences for all of the children and to prevent learning opportunity and achievement gaps? How can they better support teachers and families in this effort? Will they need to discover, modify, or invent new tools to assess the quality of first and second grade learning environments and instruction, accredit classrooms, and hone professional development?

How can they do a better job of reaching out to the programs that serve four-year-olds who don't attend K1 and of supporting their success? Should they be reaching down, expanding their community partnerships to strengthen programming and supports for children birth through three and their families? How might they reach up even further, to align with, and perhaps transform, children's educational experiences in grade 3 and beyond? And how can they assure Boston's youngest citizens the respect and care of their community, including their right to a high-quality education?

It is fitting that this account of the DEC's ongoing journey ends with questions. Asking hard questions is central to the work of this group of educators, as they constantly inquire, push, explore, and work harder on behalf of the children of Boston. Despite their many accomplishments, the DEC team is acutely aware of how much they still need to do. And in today's political climate, funding, resources, and support for public schools and programs that support young children and their families are uncertain.

What is certain is that the DEC will continue to draw on the richness of its team's experiences and perspectives, tap talents of critical friends, and use data to guide decisions. Most centrally, it will remain true to its core principles, guided by strong beliefs in both children and teachers as citizens of the Boston community.

Epilogue

A Park Where Parents Play with Their Kids

A Visit to City Hall

The incidents in this chapter are real, as is the children's dialogue. Children's names have been changed to protect their privacy. As you read this story, you may notice how it embodies the DEC's core principles of active, cognitively-challenging, and emotionally engaging learning, supported by strong relationships and sparked by a flexible, hands-on curriculum that addresses the whole child, offers a range of activities, and respects each child's learning strengths, pace, and interests. Most of all, though, we hope that you will notice the children themselves: eager, empathetic, and wise citizens of a democratic classroom and a caring community.

On the first Saturday in May 2016, five-year-old Ayana stands before two hundred people who have assembled at Boston City Hall to view an exhibition of work created by kindergarteners from across the Boston Public School district. Ayana describes "A Park Where Parents Play with Their Kids," a three-dimensional model she and her classmates at the William Trotter School have created:

We decided to make a park where parents have to play with their kids. They have some lockers so they can put their phones in when they are at the park and not use them and signs to tell them there are no phones allowed unless it's an emergency.

Her classmate Malik then tells the audience that the park is not just about limits. It also features ways to make the play experience more appealing to adults:

We made a lot of big equipment in the park so the grown-ups can play with the kids and the stuff isn't too small for them. We made a big adult slide and monkey bars and swings for them next to the kid equipment.

This event is the culmination of the *Focus on K2* "Construction" unit. In a sense, the children have been working toward it all year: collecting "beautiful stuff" that may become part of their models; learning about communities and habitats and the people and animals who live in them; and mastering skills for researching and writing, planning and measuring, drawing, crafting, building, and public speaking and storytelling. Most important, they have been learning to work together: to take their own and each other's ideas seriously; to observe, listen, ask good questions, and give helpful feedback; to consider other's perspectives along with their own; and to collaborate, compromise, and problem solve.[1]

Three months earlier, BPS's four thousand kindergarteners, had received the letter from mayor Marty Walsh featured in the introduction to this book, in which Walsh asks, "What suggestions do you have about construction in our city to make Boston fairer and a more interesting place for children?" After expressing confidence in the children's ability to answer this question, Mayor Walsh concludes:

This is a big question, so take your time in answering it. Talk to your classmates, your teacher and your family. Do research to get ideas. Write your ideas and please make a model to help me understand your ideas better. I look forward to learning about your ideas and seeing your model.[2]

Children did get to take their time in answering Mayor Walsh's question. For example, in Calla Freeman's kindergarten class, Ayana and Malik, along with their classmates, engaged in a five-week design process that involved envisioning possibilities, selecting a topic, making plans for their construction, and building their model.

Following the model set forth in *Focus on K2*, the process begins with the twenty-three kindergarteners discussing what "fair" and "more interesting" mean.[3] They decide that *fair* means "everyone has or can do the same thing," while *interesting* involves "what you love to do" or "what you want to learn more about." With this in mind, the children spend several days brainstorming ideas in whole and small group conversations. Their ideas of what to build include:

- A basketball court for little kids (because big kids are always using the other courts and the hoops are too high for kindergarteners to dunk on)
- Ice cream and candy shops in every apartment building
- A free amusement park that you could go to whenever you wanted
- Clean homes with no bugs or mice

While each of these ideas are of interest to some, none captures the imagination of the entire group. Then, at a group meeting time on the fourth day of discussion, Jamal shares an idea: a park where parents have to play with their kids. The group embraces it as exactly right. In their excitement, the children forget their classroom norms for conversation; everyone is talking at once.

With interest so high, Freeman breaks the children break into small groups to discuss what such a park might involve. At one table, Ayana suggests banning cell phone use. Other suggestions soon follow, and Freeman documents them:

AYANA: We need lockers so that parents can put their phones away in a safe place. They don't want their stuff to get stolen because they would get mad and not be in the mood to play.

SAMANTHA: There should be keys for the lockers with a number on it so that they know which locker it went in.

SAWYER: Maybe no iPads or electronics either because then they might just FaceTime their friends on an iPad instead of their phone.

REGGIE: We can put signs up that say "No phones allowed."

AMARA: Yeah, but what if there is an emergency and they need to use
the phone for help?

AYANA: Okay. Well then maybe it can say, "No phones allowed unless it
is an emergency."

At another table, Jean-Paul comments, "My dad does like to play with me,
but he always says the playground is too little for him and like he can't fit on
the slide." This starts another line of conversation:

ANGEL: Yeah, if my dad tries to do the monkey bars with me, then his
feet can just touch the ground.

MALIK: Maybe then we need to have big equipment for the grownups
like big slides and big swings and monkey bars so that they can use it.

AMARA: My mom is always hot at the park, so maybe we can have a
water part too, so if the grownups get hot, they can go there.

That night, Freeman identifies two main threads from the small group
conversation: setting rules about technology use, and making a park that is
more appealing to parents. The next day, she shares this observation with the
children and, in a whole class conversation, they quickly agree on the rule that
cell phones should be used only in emergencies. But how to make the park
more appealing to grownups is subject to much longer deliberation.

These deliberations begin during Center Time. Freeman sets up an area with
paper and drawing implements. Over three days, Ayana, Sylvie, Samantha, and
Ciara spend long stretches of time discussing their ideas and drawing possibilities.

*Notice how the children built on each other's ideas as they brainstormed, and that
the teacher was absent or silent during the children's conversations. Did you notice
also how intentional she was in elongating the process, abstracting the key ideas
and feeding them back to the children for deeper reflection and discussion? The
children in this class are not just learning to come to consensus on ideas or cooper-
ate on a project. They are learning and practicing an iterative process for arriving
at innovative solutions. As kindergarteners, they are engaging in what architects
and city planners call "design thinking," a process that has proven invaluable in
incorporating diverse community perspectives into major building projects.[4]*

While Freeman is happy about the girls' engagement and collaboration, she is uncomfortable with the possibility that just a few children's ideas might represent the entire class's answer to the mayor. She shares this concern with her coach, Melissa Tonachel. Tonachel suggests that the girls bring their ideas to the whole class during Thinking and Feedback.[5]

The result of the girls' presentation is twofold. First, two new ideas for making the park more appealing to adults are generated: having food stands ("Then we don't have to leave early if it is time for lunch because there is food and tables there for a picnic") and building a racetrack. In addition, other children become interested in visiting the planning area during Center Time.

Additional plans are presented at subsequent Thinking and Feedback sessions. During one conversation about the food stands, the children agree that all items for sale be priced at one dollar in order to be affordable. Freeman points out there cannot be too many stands or else there will not be room in the park for anything else. The children decide there should be four stands: hot dogs, popcorn, ice cream, and fruits and vegetables. Trevor gives the rationale for the fruit and vegetable stand: "My mom will make me go home for lunch if there is no healthy food to buy." Freeman is impressed that children who typically hold tight to their ideas are able to compromise. Angel, for example, gives up on his proposal for a pizza stand.

After a week of discussion, it is time to settle on a final plan, which requires merging the ideas from several groups. There are several challenges. First, the groups' ideas are not always in agreement. For example, Reggie's plan for the park had four entrances, while the other groups have just one. The following discussion ensues:

AMARA: I like four different doors so no matter what direction you come from there is a way to get in.

AYANA: But then the parents might not remember what door they left their cell phone.

TREVOR: We can put a number on each door—1, 2, 3, 4—and the key will say what entrance.

Freeman suggests that the children cut out features from each of their plans and place them on a large piece of butcher paper. This makes it apparent that there are redundancies, raising questions such as which group's swings should be used for the final plan. Aesthetics seem to guide most choices. As Jonah explains, "I like Sylvie's pool the most." Similar conversations guide whose popcorn stand will be used. But Jade, who does not have strong fine motor skills, notes that none of her work is included in the master plan. In response, Amara invites her to join her in drawing a garden around the periphery of the park. Jade accepts, but still wants something from her plan included. At this point, Jonah gently asks Sylvie if they can swap Jade's slide for hers. Sylvie generously agrees.

With final plans completed, the children spend a week using craft and recycled materials to make a 3D model of their park. There is much to build: flowers, slides, sprinklers, cell phone lockers, and more. Children use paint, glue, paper, crayons, pipe cleaners, and milk cartoons to construct their model. Drawing on what they've learned in their observations of buildings and places in their city, one group creates a skyline backdrop.

As they work, children bring their constructions to Thinking and Feedback for input from the whole group. In a class with several highly verbal, outgoing children, Freeman worries that quieter voices may not be heard. At the same time, she knows that if she asks the verbal children to hold back, they might disengage, and perhaps disrupt the conversation. She doesn't want to dampen any child's enthusiasm. She raises the issue with Tonachel, and they decide on a strategy. Freeman chooses some times when she asks the more verbal children to be in "listening mode," where their job is to summarize the conversation at the end. This strategy works well, and the majority of children contribute to the conversations.

As their model nears completion, the children decide that they need signs to label each section of the park, "So that people who are looking at our model would know what everything is that is important." After five weeks of conversation, planning, and making, the model is completed (see figure E.1). It portrays a very detailed, thoughtfully designed park that almost any parent would enjoy.

Look closely at the model (Figure E.1), and at the signs and dictated words that accompany it. What do you notice about the children's use of materials and artistic

FIGURE E.1 Children's model of their park

expression? What do you notice about how they took users' needs into consideration? What details do you notice that you might not have expected? Would you find this park a "fair" and "interesting" addition to your city? Would you like to play in it?

Now that you've seen the park model and the process that the children went through to create it, take a moment to appreciate the children's ideas and their concern for each other and for their community. Think back to how Ayana and Malik described the project as they spoke for the group:

> *We decided to make a park where parents have to play with their kids. They have some lockers so they can put their phones in when they are at the park and not use them and signs to tell them there are no phones allowed unless it's an emergency.*
>
> *We made a lot of big equipment in the park so the grown-ups can play with the kids and the stuff isn't too small for them.*

Their use of "we" reflects the progress the class has made this year. A group of individuals—sometimes competing for attention, hogging the floor, or forming exclusive small groups—has become a "we." Guided by their teacher, these kindergarteners have made impressive progress in learning how to collaborate, come to consensus, and find ways to include everyone's contributions.

Remember the original charge: "What suggestions do you have about construc-
tion in our city to make Boston fairer and a more interesting place for children . . .
Write your ideas and please make a model to help me understand your ideas better."
Clearly, the children have balanced their desires for a place that children would
find interesting with a concern for fairness, both in their attention to parents' needs
in their final product and in their consideration for each other's ideas and feelings
in the process of building it. Having taken the time to listen, explore, research,
draft, and repeatedly redraft and get feedback, they have written their ideas clearly
and made a model that helps their mayor and fellow citizens to understand them.

Our Boston

The story you just witnessed is part of a larger context. The "Our Boston"
projects inspired by the mayor's challenge are an important part of the *Focus*
on K2 curriculum, and could easily be adapted in other cities.[6] Our Boston is
a concrete embodiment of the DEC's first core principle: *Schools must promote*
our democratic society and support children's and teachers' sense of citizenship
though multiple connections to families and community.

Each year, the mayor's staff hosts an exhibit at City Hall or in another public
space where the kindergarteners' ideas and learning can be made visible to the
citizens of their city. The 2016 exhibit includes twenty-nine models created
across the city. Not surprisingly, these include a number parks and other places
for children to play, including a tree house park created by Michael Kenney's
class at the Condon School. Inside this park is a Library, a Fun Toy room, an
Art Studio, a Kitchen (where people can cook food or sell it) and a Relaxing
Room (for children to have sleepovers with old friends or with new friends
who have lost their homes).

An awareness and sensitivity for people in need—in this case people who
lost their homes—has appeared in a significant number of other models. The
children in Kelly Stevens's class at the Curtis Guide School, for example,
wanted to give children equal access to books. Their solution is the "Boston
Book Bus," which, "picks up books from children who have a lot and don't
want them anymore and gives them to children who have none, to keep."
Mary Wilder's class at the Kenny School has built a tower with apartments

for homeless families. It has areas where the families can get clothes and food. There is also a school, a library, and a place where adults can learn about jobs.

At the May 2016 celebration, attendance is much higher than at typical school functions. Following Ayana's speech, Boston's chief of education, Rahn Dorsey, addresses the children and their families:

> This is what learning looks like when learning comes to life. Certainly, learning looks like reading and writing, but it also looks like kids using their hands. It looks like cutting boxes and playing with egg crates and glue. It looks like working with your friends.[7]

The learning inspired by the Our Boston project continues beyond the City Hall exhibition. At a teacher seminar about the *Focus on K2* curriculum that the Our Boston project is part of, Melissa Tonachel facilitates a conversation with Freeman and her kindergarten teacher colleagues about struggles and success with the project. Plans are made for next year; for example, Freeman wants to spend more time on building so children can have even more ownership over the process. Tonachel asks teachers to write a letter to children from another classroom about their models. The next day, Freeman reads the letter to her children. Aligning with a Writing Workshop unit on letter writing, the note sparks a real correspondence.

We bookended our journey with this story to illustrate how Boston's early education programs "promote our democratic society and support children's and teachers' sense of citizenship though multiple connections to families and community." To the children who built it, the Park Where Parents Play with Their Kids was an idea that mattered. They worked to get the details right. It was also an experience of democratic decision making and an affirmation of their connections to each other, their families, and the larger community. Their message to the adults in their lives comes through loud and clear.

The park that Calla Freeman's kindergarteners designed also serves as a metaphor for the DEC's vision: A place where adults and children pay attention to each other and have fun together. Where they play with ideas, materials, and equipment that are just the right size and offer the right level of challenge. An integration of adults' agendas (academics, adult obligations) with children's (play-based and exploratory learning, physical and fantasy play, adults' full attention). A setting for joyful learning and healthy play. When you are four or five or six or seven, isn't that what school should be?

The Role of Data, Research, and Evaluation in the Process of Change

Christina Weiland and Jason Sachs

The use of research and data to drive change in the BPS Department of Early Childhood got off to what many would consider an inauspicious start. In our first year, the DEC contracted an outside research firm to perform a needs assessment to provide baseline data to guide our quality-building efforts. But the most concerning findings were soon prominently displayed on the first page of the *Boston Globe*: "Boston Preschools Falling Far Short of Goals, Study Says: Teacher Quality, Site Safety Faulted." That headline was a scary one for a program in its infancy. And the article's first line was even worse: "Boston's public preschool and kindergarten programs are hobbled by mediocre instruction, unsanitary classrooms, and dangerous schoolyards, according to a first-ever study of the programs."[1]

We had spent that first year trying to open as many K1 classrooms as we could while meeting basic quality standards. Compared with what was available in the private market—especially for families with low or moderate incomes whose children didn't qualify for or get into Head Start—many of our classrooms were quite good, but we knew that most were not as good as they needed to be, and some had serious problems that we had only just begun to address. So we weren't surprised by the findings. Still, the safety and sanitary practices findings were worrisome. We were beginning to figure out our course of action when the report was made public.

That newspaper article could have sounded the death knell for public preschool in Boston. But it didn't. In retrospect, it may have been one of the best things to happen to our program. Those findings, and their very public airing, sparked fundamental changes in our model that would shape our focus on supporting teachers through common curricula, professional development, and coaching—and ultimately enable our programs to be seen as a national model. At that critical early juncture, we used data to engage with teachers, administrators, policy makers, outside funders, and the public to understand and articulate what we needed. Data shaped a departmental culture committed to transparency and to using evaluation to inform and drive change. We honestly wanted to know what was working well and where we could improve.

As our project grew, we collected data for many purposes: not only to evaluate classroom quality and track child outcomes, but to also to assess teacher and family satisfaction; plan professional development; evaluate specific programmatic elements; communicate to multiple audiences, including teachers and school committee members; inform strategic decisions related to focus and resource allocation; and shape conversations as to whether to change or stay our course. We built regular data collection, rigorous evaluations, and research intended to inform our next steps into our strategic plans. But we have always been careful about what data we collect or ask teachers for—how, when, why, and especially how much.

When we showed those first needs assessment results to our K1 and K2 teachers, some told us that one of the problems they faced was that they had to spend too much time on mandated assessments, to the detriment of teaching. We also learned that many of the K2 teachers felt they were spending too much time on whole group literacy work and skill development, pressured to prepare children for the third-grade tests.

In a time of high-stakes testing, accountability, and teach-to-the-test pressures, we stayed focused on what was best for young learners and sought age-appropriate measures that would help us assess their learning and the efficacy of our efforts to support and promote it. The videotapes, student work, and other artifacts of learning that teachers collect for their own purposes, and often reflect on with coaches, parents, specialists, or colleagues, shape instruction in real time and show us strengths and gaps in our curricula and teacher supports. Similarly, our department routinely collects, shares, and analyzes coaching notes, PD evaluations, and artifacts of adult learning in order to improve our own practice and plan our next steps.

What has set Boston's early learning program apart has been a deep philosophical difference about the purpose of data in education. For us, *data is a tool for* building *the program, not merely for grading it.*

That belief has shaped a robust research-practice partnership, grounded in inclusiveness, transparency, genuine curiosity, and a focus on driving change to meet the goal set forth in the DEC's mission statement: *To ensure that principals, teachers, paraprofessionals, and school support staff have the knowledge, skills, and resources they need to provide a high-quality early education experience for all students.* Our expectation is that all children will become internally driven and self-motivated learners and will read, write, and communicate effectively by third grade. One of the DEC's core principles is that varied assessments (including teacher's informal observations and their documentation of student's learning processes) provide data to inform instruction and drive change.[2] Teachers and families participate along with administrators and specialists in interpreting findings, evaluating their implications, and shaping decisions.

Research and Evaluation in the DEC, 2006–2017

Almost all the work we describe in the rest of this appendix has been conducted in the context of our research-practice partnership. We view our partnership as a key element of what has worked in the program to date—a "key lesson" we expound on later.

Overview of Data Types

Over the DEC's history, we have collected and used data in a variety of ways. Table A.1 gives an illustrative snapshot of the data types we have used, how frequently each has been collected, its purpose, and how we have used it to drive change. The table provides an overview of our approach without capturing the details of each wave of data collection. As an example, observational classroom quality data have been collected on a random sample of classrooms approximately every two years, usually via a contract with the Wellesley Centers for Women or with Abt Associates. The researchers produce a report with central findings and also provide a dataset for the district's use. We use these findings to inform DEC programmatic and district policy decisions and also perform our own analyses, often linking a contractor's dataset to internal data such as administrative data on program demographics.

Partnerships with researchers, such as those at Wellesley Centers for Women and Abt Associates, have been key. The DEC has not had the capacity to collect all the data we need on our own and reports from outside researchers bring an additional perspective into what the results mean. Importantly, we are careful in our contracts with outside firms to always retain full access to the identified data so that we are not limited in the kinds of internal research that are subsequently possible. Although some outside firms or their IRB's may balk at first, this is a nonnegotiable DEC policy.

Funding availability and funders' agendas have also influenced data collection. Partners such as the Barr Foundation both expected and supported evaluations, helping the DEC to learn what was working and hold itself accountable for results. State and federal grants often came with specific requirements, such as tracking NAEYC accreditation or investigating particular research questions. Weiland has led large-scale grants that have funded additional data collection, including work to create and use curriculum fidelity measures in district classrooms and to expand child outcome data to important domains beyond language and literacy, such as mathematics and executive function.

Measuring Instructional Quality and Child Outcomes

Whenever possible, we use state-of-the-art instruments to assess the quality of learning environments and instructional supports. This has meant not only

TABLE A.1 Summary of types of data collected, frequency of collection, purpose, and use

Data source	Collected	Purpose	Use
Artifacts of learning (teacher-collected pedagogical documentation)	Frequently during each unit	To make learning visible to children and to adult stakeholders	To spark teachers' reflective conversations with coaches, parents, and colleagues and influence instruction in real time
Classroom quality and curriculum fidelity observational scores	About every two years	Changes as program evolves; in 2012, for example, data collection focused on K–2 due to concerns about quality of education after prekindergarten	Determine program gaps, needs, and strengths; guide professional development and programmatic decisions
Administrative data	Ongoing	Tracking important programmatic data like child attendance, enrollment, and demographics; teacher education, certification, and experience	Answer questions about programmatic use and take up; describe population and how it changes over time. The data also are used as control variables in analyses, limiting participant burden
Teacher survey	About every two years	Gather richer data on teacher background, experience of professional development, and opinions/desires related to current offerings	Understand teacher population in more depth; guide professional development and programmatic decisions
K0–K2 child vocabulary; K1–2 early reading skills	Three times per year by teachers	Monitor children's early language and literacy skill development; identify supports as needed	Describe BPS population; useful as outcomes in evaluation studies
Broader set of child outcomes	When external funding is available or when a research study requires them	Examine children's levels and growth on a broader set of important outcomes, like math, executive function, and socio-emotional skills	Describe BPS population; used as outcomes in evaluation studies

using the most recent versions of widely accepted tools like the ECERS and newer ones like the CLASS, but seeking out less commonly used tools like the SELA and ELLCO for literacy, the COEMET for math, and the Early Childhood Classroom Observation Measure (ECCOM), which includes two scales that measure the extent to which teachers employ child-centered *constructivist* practices that promote active learning and knowledge construction, and the extent to which they use teacher-centered *didactic* practices.[3] Working with coaches, teachers, and researchers in an iterative process, we are also designing our own measures and benchmarks of curriculum implementation fidelity so that we can learn what modifiable elements and strategies are most predictive of the outcomes we seek.

Similarly, measures of child outcomes in multiple domains are selected to both meet rigorous research standards and reflect the DEC's developmentally grounded and research-informed vision of what is important to learn, develop, and master. Because group testing is often unreliable for young children, these assessments need to be administered individually, which can be quite time-consuming. So as not to burden teachers, children, and budgets, we use sampling rather than whole-cohort assessments for most of our needs assessments and research studies.

Multipurposed Data Use

As table A.1 illustrates, data have been used for a variety of purposes in the DEC. Classroom observational data, for example, have been used to identify systematic weaknesses across classrooms and target professional development accordingly. For example, K1 and K2 classroom quality data collected in 2008 and again in 2010 revealed that our teachers were not doing enough to support children's conceptual development.[4] Professional development was subsequently modified to target best practices in this area. We also created a teacher-friendly template that displays individual teachers' results and compares them with district averages. The reports, which we shared directly with teachers, highlighted specific strengths along with areas for growth. Coaches worked with teachers to help them interpret their scores and reflect on implications for their practice.

Data have also been used to link children's learning to their program experiences. For example, BPS elementary schools vary in how mixed they are in their income demographics. Some schools are nearly all low-income while others have approximately equal representation of students from higher- and lower-income backgrounds. Accordingly, Sachs asked Weiland and Hirokazu Yoshikawa to examine whether the percentage of low-income peers was related to children's gains in their prekindergarten year. Sachs's reasoning was that preschool classrooms are structured so that children spend a lot of time interacting with each other and that they learn a lot from each other. Higher-income children on average come to school with stronger language skills and more world knowledge than their low-income peers. Weiland and Yoshikawa found that, as Sachs suspected, having more mixed-income peers (versus low-income only) did predict gains in children's vocabulary skills during the preK year.[5] These results have not (yet) affected BPS policy; children are still assigned to schools via a centralized parent choice system within geographic areas, with no attempt to balance schools by children's family income status. But they did enhance the DEC's understanding of drivers of child gains in early childhood classrooms and contribute to conversations in the early childhood field.

The mixed-income peers study was published in an academic journal. We have viewed this as desirable when possible because feedback from reviewers helps our work be as rigorous as possible and peer-reviewed publication adds to its credibility. However, the work we have done with the data sources in table A.1 has often not been publishable in peer-reviewed journals, because available data has not always been complete enough or captured the full story enough to meet publication standards. Consider the following example. In 2010, BPS had to decide whether to continue to offer a summer reading program to kindergarten and first-grade students and whether to extend the program to prekindergarteners. The district was well aware of research showing that low-income children commonly experience summer learning loss and that high-quality summer enrichment programs have been effective in combating this problem.[6] In late fall 2010, within the structure of our research-practice partnership, we framed the key research questions and identified key data from the summer 2009 district summer program (which children chose to attend the program, attendance data, and student outcome data) that could help inform the decision.

The challenge in answering the research questions rigorously was that students had selected into the program; that is, any results, positive or negative, could have had to do with the students themselves and not the program. The research team decided to create two quasi-experimental control groups to increase the study's rigor: (1) students who applied to the program but did not attend and (2) all other students attending the same regular-school-year schools as summer-program attenders. Analyses showed that program attendance was strong—80 percent of students had attendance rates of 73 percent or higher. The program also reached children more in need of help than their peers; participants had lower literacy skills than their peers before they entered the program and were significantly more likely to have previously repeated a grade. Students who attended the program had stronger post-program literacy skills scores than children in either of the two control groups. Weiland was careful to make sure that the study's limitations were clearly communicated, so that the results were seen as just one piece of evidence to inform the decision and not as decisive. The district solicited feedback from teachers involved in the program and, based on the evidence it had, decided to continue offering the program and eventually to expand it to include incoming pre-kindergarteners.

Notably, not enough data was available at the time on the program in practice—i.e., valid, descriptive observational data on its components and quality of delivery—to make the study publishable. But through the research, the district made a more informed decision that it would have otherwise. As the Summer Early Focus program matured, it became an important place for the DEC to pilot new curricula. And children in the program continued to make summer literacy gains.

As we've used data to build our program, our questions and data sources have evolved. For example, in 2010, the district learned that the Boston program had the highest instructional quality of any large-scale preK program examined with the CLASS to date. As shown in figure A.1, Boston, like the other preK programs, scored at the "Good" level on the Emotional Support section of the CLASS.[7] Nationally, Instructional Support measured "Barely Adequate." After just two years of the coaching and curricula described throughout this

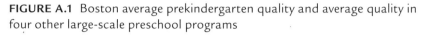

FIGURE A.1 Boston average prekindergarten quality and average quality in four other large-scale preschool programs

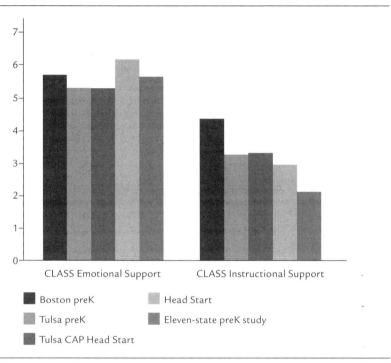

Source: Reproduced by permission from Chaudry et al., *Cradle to Kindergarten: A New Plan to Combat Inequality* (New York: Russell Sage Foundation, 2017).[7]

book, Boston was the only place where average instructional supports scores neared the "Good" benchmark. Compared with the lowest instructional quality level observed across these contexts (an eleven-state study that had used an earlier, but very similar, version of the CLASS), Boston's instructional quality was a very large 2.7 standard deviations higher.

Given this evidence, the DEC decided in 2012 to break with past policy and not to measure preK quality in its biannual observational quality monitoring. What appeared to be fadeout, or convergence, of the literacy edge that K1 graduates showed over children who entered BPS at K2, as well as differences in approach and emphasis between OWL and *Reading Street*, raised concern that children were transitioning from high-quality preK to lower-quality K–3 experiences. Resources were too limited to do a thorough job of assessing the quality of preK–3 classrooms. The K–3 data revealed that the quality in K–3 settings was 0.23 to 0.87 standard deviations lower than the quality of the preK classrooms that were assessed in 2010.[8]

Lessons Learned

From more than a decade of work connecting research to practice, we have drawn a set of key lessons that may be of use to other programs, which we describe below.

Effective Research-Practice Partnership Develops over Time— Longevity Matters

As we explained at the outset of this appendix, almost all of the work we describe has been conducted in the context of our research-practice partnership. We have had great success working with organizations such as the Wellesley Centers for Women, Abt Associates, and most recently, MDRC. But key in the district's use of data and reports from these organizations has been Weiland's depth of knowledge of the BPS data, schools, context, and DEC staff. Her start as an intern who learned from, took orders from, and worked hard to understand others in the DEC has been invaluable, helping her learn how to be helpful to the DEC. Her deep understanding of DEC practice has prompted research questions that she might not have framed otherwise—like the impact of learning with low-income versus mixed-income peers.

We view it as an extremely positive development for the field that in the last few years research-practice partnerships have become a key recommendation for how research should happen. For example, the Society for Research in Educational Effectiveness, which focuses on rigorous educational evaluation, is devoting its Spring 2018 conference to research-practice partnerships. The W.T. Grant Foundation and other leading funders have been publicizing the model as the way to move forward as a field. New York City's preK program is being evaluated and improved via this model as well, through Pamela Morris and her colleagues' partnership with the city.[9] There is also now a pipeline for training researchers steeped in practice; the Society for Research in Child

Development in 2017 launched a fellowship program that places promising postdoctoral and predoctoral students in city and state early learning departments around the country.

Acknowledge the Natural Tensions in a Research-Practice Partnership

Despite our cheerleading for the research-practice partnership model, we want be clear that there are inevitable tensions that have to be addressed and managed. For example, rigor and timeliness often conflict; careful studies can take years while policy and practice decisions are often made in a matter of weeks or months. We call this the "academic time versus BPS real time" dilemma. For example, around 2010, the district faced a critical decision of whether to pursue NAEYC accreditation for all district elementary schools. Though NAEYC accreditation is widely considered a marker of quality by the early childhood field, Weiland's literature review revealed limited empirical evidence on its effects on classroom quality and child outcomes.[10] Accordingly, in 2008 we used data from the needs assessment study conducted by the Wellesley Centers for Women to examine whether undertaking accreditation was associated with higher classroom quality in the group of early adopters in the district versus other district classrooms.[11] Importantly, schools had selected into accreditation, and the level of rigor we would have preferred was not possible in time to inform the district's decision-making process. As shown in figure A.2, we found that achieving or even seeking NAEYC accreditation was associated with meaningful improvements in classroom quality.[12] The district subsequently used results of this analysis as one piece of evidence in informing its decision to expand NAEYC accreditation to more district schools. Analyses in 2010 and 2015 also examined the role of accreditation in the district; the 2015 results led to a shift in NAEYC work to emphasize cognitively demanding tasks for students.

Tensions can also arise around the choice of research questions. The DEC turned down some of Weiland's (and others') proposals as "too academic"— that is, likely to advance the field but create burden without benefit for the district. Conversely, sometimes the DEC has had a question or a "need to know" that is not of interest to academics or not publishable. Weiland and her team have generally taken these studies on nonetheless, viewing them as

FIGURE A.2 The relationship between NAEYC Accreditation and classroom quality in Boston Public Schools prekindergarten and kindergarten classrooms

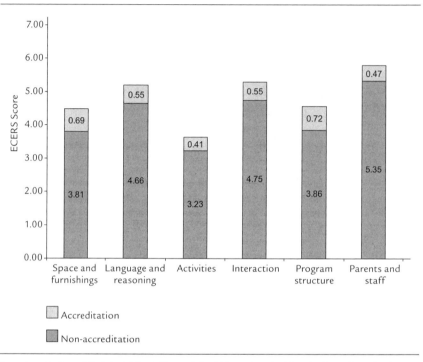

Source: Jason Sachs and Christina Weiland, "Boston's Rapid Expansion of Public School-Based Preschool: Promoting Quality, Lessons Learned," *Young Children* 65, no. 5 (2010): 74–77; internal analysis, 2008.

important for being good citizens and partners and for learning as much about the district as possible. Finally, a common issue in our work has been that funders are usually interested in either the research or the program, supporting one but skimping on the other. Research-practice partnership generally requires strong support for both. Managing this issue has meant cobbling together various sources of support as best we can.

Strategic Planning Matters

In September 2007, after three months working with the DEC, Weiland prepared a memo with a list of all data collected by the district relevant to the DEC, study designs that could be appropriate for answering different kinds of questions, and needs for external funding to collect other types of data. This early exercise—shared and discussed with the DEC and the BPS director of research—helped create a strategic plan for the kinds of questions our research-partnership would address and when. A key question, for example, was whether the program was ready for an impact study and what funding would be available to carry it out. We jointly determined that two years after the implementation of the district's curricula and every-other-week coaching was—in accordance with the literature—an optimal time to determine if the new model was working.

The subsequent study—funded by the Institute of Education Sciences and using a rigorous regression discontinuity design—showed that the model had the largest impacts of any large-scale public preK program evaluated to date.[13] As shown in figure A.3, these impacts covered both outcomes directly targeted by the program—language, literacy, math, and social-emotional skills—and a domain that was not directly targeted (executive function) but is developmentally linked to growth in the other domains.[14] It was critical that this evaluation was conducted when the program was ready and not before the new changes had time to take root.

A research strategic plan also helped us to be clear which data would be used for continuous quality improvement and how, as well as be clear how the research and data pieces fit together.

What You Don't Do Is As Important As What You Do

We actually collect *less* data than many programs do, particularly teacher-collected data. The DEC philosophy is that teachers should stay focused on teaching. The DEC has pushed back against state requirements for teachers to collect data via the formative assessment systems used in most preK contexts nationally. Sachs had Weiland review the literature on these systems; there is very little rigorous evidence that they provide reliable, valid data or that they change teachers' practice. What they *do* do is require teachers to collect lengthy data on every child in their classroom, several times a year, generally while paying a fee to the licensing company. We have relied instead on a sampling approach and have limited teacher-collected data to short direct assessments of child language and literacy on well-validated, reliable measures.[15] Of course,

FIGURE A.3 Boston prekindergarten impacts on children's school readiness

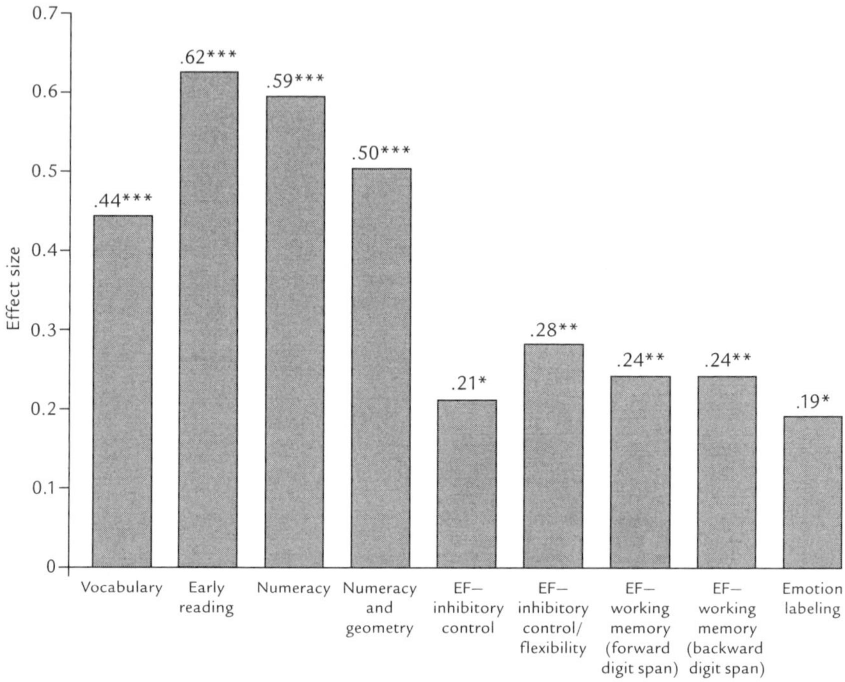

*p<0.05; **p<.01; ***p<.001

we encourage and support our teachers to collect data on student work and learning processes on an ongoing basis, and to use these authentic artifacts of learning to reflect on their practice (alone and with others) and shape their teaching strategies in real time.

Data Helps You Work Smarter

We opened this chapter with a discussion of the inauspicious beginning of data use in the DEC. The *Boston Globe*'s very public criticism caused the DEC to slow down the pace of its expansion and invest in quality. Thus in 2012, when the DEC was asked to expand its model to community-based preschools in Boston, it started small, in order to understand the challenges and opportunities of this new context. The pilot study included observational quality measures, surveys, and interviews of key stakeholders. After two and a half years, the results were disappointing. While quality initially increased after coaching and curricula were implemented in the first year and a half, these gains were not sustained through the full two and a half years. The CBOs' results remained lower quality than BPS classrooms, although some gains endured, particularly for classrooms that had scored low on the initial quality assessment.[16] The pilot study identified specific barriers that contributed to implementation failure, including lack of common planning time, teachers retaining old curricula, teacher and director turnover, too many three-year-olds in a program targeted to four-year-olds, insufficient instructional support for teachers from center leaders, and an extended but flexible childcare day with overlapping shifts that made it challenging to schedule the large blocks of common instruction and learning time that the BPS curricula demanded.

These barriers were addressed in subsequent work in the CBOs—data helped us get smarter. For example, the DEC capped the number of three-year-olds allowed in each classroom to approximately five out of twenty students, standardized the pay increases across CBOs so that participating CBO lead teachers received salaries equivalent to BPS preK teachers, and required common planning time. Also, the DEC modified CBO professional development to better incorporate CBO teachers into district trainings. Another research team (Abt Associates) is currently evaluating this new model and new expansion effort and sharing data back with the DEC. Findings from the first year of implementation were encouraging and research is ongoing.[17] The pilot project and its associated research components operated as intended in this respect—that is, as part of a continuous quality improvement system—despite somewhat disappointing overall quality changes in the CBOs in the pilot project. In our view, improving the preschool landscape nationally requires more such careful program piloting, with research that can pinpoint specific, addressable barriers to program quality improvement efforts.

Conclusion

Our research-practice partnership included both a strategically planned program of data collection, tracking of key metrics and benchmarks over time, research, and evaluation and real-time responses to funding opportunities and decision-making needs. It has been an ongoing learning experience for both of us. We have been confirmed in our beliefs and intuitions, and also surprised. Our work together has improved local practice, informed national academic and policy conversations, and highlighted new questions. It continues to evolve. The preK–2 curriculum reform work, for example, is currently being studied via large scale grants, in partnership with researchers at MDRC, Harvard University, and the University of Michigan (Weiland's current employer). We are committed to using data just as we ask our youngest students in BPS to do—to test our hypotheses, draw new insights, and get better.

Notes

Chapter 1

1. Massachusetts Department of Elementary and Secondary Education, School and District Profiles, 2017), http://profiles.doe.mass.edu/profiles/student.aspx?orgcode=00350000&orgtypecode=5&leftNavId=300.

2. Christina Weiland and Hirokazu Yoshikawa, "Impacts of a Prekindergarten Program on Children's Mathematics, Language, Literacy, Executive Function, and Emotional Skills." *Child Development* 84, no. 6 (2013): 2112–2130.

3. In this book, the term *twenty-first-century skills* refers to critical thinking and problem solving, collaboration, creativity, and communication. With respect to literacy and mathematics, they include the capacities to integrate information from multiple sources and perspectives, solve novel problems, and communicate effectively with diverse audiences orally and in writing.

4. See Mara Krechevsky et al., *Visible Learners: Promoting Reggio-Inspired Approaches in All Schools* (New York: John Wiley & Sons, 2013).

5. Carol Garhart Mooney, *Theories of Childhood: An Introduction to Dewey, Montessori, Erikson, Piaget, and Vygotsky* (St. Paul MN: Redleaf Press, 2013).

6. Lella Gandini, "History, Ideas, and Basic Principles: An Interview with Loris Malaguzzi," in *The Hundred Languages of Children: The Reggio Emilia Experience in Transformation* 3rd edition, eds. Carolyn Edwards, Lella Gandini, and George Forman (Santa Barbara, CA: ABC-CLIO, 2012), 27–71.

7. Mary Ann Biermeier, "A Tale of Two Kindergarten Programs: Language and Literacy Assessment in the Era of Common Core Standards," (paper presented at the INSPIRE Early Childhood Leadership Series, Phoenix, Arizona, May, 2015), https://www.researchgate.net/publication/276205942_A_Tale_of_Two_Kindergarten_Programs_Language_Literacy_Assessment_in_the_Era_of_Common_Core_Standards.

8. This view of young children is reflected, for example, in the work of developmental theorists Jean Piaget, Lev Vygotsky, and T. Berry Brazelton; early educators Loris Malaguzzi, Maria Montessori, John Dewey, Susan Neuman, and Kathleen Roskos; researchers Kathy Hirsh-Pasek and Allison Gopnik; and the title and contents of the National Research Council's *Eager to Learn: Educating Our Preschoolers* (National Academies Press, 2001).

9. See *The Hundred Languages of Children: The Reggio Emilia Experience in Transformation*, 2nd edition, eds. Carolyn Edwards, Lella Gandini, and George Forman (Greenwich, CT.: Ablex Pub. Corp., 1998), 202.

10. Harry Hendrick, *Children, Childhood and English Society, 1880–1990*, vol. 32 (Cambridge: Cambridge University Press, 1997).

11. Sheryl Gilman, "Including the Child with Special Needs: Learning from Reggio Emilia." *Theory into Practice* 46, no. 1 (2007): 23–31.

12. Patricia Cantor, "Elizabeth Peabody: America's Kindergarten Pioneer," *Young Children*, May 2013, 92–93.

13. National Center for Educational Statistics. *The Nation's Report Card*, https://www.nationsreportcard.gov/profiles/stateprofile?chort=3&sub=MAT&sj=AL&sfj=NP&st=MN&year=2009R3.

14. William T. Gormley and Ted Gayer, "Promoting School Readiness in Oklahoma: An Evaluation of Tulsa's Pre-K Program," *Journal of Human Resources* 40, no. 3 (2005): 533–558.

15. Geoff Marietta, "Lessons in Early Learning: Building an Integrated Pre-K–12 System in Montgomery County Public Schools," Education Reform Series, Pew Center on the States (2010), http://www.pewtrusts.org/~/media/legacy/uploadedfiles/pcs_assets/2010/mcpsreportpdf.pdf.

16. W. Steven Barnett et al., Abbott Preschool Program Longitudinal Effects Study: Fifth Grade Follow-Up (New Brunswick, NJ: National Institute for Early Education Research, 2013), http://nieer.org/publications/latest-research/abbott-preschool-program-longitudinal-effects-study-fifth-grade-follow.

17. The Perry Preschool Project has served as an inspiration, model, and advocacy tool for both Head Start and preK. Begun in 1962, the forty-year study followed 123 children who had been born into poverty. About half of the children had been randomly assigned to participate in a high-quality early learning program as three- and four-year olds. The highly educated and well-supported teachers used HighScope's participatory learning curricular approach. They also engaged with parents, who they viewed as essential partners in their children's learning, At age forty, program participants showed higher education levels, employment rates, and earnings and lower likelihood of having committed a crime than their counterparts in the comparison group (Lawrence J. Schweinhart, *Lifetime Effects: the HighScope Perry Preschool Study through Age 40*, no. 14 (Ypsilanti, MI: HighScope Foundation, 2005.

18. Zongping Xiang and Lawrence J. Schweinhart, "Effects Five Years Later: The Michigan School Readiness Program Evaluation through Age 10." (paper prepared for the Michigan State Board of Education, High/Scope Educational Research Foundation, Ypsilanti, Michigan, January 2002), https://www.brookings.edu/blog/brown-center-chalkboard/2017/01/25/high-quality-statewide-preschool-is-possible-just-look-to-michigan/.

19. Mike Puma et al., "Third Grade Follow-Up to the Head Start Impact Study: Final Report," OPRE Report 2012-45 (Washington, DC: Office of the Administration for Children and Families, 2012), https://www.acf.hhs.gov/sites/default/files/opre/head_start_report.pdf.

20. Noreen Yazejian et al., "Child and Parenting Outcomes After 1 Year of Educare," *Child Development*, 88 (2017): 1671–1688, doi:10.1111/cdev.12688.

21. Between November 2013 and November 2017, the DEC hosted visiting teams from more than fifty organizations, including school districts, departments of education, and preK and preK–3 initiative teams from fifteen states, Washington, DC, and seven foreign countries. Boston Public Schools Department of Early Childhood, "Site Visit Tracker and Collab Log," internal document, 2017.

22. Lillian Mongeau, "What Boston's Preschools Get Right," *The Atlantic,* August 2, 2016, https://www.theatlantic.com/education/archive/2016/08/what-bostons-preschools-get -right/493952/.

Chapter 2
We ask our readers to list Melissa Rivard and Jodi Doyle Krous as first authors when citing material from this chapter.

1. Melissa Rivard, a specialist in pedagogical documentation with the Making Learning Visible Project at Project Zero (http://www.pz.harvard.edu), worked with Jodi Doyle as part of a Commendation Grant that the DEC received to highlight the work of exemplary teachers. As part of this grant, Melissa visited Doyle's classroom weekly for several months to support Doyle in collecting and using Reggio-inspired documentation, including video, photographs, notes, and children's work. These artifacts were collected during the learning process to support formative assessment, deepen learning for those directly involved in the experience, and make learning visible to others to build collective knowledge about quality teaching and learning. Throughout the project, Rivard, Doyle, and other colleagues reviewed documentation together to determine next steps. A video based on this work is available on the DEC website, and has been used in professional development workshops. See https://sites.google.com/bostonpublicschools.org/early childhood/proven-practices-beyond-pd/making-learning-visible. For a related Teachers' Guide, see https://drive.google.com/file/d/0B3qKorUGb2mHaXdUVUp5dlpsT3M /view.

2. All BPS K0 and K1 classrooms have a full-time paraprofessional. They play various roles, including working with one group while the teacher works with another on a similar activity, working one-to-one with a child who needs extra support during a whole class activity, and working with a small group on one activity or lesson while other children work independently or with the teacher in other centers. Sometimes, as we see in this example, the majority of the children work independently or with the paraprofessional, enabling the teacher to work intensively with an individual or small group.

3. Judy Schickedanz and David Dickinson, *Opening the World of Learning: A Comprehensive Literacy Program* (New York: Pearson Early Learning, 2006).

4. Clearly, both Jodi Doyle and the developers of the curriculum she is using see the children as curious, active, capable learners and seek to engage and support all areas of their development, in accordance with core principles 2 (Young children are curious, active learners who are capable of high level thinking processes, empathy, and taking multiple perspectives) and 4 (Early learning programs must support children's physical, intellectual, language, and social-emotional development, along with their curiosity, creativity, persistence at challenging tasks, and academic learning), as you'll see throughout this chapter.

5. Margie Carter et al., "Becoming a Reflective Teacher." *Teaching Young Children* 3, no. 4 (2010): 1–4.

6. In accordance with core principle 9 (Varied assessments provide data to inform instruction and drive change. Teachers and families participate along with administrators and specialists in interpreting findings, evaluating their implications, and shaping resultant decisions).
7. Core principle 2.
8. Core principles 2, 4, and 6 (Basic literacies, knowledge, and higher-level skills can be furthered through pretend play, projects, extended conversation, and thoughtful instruction).
9. Core principle 3 (Strong relationships are at the center of powerful learning experiences).
10. Core principle 7 (Because young children learn and develop at different rates and exhibit a wide range of interests, strengths, and learning styles, teachers need the time, flexibility, information, and resources to tailor learning experiences and engage all children, including dual language learners and children with special needs, as full participants in the classroom community).
11. Core principles 5 (Flexible, hands-on curricula that align with prior and future experiences foster mastery of learning standards and achievement of twenty-first-century goals) and 7.
12. Core principle 8 (The adult and child learning environment are connected and mirror one another through respectful processes of inquiry and differentiation).
13. Core principle 7.
14. Core principle 3.
15. Seeing children's developmental progressions, and having a sense of what's coming next, helps Doyle align her instruction with prior and future experiences foster mastery of learning standards and achievement of twenty-first-century goals, as she uses a flexible, hands-on curriculum (core principle 6).
16. Core principles 2, 4, 5, and 6.
17. Core principle 1 (Schools must promote our democratic society and support children's and teachers' sense of citizenship though multiple connections to families and community).
18. Core principle 6.

Chapter 3

1. Laurie Bozzi et al., *Boston Public Schools 2015 Needs Assessment. A Report Prepared for Jason Sachs, Boston Public Schools* (Cambridge, MA: Abt Associates with Wellesley Centers for Women, Wellesley College, 2015); measures used included the CLASS (Robert Pianta et. al., *Classroom Assessment Scoring System Manual, Pre-K* Baltimore: Paul H. Brookes Publishing Co, 2008); ELLCO (Mariam Smith and Joanne Brady, *The Early Language & Literacy Classroom Observation, Research Edition, Pre-K* (Baltimore: Paul H. Brookes Publishing Co., 2008); and COEMET (Julie Sarama and Doug Clements, *Classroom Observation of Early Mathematics: Environment and Teaching,* version 4 (Buffalo, NY: University at Buffalo SUNY, 2010); see https://www.du.edu/marsicoinstitute/whatwedo/pd.html for training on using this instrument.
2. Throughout this book, we will cite both data and peer-reviewed research on quality and child outcomes in BPS early childhood classrooms over time. Chapter 10 describes the research and evaluation program.

3. The DEC works hard to hire expert practitioners from varied sectors of the early childhood field. Interviews are rigorous; candidates are asked not only about their experiences with low-income children and their families, dual language learners and children with special needs, and teaching early literacy and interdisciplinary curricula, but also what approaches they have tried, how they make connections across content areas, how they interpret and apply "developmentally appropriate practice," and what they believe is most important. Questions about experiences with teaching and coaching adults include: *What ideas do you have about most effective ways to pass on professional knowledge? How do you advise a teacher who recognizes the interest of an individual child or group of children that strays from the path of the established curriculum? What is your approach to moving a teacher's practice? What do you do when your perspective differs from the perspectives of others?*

4. Boston Public Schools at a Glance, 2016–2017, BPS Communications Office. https://www.bostonpublicschools.org/cms/lib/MA01906464/Centricity/Domain/238/BPS%20at%20a%20Glance%202016-17_online.pdf.

5. Countdown to Kindergarten was founded in 1999. For information about the program and its development, see chapter 6 and http://www.countdowntokindergarten.org.

6. See three comprehensive compilations of the science of early learning and its implications for practice and policy published by the National Academy of Sciences: *Preventing Reading Difficulties in Young Children* (Catherine E. Snow, M. Susan Burns, and Peg Griffin, eds. [Washington, DC: National Academies Press, 1998]); *From Neurons to Neighborhoods: The Science of Early Childhood Development* (Deborah A. Phillips and Jack P. Shonkoff, eds. [Washington, DC: National Academies Press, 2000]); and *Eager to Learn: Educating Our Preschoolers* (Barbara T. Bowman, W. Suzanne Donovan, and M. Susan Burns, eds, [Washington, DC: National Academies Press, 2001]). Collectively, they highlight the importance of positive early relationships; rich language environments and responsive, cognitively challenging conversations; high-quality early learning programs that address all developmental domains in an integrated way; and an integrated approach to teaching reading that focuses on oral language, background knowledge, and interactive read-aloud experiences as well as code-focused skills.

7. Early Learning Services unit in the Massachusetts Department of Education, "Community Partnerships for Children: Building a System of Early Childhood Education in Massachusetts," Massachusetts Department of Early Education and Care, 2005, http://www.eec.state.ma.us/docs/tacpcfactsheet.pdf.

8. Barr Foundation, "About Us," https://www.barrfoundation.org/about.

9. "Boston Public Schools at a Glance, 2010–2011," BPS Communications Office, http://bpsom-presentation.wikispaces.com/file/view/bps_at_a_glance_11-0428_4.pdf.

10. Research and Massachusetts experience had demonstrated a link between seeking and achieving NAEYC accreditation and sustained improvement in observed program quality. See Marcy Whitebook, Laura M. Sakai, and Carollee Howes. "Improving and Sustaining Center Quality: The Role of NAEYC Accreditation and Staff Stability," *Early Education and Development* 15, no. 3 (2004): 305–326.

11. Assessments included the Early Childhood Environment Rating Scale- Revised (ECERS-R); the Classroom Assessment Scoring System (CLASS); and the unpublished but widely used SELA (Sheila Smith, Sherry Davidson, and Georgeanne Weisenfeld, *Supports for Early Literacy Assessment* [New York: New York University School of Education, 2001]).

12. Nancy L. Marshall, Joanne Roberts, and Linda Mills, *Boston Public Schools K1 and K2 Needs Assessment* (Wellesley, MA: Wellesley Centers for Women, 2007).

13. Tracy Jan, "Boston Preschools Falling Far Short of Goals, Study Says," *Boston Globe*, April 7, 2007.

14. Marshall, Roberts, and Mills, *Boston Public Schools K1 and K2 Needs Assessment.*

15. Note how the DEC's commitment to democratic processes (core principle 1) applies to adults as well as children (core principle 8), and how they intentionally seek multiple perspectives as they employ varied assessments and engage with teachers in forthright, democratic discussions of their interpretation and implications (core principle 9.)

16. As children listen to storybooks and pursue activities in learning centers, OWL curriculum coaches encourage teachers to ask open-ended questions that prompt children to hypothesize, reason, make inferences and connections, rethink ideas in light of new evidence, empathize with characters, consider new perspectives, and ask new questions, in accordance with core principle 2 (Young children are curious, active learners who are capable of high-level thinking processes, empathy, and taking multiple perspectives).

17. In line with core principle 4, systematic daily attention to all learning domains (physical, intellectual, language, and social-emotional development, along with curiosity, creativity, persistence at challenging tasks, and academic learning) is built into the OWL.

18. Snow, Burns, and Griffin, *Preventing Reading Difficulties*; Susan B. Neuman, "Lessons from My Mother: Reflections on the National Early Literacy Panel Report," *Educational Researcher* 39, no. 4 (2010): 301–304.

19. Catherine E. Snow et al., *Is Literacy Enough? Pathways to Academic Success for Adolescents* (Baltimore, MD: Paul H. Brookes Publishing, 2007).

20. Note how OWL aligns with core principle 6 (Basic literacies, knowledge, and higher-level skills can be furthered through pretend play, projects, extended conversation, and thoughtful instruction).

21. Deborah J., Leong and Elena Bodrova, "Assessing and Scaffolding: Make-Believe Play," *Young Children* 67, no. 1 (2012): 28.

22. Elena Bodrova and Deborah Leong, *Tools of the Mind: The Vygotskian Approach to Early Childhood Education*, 2nd edition (New York: Pearson, 2006). See also Kathleen Roskos, and James Christie, "The Play-Literacy Nexus and the Importance of Evidence-Based Techniques in the Classroom," *American Journal of Play* 4, no. 2 (2011): 204–224.

23. Neuman, "Lessons from My Mother," 301–304.

24. W. Steven Barnett et al., "Educational Effects of the Tools of the Mind Curriculum: A Randomized Trial," *Early Childhood Research Quarterly* 23, no. 3 (2008): 299–313.

25. David K. Dickinson and Kimberley. E. Sprague, "The Nature and Impact of Early Childhood Care Environments on the Language and Early Literacy Development of Children from Low-Income Families," in *Handbook of Early Literacy Research*, ed. Susan B. Neuman and David K. Dickinson (New York: Guilford Press, 2001), 283–280.

26. Julie Sarama and Douglas H. Clements, "Building Blocks for Early Childhood Mathematics," *Early Childhood Research Quarterly* 19, no. 1 (2004): 181–189.

27. Especially core principles 2, 5 (Flexible, hands-on curricula that align with prior and future experiences foster mastery of learning standards and achievement of twenty-first-century goals), and 9.

28. TERC, *Investigations in Number, Data, and Space* (New York: Pearson, 2008), https://investigations.terc.edu/.

29. Jason Sachs, unpublished report to the Barr Foundation, October 2007.
30. Douglas M. Dunn and Lloyd M. Dunn, *Peabody Picture Vocabulary Test: Manual* (New York: Pearson, 2007).
31. Note how Boni describes *Building Blocks* as a flexible, hands-on curriculum that is consonant with core principle 2. *Building Blocks* is also an exemplar of core principle 5, as it is built on an understanding of children's developmental trajectories in mathematical understanding. See Douglas H. Clements and Julie Sarama, "Learning Trajectories in Mathematics Education," *Mathematical Thinking and Learning* 6 (2004): 81–89.
32. Core principle 9.
33. Core principle 7.
34. Nancy L. Marshall and Joanne Roberts, *Boston Public Schools Early Childhood Quality Study*, internal report to the Boston Public Schools (Wellesley, MA: Wellesley Centers on Women, 2008).

Chapter 4

1. Douglas H. Clements and Julie Sarama, "Experimental Evaluation of the Effects of a Research-Based Preschool Mathematics Curriculum," *American Educational Research Journal* 45, no. 2 (2008): 443–494; Christina Weiland and Hirokazu Yoshikawa, "Impacts of a Prekindergarten Program on Children's Mathematics, Language, Literacy, Executive Function, and Emotional Skills," *Child Development* 84, no. 6 (2013): 2112–2130.
2. Weiland and Yoshikawa, "Impacts of a Prekindergarten Program," 2112–2130.
3. Core principle 2 (Young children are curious, active learners who are capable of high level thinking processes, empathy, and taking multiple perspectives).
4. See Justin Markussen-Brown et al., "The Effects of Language- and Literacy-Focused Professional Development on Early Educators and Children: A Best-Evidence Meta-Analysis," *Early Childhood Research Quarterly* 38 (2017): 97–115.
5. Nancy Marshall and JoAnne Roberts, *Boston Public Schools Early Childhood Quality Study 2010*, internal report to the Department of Early Childhood, Boston Public Schools (Wellesley, MA: Wellesley Centers for Women, Wellesley College., 2010).
6. Core principle 9 (Varied assessments provide data to inform instruction and drive change. Teachers and families participate along with administrators and specialists in interpreting findings, evaluating their implications, and shaping resultant decisions).
7. Begun in 2010, the BPS Circle of Promise initiative focused on turnaround schools and their surrounding neighborhoods. It sought to collaborate with early education providers, health centers, businesses, faith-based groups, families, and residents to strengthen children's early and ongoing learning opportunities.
8. Charlotte B. Kahn, Tim H. Davis, and Jessica K. Martin, *Boston's Education Pipeline: A Report Card* (Boston: The Boston Foundation, 2008), http://www.tbf.org/~/media/TBFOrg/Files/Reports/EdReportCard_Final5.pdf.
9. See Davida McDonald, *Elevating the Field* (Washington, DC: NAEYC, 2009) for a summary of contemporary studies linking NAEYC Accreditation to improved program and classroom quality and better child outcomes. For a more recent study, see Laura H. Dinehart et al., "Associations Between Center-Based Care Accreditation Status and the Early Educational Outcomes of Children in the Child Welfare System," *Children and Youth Services Review* 34, no. 5 (2012): 1072–1080.

10. CAYL stands for Community Advocates for Young Learners. The CAYL Institute equips early education professionals to be architects of change and brings leaders together to advocate for systemic and policy improvements. Its fellowships for principals would be offered through school districts in Massachusetts and beyond following their Boston pilot.

11. Core principle 3 (Strong relationships are at the center of powerful learning experiences).

12. Notice how coaching for accreditation, curriculum, and curriculum coaching come together to strengthen implementation of core principle 6 (Basic literacies, knowledge, and higher level skills can be furthered through pretend play, projects, extended conversation, and thoughtful instruction).

13. *NAEYC Early Learning Program Standards and Accreditation Standards and Assessment Items*, Standard 3 G (Washington, DC: National Association for the Education of Young Children, https://www.naeyc.org/sites/default/files/globally-shared/downloads/PDFs /accreditation/early-learning/naeyc_early_learning_program_accreditation_standards _and_assessment_items.pdf.

14. Core principles 3, 2, 9, and 7 (Because young children learn and develop at different rates and exhibit a wide range of interests, strengths, and learning styles, teachers need the time, flexibility, information, and resources to tailor learning experiences and engage all children, including dual language learners and children with special needs, as full participants in the classroom community).

15. Marshall and Roberts, "BPS Early Childhood Quality Study 2010."

16. Jason Sachs and Christina Weiland, "Boston's Rapid Expansion of Public School–Based Preschool: Promoting Quality, Lessons Learned," *Young Children* 65, no. 5 (2010): 74–76.

17. Sachs and Weiland, "Boston's Rapid Expansion."

18. Miriam W. Smith and David K. Dickinson, "Describing Oral Language Opportunities and Environments in Head Start and Other Preschool Classrooms," *Early Childhood Research Quarterly* 9, no. 3–4 (1994): 345–366.

19. Gary T. Henry and Dana K. Rickman, "Do Peers Influence Children's Skill Development in Preschool?" *Economics of Education Review* 26, no. 1 (2007): 100–12; Caroline Hoxby, "Peer Effects in the Classroom: Learning from Gender and Race Variation," NBER Working Paper 7867 (Washington, DC: National Bureau of Economic Research, 2000).

20. Jeanne E. Montie, Zongping Xiang, and Lawrence J. Schweinhart, "Preschool Experience in 10 Countries: Cognitive and Language Performance at Age 7," *Early Childhood Research Quarterly* 21, no. 3 (2006): 313–331.

21. Catherine E. Snow et al., *Is Literacy Enough? Pathways to Academic Success for Adolescents* (Baltimore: Paul H. Brookes Publishing, 2007).

22. Notice how core principle 9 (using varied assessments to inform instruction and drive change) integrates with core principle 7 (assuring that teachers have the time, flexibility, information, and resources to tailor learning experiences and engage all children).

23. Elena Bodrova and Deborah Leong, *Tools of the Mind: The Vygotskian Approach to Early Childhood Education*, 2nd edition (New York: Pearson, 2006); W. Steven Barnett et al., "Educational Effects of the Tools of the Mind Curriculum: A Randomized Trial," *Early Childhood Research Quarterly* 23, 3 (2008): 299–313.

24. *Reading Street* (New York: Pearson, 2011).

25. http://www.pearsonschool.com/index.cfm?locator=PS1dH9.
26. As BPS longitudinal data would show, students who had attended K1 in 2007–2008 would outperform peers on the Massachusetts English Language Arts and Mathematics tests (MCAS) given in the third and fifth grades.

Chapter 5
We ask our readers to list David Ramsey and Abby Morales as first authors when citing material from this chapter.
1. Kathy Tucker and Grace Lin (illus.), *The Seven Chinese Sisters* (Park Ridge, IL; Albert Whitman & Company, 2003).
2. Core principle 3 (Strong relationships are at the center of powerful learning experiences).
3. In her longitudinal studies of Chicago children who faced extreme adversities, Delores Norton found that predictable routines, frequent talk about the past, talk about what would or might happen, and taking time to explain with young children promoted their ongoing resilience. See Delores Norton, "Early Linguistic Interaction and School Achievement: An Ethnographical, Ecological Perspective" *Zero to Three* 16 (1996): 8–14.
4. Core principles 6 (Basic literacies, knowledge, and higher-level skills can be furthered through pretend play, projects, extended conversation, and thoughtful instruction) and 4 (Early learning programs must support children's physical, intellectual, language, and social-emotional development, along with their curiosity, creativity, persistence at challenging tasks, and academic learning).
5. According to Doug Clements and Julie Sarama's map of mathematics learning trajectories, this skill is typically mastered at age six or seven; see http://ncscdfoundationsof mathematics.ncdpi.wikispaces.net/file/view/Building+Block+Learning+Trajectories.pdf. The concept in the book is particularly challenging: the children have to understand both that the total number of trees remains the same whether you count by ones or twos and that counting by twos is twice as fast. Many four-year-olds can recite the pattern: two, four, six, eight, but are just beginning to grasp the concept of "counting by," the basis of multiplication.
6. Amy L. Dombro, Judy Jablon, and Charlotte Stetson, *Powerful Interactions: How to Connect with Children to Extend Their Learning* (Portland, ME: Stenhouse Publishers, 2011).
7. Core principle 6.
8. Core principles 3 (Strong relationships are at the center of powerful learning experiences), 5 (Flexible, hands-on curricula that align with prior and future experiences foster mastery of learning standards and achievement of twenty-first-century goals), and 7 (Because young children learn and develop at different rates and exhibit a wide range of interests, strengths, and learning styles, teachers need the time, flexibility, information, and resources to tailor learning experiences and engage all children, including dual language learners and children with special needs, as full participants in the classroom community).

Chapter 6
1. Jason Sachs and Christina Weiland, "Boston's Rapid Expansion of Public School–Based Preschool: Promoting Quality, Lessons Learned," *Young Children* 65, no. 5 (2010): 74–76.
2. William T. Gormley and Ted Gayer, "Promoting School Readiness in Oklahoma: An Evaluation of Tulsa's Pre-K Program," *Journal of Human Resources* 40, no. 3 (2005):

533–558; Gary T. Henry, and Dana K. Rickman, "Do Peers Influence Children's Skill Development in Preschool?" *Economics of Education Review* 26, no. 1 (2007): 100–112.

3. Countdown to Kindergarten Boston, "Talk, Read, Play," http://www.countdownto kindergarten.org/talk-read-play.

4. Martin J. Walsh and Michael Durbin, "Every Child Given Every Opportunity to Thrive: Advancing Early Childhood and School Readiness in Boston" (introductory letter to Thrive in Five impact report), http://thrivein5boston.org/wp-content/uploads/2016/08 /T5_Impact-Report_082516.pdf.

5. Jane Squires, Diane Bricker, and Elizabeth Twombly, *Ages and Stages Questionnaires* (Baltimore, MD: Paul H. Brookes Publishing, 2009).

6. In 2013, Smart from the Start reported ASQ data on all of their entering kindergarteners. All children met the school readiness benchmarks for gross motor development and for problem solving, 98 percent met those for communication and personal/social development, and more than 88 percent met the social-emotional benchmarks on the ASQ-SE. The one area of apparent weakness was fine motor development, where only 82 percent of the children met the kindergarten readiness benchmark ("Smart from The Start Outcomes," http://smartfromthestartinc.org/programs/outcomes/).

7. Brian Gold, internal analysis of Boston Public Schools data, cited in Jason Sachs, "New P-2 Early Childhood Strategic Plan and Update on Boston Universal Preschool" (presentation to the BPS School Committee, Boston, MA, April 26, 2017), https://www.bostonpublic schools.org/cms/lib/MA01906464/Centricity/Domain/162/Early%20Childhood%20 Strategic%20Plan%2020172022School%20Committee%20presentation.pdf.

8. Massachusetts Department of Elementary and Secondary Education, *Massachusetts Curriculum Framework for English Language Arts and Literacy Grades Pre-Kindergarten to 12* (2011) 7. This framework was changed in 2017, but the 2011 version is currently available at http://www.hanoverschools.org/curriculum/pdf/dese/2011%20Massachusetts %20Curriculum%20Framework%20for%20ELA.pdf.

9. Rima Shore, "The Case for Investing in Pre-K to 3rd Education: Challenging Myths About School Reform," *PreK to 3rd Policy to Action Brief*, no. 1 (New York: Foundation for Child Development, 2009), 6, https://www.fcd-us.org/assets/2016/04/TheCaseFor Investing-ChallengingMyths.pdf.

10. Massachusetts Department of Elementary and Secondary Education, "Improving the Early Years of Education in Massachusetts: The P-3 Curriculum, Instruction, and Assessment Project," 2011, http://www.doe.mass.edu/kindergarten/PK-3report.txt.

11. Megina Baker, Beth Benoit, Ben Mardell, and the Boston Public Schools Department of Early Childhood, *Focus on K2: An Integrated Approach to Teaching and Learning* (Boston: Boston Public Schools, 2014).

12. Marcia T. Edson, *Starting with Science: Strategies for Introducing Young Children to Inquiry* (Portland, ME: Stenhouse Publishers, 2003.)

13. Core principles 2 (Young children are curious, active learners who are capable of high level thinking processes, empathy, and taking multiple perspectives), 4 (Early learning programs must support children's physical, intellectual, language, and social-emotional development, along with their curiosity, creativity, persistence at challenging tasks, and academic learning), and 6 (Basic literacies, knowledge, and higher level skills can be furthered through pretend play, projects, extended conversation, and thoughtful instruction).

14. These materials are available to all on the DEC's website, https://www.bostonpublic schools.org/earlychildhood

15. *Focus on K2*, Unit 1: Our Community, https://drive.google.com/drive/folders/0B2b6s1X MQiU7T2pNSlpOcUMzS1U.

16. Ed Young, *Lon Po Po: A Red-Riding Hood Story from China* (New York: Philomel Books, 1989).

17. *Focus on K2*, Unit 2: Animals and Habitats, https://drive.google.com/drive/folders/0B2b 6s1XMQiU7dDhkcWk5T1pibzg.

18. *Focus on K2*, Unit 3: Construction, https://drive.google.com/drive/folders/0B3qKorUGb 2mHeG5vYW5ZZUk0cUk

19. *Focus on K2*, Unit 4: Our Earth, https://drive.google.com/drive/folders/0B3qKorUGb2 mHaXhvNFg0YlRwc00.

20. "Implementing the Common Core State Standards," Common Core State Standards Initiative, (2013), http://www.corestandards.org/.

21. Adele Diamond and Kathleen Lee, "Interventions Shown to Aid Executive Function Development in Children 4 to 12 Years Old," *Science* 333 (2011) 959–964.

22. For examples and summaries of research on the benefits of reading aloud with children, see Isabel L. Beck and Margaret G. McKeown, "Text Talk: Capturing the Benefits of Read-Aloud Experiences for Young Children," *The Reading Teacher* 55, no, 1 (2001): 10–20; Jim Trelease, *The Read-Aloud Handbook*, 7th edition (New York: Penguin Books, 2013); and Nonie K. Lesaux, *Turning the Page: Refocusing Massachusetts for Reading Success* (Boston: Strategies for Children, Inc., 2010).

23. Mariela M. Páez, Kristen Paratore Bock, and Lianna Pizzo, "Supporting the Language and Early Literacy Skills of English Language Learners: Effective Practices and Future Directions," *Handbook of Early Literacy Research* 3 (2011): 136–152; Ellen Oliver Keene and Susan Zimmermann, *Mosaic of Thought: The Power of Comprehension Strategy Instruction*, 2nd edition (Portsmouth, NH: Heinemann, 2007).

24. Core principle 7 (Because young children learn and develop at different rates and exhibit a wide range of interests, strengths, and learning styles, teachers need the time, flexibility, information, and resources to tailor learning experiences and engage all children, including DLL's and children with special needs, as full participants in the classroom community).

25. This component was originally called "Literacy Circles." Like Working on Words, Literacy Circles incorporated a balanced approach to literacy and engaged children in a variety of reading, writing, listening, and talking activities. All of these were connected to the unit themes and Read Aloud texts. The Working on Words variation was developed in 2016 in order to include more explicit whole group instruction and to accommodate school and district skill-building initiatives.

26. Core principle 7.

27. Gail E. Tompkins, *Sharing the Pen: Interactive Writing with Young Children* (Upper Saddle River, NJ: Pearson, 2003).

28. Barbara A. Wilson, *Fundations: Wilson Language Basics* (Oxford, MA: Wilson Language Training, 2012), http://www.wilsonlanguage.com/programs/fundations/.

29. TERC, *Investigations in Number, Data, and Space* (New York: Pearson), https://investigations.terc.edu/.

30. This practice was pioneered and honed by Vivian Paley; see Vivian Paley, *The Boy Who Would Be a Helicopter: The Uses of Storytelling in the Classroom* (Cambridge MA: Harvard

University Press, 1990). See also Angeliki Nicolopoulou et al., "Using a Narrative- and Play-Based Activity to Promote Low-Income Preschoolers' Oral Language, Emergent Literacy, and Social Competence," *Early Childhood Research Quarterly* 31(2015): 147–162.

31. Ben Mardell, "Boston Listens: Vivian Paley's Storytelling/Story Acting in an Urban School District," *New England Reading Association Journal* 49, no. 1 (2013): 58.

32. "Storytelling and Story Acting," Boston Public Schools Department of Early Childhood, https://sites.google.com/bostonpublicschools.org/earlychildhood/storytelling-story -acting.

33. Lynne Cherry, *The Great Kapok Tree: A Tale of the Amazon Rain Forest* (Boston: HMH Books for Young Readers, 2000).

34. Baker et al., *Focus on K2.*

Chapter 7

1. Laura M. Justice et al., "Accelerating Preschoolers' Early Literacy Development Through Classroom-Based Teacher–Child Storybook Reading and Explicit Print Referencing." *Language, Speech, and Hearing Services in Schools* 40, no. 1 (2009): 67–85.

2. Patricia M. Cooper, *The Classrooms All Young Children Need: Lessons in Teaching from Vivian Paley* (Chicago: University of Chicago Press, 2009).

3. Principle 6 (Basic literacies, knowledge, and higher-level skills can be furthered through pretend play, projects, extended conversation, and thoughtful instruction).

4. Principle 3 (Strong relationships are at the center of powerful learning experiences).

5. Principle 1 (Schools must promote our democratic society and support children's and teachers' sense of citizenship though multiple connections to families and community).

6. Marcia Talhelm Edson, *Starting with Science: Strategies for Introducing Young Children to Inquiry* (Portland, ME: Stenhouse Publishers, 2013); *NGSS Lead States 2013, Next Generation Science Standards: For States, by States* (Washington, DC: The National Academies Press, 2013).

7. Dr. Seuss, *The Lorax* (New York: Random House Books for Young Readers, 1971).

8. For insight into the social worlds of kindergarteners, see Vivian G. Paley, *You Can't Say You Can't Play* (Cambridge, MA: Harvard University Press, 1996), and Marilyn Segal and Betty Bardige, *Your Child at Play: Five to Eight Years: Guiding Friendships, Expanding Interests, and Resolving Conflicts* (New York: William Morrow, 2000.)

9. Core principle 4 (Early learning programs must support children's physical, intellectual, language, and social-emotional development, along with their curiosity, creativity, persistence at challenging tasks, and academic learning).

10. See *Preventing Reading Difficulties in Young Children* and its companion volume, *Learning to Read and Write*, ed. Catherine Snow, M. Sidan Burns, and Peg Griffin (Washington, DC: National Academies Press, 1998). A 2008 intervention study found that "invented spelling coupled with feedback encourages an analytical approach and facilitates the integration of phonological and orthographic knowledge, hence facilitating the acquisition of reading" (Gene Ouellette and Monique Sénéchal, "Pathways to Literacy: A Study of Invented Spelling and Its Role in Learning to Read," *Child Development* 79, no. 4 [2008]: 899–913.)

11. Lynne Cherry, *The Great Kapok Tree: A Tale of the Amazon Rainforest* (Boston: HMH Books for Young Readers, 2000).

12. Core principle 9 (Varied assessments provide data to inform instruction).

13. Common Core State Standards Initiative (2013), "Implementing the Common Core State Standards," https://www.achieve.org/files/RevisedElementaryActionBrief_Final_Feb.pdf.

14. *Making Learning Visible: Children as Individual and Group Learners*, Project Zero and Reggio Children. (Reggio Emilia, Italy: Reggio Children, 2001); also see "Austin's Butterfly Drafts," *Models of Excellence*, 2015, http://modelsofexcellence.eleducation.org/projects/austins-butterfly-drafts. Note that children are being engaged as curious, active learners as they use and develop twenty-first-century skills of communication, collaboration, critical thinking, and creativity, in accordance with core principles 2 and 5.

15. Core principle 1.

16. Patton O. Tabors, *One Child, Two Languages: A Guide for Early Childhood Educators of Children Learning English as a Second Language*, 2nd edition (Baltimore, MD: Paul H. Brookes, 2008), 124.

17. Coe principle 7 (Because young children learn and develop at different rates and exhibit a wide range of interests, strengths, and learning styles, teachers need the time, flexibility, information, and resources to tailor learning experiences and engage all children, including dual language learners and children with special needs, as full participants in the classroom community).

18. Gail Gibbons, *From Seed to Plant* (New York: Holiday House Books, 1991); Alvin Tresselt and Henri Sorensen (illus.), *The Gift of the Tree* (New York: Harper Collins, 1992).

Chapter 8

This chapter is based on and quotes extensively from Melissa Tonachel's unpublished white paper, "The Boston Public Schools Early Childhood Professional Development Model." Tonachel has granted us permission to use this material, and we ask our readers to cite this white paper when quoting from this chapter.

1. Note here and throughout how the PD program that Tonachel describes centers around two DEC core principles: 3 (Strong relationships are at the center of powerful learning experiences) and 8 (The adult and child learning environment are connected and mirror one another through respectful processes of inquiry and differentiation).

2. Vivian Paley, *The Boy Who Would Be a Helicopter* (Cambridge, MA: Harvard University Press, 1990).

3. Shirley Brice Heath, *Ways with Words: Language, Life and Work in Communities and Classrooms* (Cambridge, UK, Cambridge University Press, 1983); Terry Meier, *Black Communications and Learning to Read: Building on Children's Linguistic and Cultural Strengths* (Abington, UK: Routledge, 2007).

4. Nicole Gardner-Neblett and John Sideris, "Different Tales: The Role of Gender in the Oral Narrative–Reading Link Among African American Children," *Child Development* (April2017), doi:10.1111/cdev.12803.

5. Core principles 3 and 8.

6. Core principles 1 (Schools must promote our democratic society and support children's and teachers' sense of citizenship though multiple connections to families and community) and 2 (Young children are curious, active learners who are capable of high-level thinking processes, empathy, and taking multiple perspectives).

7. Note that teachers and paraprofessionals are engaged in the decision-making process as democratic participants, consistent with core principles 1 and 8.

8. Project Zero, "See-Think-Wonder," http://pz.harvard.edu/resources/see-think-wonder.
9. Core principle 8.
10. See, for example, Marilyn Cochran-Smith and Susan L. Lytle, "Relationships of Knowledge and Practice: Teacher Learning in Communities," *Review of Research in Education* 24 (1999): 249–306.
11. Note how this mirrors on an adult level the active learning, inquiry, perspective-taking, relationship-building, and collaboration that the DEC encourages teachers to engage and foster in children, in accordance with core principles 2 (treating children as curious, active learners), 3 (strong relationships as central to powerful learning experiences), and 5 (building twenty-first-century skills through flexible, hands-on curricula).
12. Ron Ritchhart, Mark Church, and Karin Morrison, *Making Thinking Visible: How to Promote Engagement, Understanding, and Independence for All Learners* (New York: John Wiley & Sons, 2011).
13. Project Zero, "See-Think-Wonder," http://pz.harvard.edu/resources/see-think-wonder; Making Learning Visible, "Ladder of Feedback," https://makinglearningvisibleresources.wikispaces.com/Ladder+of+Feedback.
14. Carollee Howes, Bridget K. Hamre, and Robert C. Pianta, eds., *Effective Early Childhood Professional Development: Improving Teacher Practice and Child Outcomes* (Baltimore, MD: Paul H. Brookes Publishing Company, 2012).
15. Bob Tschannen-Moran and Megan Tschannen-Moran, *Evocative Coaching: Transforming Schools One Conversation at a Time* (New York: John Wiley and Sons, 2010), 234–235.
16. Boston Public Schools Department of Early Childhood, "Focus on Coaching," internal document.
17. Melissa Tonachel, "The Boston Public Schools Early Childhood Professional Development Model."

Chapter 9

1. As a learning organization, the DEC nurtures the strong personal relationships that they believe are at the center of powerful learning experiences (principle 3).
2. In 2017, the DEC staff included seventeen program directors, whose primary responsibility is coaching; two senior managers (for NAEYC accreditation and school readiness); three project managers (for the Coordinated Family and Community Engagement Grant, the Preschool Expansion Grant, and general administration), an operations analyst, and the director.
3. As DEC members work together, using a protocol to ensure that all voices are heard, they mirror the respect, transparency, and tools that they hope the directors they work with will use in their own ways as they supervise, support, and learn with teachers, who will then use them in their own ways as they teach, support, and learn with children (core principle 8 [The adult and child learning environment are connected and mirror one another through respectful processes of inquiry and differentiation]).
4. Notice the intentional implementation of core principles 1 (Schools must promote our democratic society and support children's and teachers' sense of citizenship though multiple connections to families and community) and 8 here and throughout this chapter.
5. Project Zero and Reggio Children, *Making Learning Visible: Children as Individual and Group Learners*. Project Zero and Reggio Children (Reggio Emilia, Italy: Reggio Children, 2001); School Reform Initiative, "Protocols," http://www.schoolreforminitiative.org/protocols/#.

6. Thelma Harms, Richard M. Clifford, and Debby Cryer, *Early Childhood Environment Rating Scale* (New York: Teachers College Press, 2014); Robert C. Pianta, Karen M. La Paro, and Bridget K. Hamre, *Classroom Assessment Scoring System: Manual K–3*, (Baltimore: Paul H. Brookes Publishing, 2008); Miriam W. Smith and David K. Dickinson, *Early Language & Literacy Classroom Observation (ELLCO) Toolkit, Research Edition* [with User's Guide] (Baltimore: Paul H. Brookes Publishing, 2002); Julie Sarama and Douglas H. Clements, *Manual for Classroom Observation of Early Mathematics—Environment and Teaching* (unpublished manuscript, 2009).

7. Core principle 9 (Varied assessments provide data to inform instruction and drive change. Teachers and families participate along with administrators and specialists in interpreting findings, evaluating their implications, and shaping resultant decisions).

8. Boston Public Schools Department of Early Childhood, "Strategic Plan," 2017–2022.

9. Boston Public Schools Department of Early Childhood, "Kindergarten Conference," https://sites.google.com/bostonpublicschools.org/earlychildhood/proven-practices -beyond-pd/kindergarten-conference.

10. The DEC's vigilant insistence on interdisciplinary, whole-child approaches that address all domains of development and on balanced approaches to building basic literacies and twenty-first-century skills that integrate play, projects, and thoughtful instruction is driven by core principles 2 (Young children are curious, active learners who are capable of high-level thinking processes, empathy, and taking multiple perspectives), 4 (Early learning programs must support children's physical, intellectual, language, and social-emotional development, along with their curiosity, creativity, persistence at challenging tasks, and academic learning), and 6 (Basic literacies, knowledge, and higher-level skills can be furthered through pretend play, projects, extended conversation, and thoughtful instruction). Their argument that this not "just for babies" takes on increased urgency as they seek to align their curricula with what children will be expected to know and given opportunities to learn in higher grades (core principle 5 [Flexible, hands-on curricula that align with prior and future experiences foster mastery of learning standards and achievement of twenty-first-century goals]).

11. Core principle 9.

Chapter 10

1. CAST, "About Universal Design for Learning," http://www.cast.org/our-work/about -udl.html#.WfSXPkzMy8o; Django Paris, "Culturally Sustaining Pedagogy: A Needed Change in Stance, Terminology, and Practice," *Educational Researcher* 41, no. 3 (2012): 93–97.

2. See Alfie Kohn, *The Homework Myth: Why Our Kids Get Too Much of a Bad Thing* (Boston: Da Capo Lifelong, 2006), for a summary of research on worksheet-type structured homework for young children. In contrast, "homework" based on family engagement can be quite powerful. Reading and talking about books activates and strengthens brain regions related to reading and higher order thinking (John S. Hutton et al., "Home Reading Environment and Brain Activation in Preschool Children Listening to Stories," *Pediatrics* 136, no. 3 (2015): 466–478). Playing board games builds number sense (Geetha B. Ramani and Robert S. Siegler, "Promoting Broad and Stable Improvements in Low-Income Children's Numerical Knowledge Through Playing Number Board Games," *Child Development* 79, no. 2 [2008]: 375–394). Dinner-table conversations that go beyond the here and now build language and storytelling skill (David K. Dickinson

and Patton O. Tabors, *Beginning Literacy with Language: Young Children Learning at Home and School* [Baltimore: Paul H. Brookes Publishing Co, 2001]).

3. Christina Weiland and Jason Sachs, unpublished Summer Learning Academy study, Boston Public Schools, 2010.

4. See, for example, Mokhtar Farhadian et al., "Theory of Mind in Bilingual and Monolingual Preschool Children," *Journal of Psychology* 1, no. 1 (2010): 39–46. http://www.krepublishers.com/02-Journals/JP/JP-01-0-000-10-Web/JP-01-1-000-10-PDF/JP-01-1-039-10-010-Farhadian-M/JP-01-1-039-10-010-Farhadian-M-Tt.pdf. For a recent review see Ellen Bialystok, "Bilingual Education for Young Children: Review of the Effects and Consequences," *International Journal of Bilingual Education and Bilingualism* (2016): 1-14 https://www.ncbi.nlm.nih.gov/pmc/articles/PMC3322418/.

5. Jennifer L. Steele et al., "Effects of Dual-Language Immersion Programs on Student Achievement: Evidence from Lottery Data." *American Educational Research Journal* 54, no. 1 (supplement) (2017): 282S–306S.

6. Virginia P. Collier and Wayne P. Thomas, "The Astounding Effectiveness of Dual Language Education for All," *NABE Journal of Research and Practice* 2, no. 1 (2004): 1–20, http://hillcrest.wacoisd.org/UserFiles/Servers/Server_345/File/Publications/ELL/Dual%20language%20survey.pdf.

7. Boston Public Schools Department of Early Childhood, *Piloting the Boston Public Schools' Prekindergarten Model in Community-Based Programs: Final Report* (Boston Public Schools, 2016), http://bpsearlychildhood.weebly.com/uploads/1/0/1/3/10131776/bps k1ds_final_report_feb2016_11.pdf.

8. Mixed-age classrooms have many benefits for both three- and four-year-olds, in terms of empathy, social responsibility, language and storytelling, and the development of mature pretend play. See, for example, Lilian G. Katz, *The Case for Mixed-Age Grouping in Early Education* (Washington, DC: National Association for the Education of Young Children, 1990). However, they can also have negative impacts on four-year-olds' school readiness skills (Arya Ansari, Kelly Purtell, and Elizabeth Gershoff, "Classroom Age Composition and the School Readiness of 3- and 4-Year-Olds in the Head Start Program," *Psychological Science* 27, no. 1 (2016): 53–63). In addition, Walter Gilliam and Golan Shahar's research on preschool expulsion in Massachusetts found that four-year-olds in classes with a high proportion of three-year-olds were at higher risk for preschool expulsion due to behavioral issues ("Preschool and Child Care Expulsion and Suspension: Rates and Predictors in One State," *Infants and Young Children* 19, no. 3 [2006]: 228–245).

9. Ann Bookman, "Cost of Early Care and Education in Boston and in Massachusetts: Is Quality Child Care Affordable?" (Presentation to the Boston City Council, April 11, 2017), https://www.boston.gov/sites/default/files/document-file-04-2017/bookman_umassboston11april2017_childcareaffordability_0.pdf.

10. Amy Checkoway et al., *Year 1 Massachusetts Preschool Expansion Grant (PEG): Evaluation Report* (Cambridge, MA: ABT Associates, 2016).

11. Suzanne Bouffard, *The Most Important Year: Pre-Kindergarten and the Future of Our Children* (New York: Penguin, 2017).

12. Kimber Bogard and Ruby Takanishi, "PK-3: An Aligned and Coordinated Approach to Education for Children 3 to 8 Years Old, *Social Policy Report*,Volume 19, Number 3," *Society for Research in Child Development* (2005), https://www.fcd-us.org/pk-3-an-aligned-and-coordinated-approach-to-education-for-children-3-to-8-years-old/; Jade M.

Jenkins et al., "Preventing Preschool Fadeout Through Instructional Intervention in Kindergarten and First Grade," working paper, Graduate School of Education, University of California, Irvine (2015), http://inid.gse.uci.edu/files/2011/03/Jenkinsetal _Fadeout_SREE.pdf.

13. Core principle 4 (Early learning programs must support children's physical, intellectual, language, and social-emotional development, along with their curiosity, creativity, persistence at challenging tasks, and academic learning.)

14. Core principles 1 (Schools must promote our democratic society and support children's and teachers' sense of citizenship though multiple connections to families and community), 5 (Flexible, hands-on curricula that align with prior and future experiences foster mastery of learning standards and achievement of twenty-first-century goals), and 6 (Basic literacies, knowledge, and higher-level skills can be furthered through pretend play, projects, extended conversation, and thoughtful instruction).

15. Core principle 8 (The adult and child learning environment are connected and mirror one another through respectful processes of inquiry and differentiation).

16. James Vanis, "Review Finds Boston Schools in Disarray: Says Lack of Harmony Among Departments Imperils Education," *Boston Globe*, May 23, 2014; John McDonough, memorandum to chairperson and members of Boston School Committee, May 21, 2014, https://www.bostonpublicschools.org/cms/lib07/MA01906464/Centricity /Domain/238/CGCS%20Academics%20Memo%20and%20BPS%20Superintendent %20Letter.pdf.

17. Nancy L. Marshall, Wendy Wagner Robeson, and Joanne Roberts, *Boston Public Schools K2–3rd Grade Needs Assessment 2012*, internal report to the Department of Early Childhood, Boston Public Schools (Wellesley MA: Wellesley Centers for Women, 2012).

18. *Reach for Reading* (website), http://ngl.cengage.com/search/productOverview.do?N=201 +4294918395&Ntk=NGL&Ntt=PRO0000000004&Ntx=mode%2Bmatchallpartial.

19. Carol Copple and Sue Bredekamp, *Developmentally Appropriate Practice in Early Childhood Programs Serving Children from Birth Through Age 8, Third Edition* (Washington, DC: NAEYC, 2010).

20. Core principle 6.

21. In a review of studies of early literacy skills and instructional practices that support their development, the 2009 report of the National Early Literacy Panel (NELP) had highlighted the importance of these decoding skills for learning to read. See Christopher J. Lonigan and Timothy Shanahan, *Developing Early Literacy: Report of the National Early Literacy Panel. A Scientific Synthesis of Early Literacy Development and Implications for Intervention* (Washington, DC: National Institute for Literacy, 2009).

22. Susan B. Neuman, "Lessons from My Mother: Reflections on the National Early Literacy Panel Report," *Educational Researcher* 39, no. 4 (2010): 301–304.

23. Massachusetts Department of Elementary and Secondary Education, 2017 English Language Arts and Literacy Framework: Grades Pre-Kindergarten Through 12, 15–16, http://www.doe.mass.edu/frameworks/ela/2017-06.pdf.

24. MA DESE, 2017 ELA and Literacy Framework, 14.

25. Core principle 6.

26. Douglas Clements and Julie Sarama, "Longitudinal Evaluation of a Scale Up Model for Teaching Math with Trajectories and Technologies: Persistence of Effects in the Third Year" (poster presented at Society for Research on Educational Effectiveness Conference

"Building an Education Science: Improving Mathematics and Science Education for All Students," Washington, DC, September 8–10, 2011), https://www.sree.org/conferences /2011/program/downloads/posters/52.pdf.

27. Core principle 5.

28. JoAnn Hsueh et al., "Boston P–3: Identifying Malleable Factors for Promoting Student Success," proposal submitted to the Supporting Early Learning from Preschool Through Early Elementary School Grades Network (Washington, DC: Institute for Education Sciences, 2015), https://ies.ed.gov/ncer/projects/grant.asp?ProgID=91&grantid=1770& NameID=49.

29. Catherine Snow, personal communication, September 27, 2017.

30. Institute of Education Sciences, National Center for Education Research, "Supporting Early Learning from Preschool Through Early Elementary School Grades Network," https://ies.ed.gov/ncer/projects/program.asp?ProgID=91.

Epilogue

1. These twenty-first-century skills may be more important to ongoing school and life success than specific academic knowledge or competencies. For example, Ellen Galinsky's book, *Mind in the Making: The Seven Essential Life Skills that Every Child Needs* (Washington, DC: National Association for the Education of Young Children, 2010), summarizes research on the importance of focus and self-control, perspective taking, communicating, making connections, critical thinking, taking on challenges, and self-directed, engaged learning.

2. Clearly, a letter from the mayor asking for their opinions is a powerful statement to children that they are valued citizens of their community (core principle 1). The letter echoes the curriculum in assuming that kindergarteners are curious, active learners, capable of doing research, thinking about big ideas, showing empathy for others and considering their perspectives, and communicating their ideas both in a collaborative project and in writing (core principle 2).

3. This close reading and discussion of the meanings and connotations of words in context is an example of a balanced approach to literacy that engages critical thinking and uses play, projects, and discussion along with focused instruction (core principle 6) to build what matters most for literacy long term; see Susan Neuman, "Lessons from My Mother: Reflections on the National Early Literacy Panel Report," *Educational Researcher* 39, no. 4 (2010): 301–304.

4. Interaction Design Foundation, "Five Stages of the Design Thinking Process," https:// www.interaction-design.org/literature/article/5-stages-in-the-design-thinking-process.

5. As they do for the DEC members and teachers whose discussions with each other mirror, without mimicking, the kinds of democratic and learning-focused discussions they will engage children in (core principle 8), protocols like Thinking and Feedback make it more likely that less vocal community members will be heard (core principles 1 and 7).

6. See Boston Public Schools Department of Early Childhood, *Focus on K2*, Unit 3: Construction for Teaching Materials and Exemplars of Children's Work and Their Creation Process. https://sites.google.com/bostonpublicschools.org/earlychildhood/focus-on-k2.

7. An affirmation of core principles 4 (Early learning programs must support children's physical, intellectual, language, and social-emotional development, along with their curiosity, creativity, persistence at challenging tasks, and academic learning) and 6.

Appendix
We ask our readers to list Jason Sachs and Christina Wieland as the authors when citing material from this appendix.

1. Tracy Jan, "Boston Preschools Falling Far Short of Goals, Study Says," *Boston Globe*, April 7, 2007.
2. Core principle 9.
3. Deborah Stipek and Patricia Byler, "The *Early Childhood* Classroom Observation Measure," *Early Childhood Research Quarterly* 19, no. 3 (2004): 375–397.
4. Nancy L. Marshall and Joanne Roberts, *Boston Public Schools Early Childhood Quality Study* (internal report to the Department of Early Childhood, Boston Public Schools) (Wellesley, MA: Wellesley Centers for Women, 2008); Nancy Marshall and JoAnne Roberts, *Boston Public Schools Early Childhood Quality Study 2010* (internal report to the Department of Early Childhood, Boston Public Schools, 2010) (Wellesley, MA: Wellesley Centers for Women, Wellesley College, 2010).
5. Christina Weiland and Hirokazu Yoshikawa, "Does Higher Peer Socio-Economic Status Predict Children's Language and Executive Function Skills Gains in Prekindergarten?" *Journal of Applied Developmental Psychology* 35, no. 5 (2014) 422–432.
6. Doris R. Entwisle and Karl L. Alexander, "Summer Setback: Race, Poverty, School Composition, and Mathematics Achievement in the First Two Years of School," *American Sociological Review* (1992): 72–84; Geoffrey D. Borman and N. Maritza Dowling, "Longitudinal Achievement Effects of Multiyear Summer School: Evidence from the Teach Baltimore Randomized Field Trial," *Educational Evaluation and Policy Analysis* 28, no. 1 (2006): 25–48; Brian A. Jacob and Lars Lefgren, "Remedial Education and Student Achievement: A Regression-Discontinuity Analysis," *Review of Economics and Statistics* 86, no. 1 (2004) 226–244.
7. Ajay Chaudry et al., *Cradle to Kindergarten: A New Plan to Combat Inequality* (New York: Russell Sage Foundation, 2017). Boston data were collected in 2010 (*N* = 83 classrooms) in Christina Weiland et al., "Associations Between Classroom Quality and Children's Vocabulary and Executive Function Skills in an Urban Public Prekindergarten Program," *Early Childhood Research Quarterly* 28, no. 2 (2013): 199–209. Tulsa data were collected in 2006 (*N* pre-k = 77 classrooms, *N* CAP = 28 classrooms) in Deborah A. Phillips, William T. Gormley, and Amy E. Lowenstein, "Inside the Pre-Kindergarten Door: Classroom Climate and Instructional Time Allocation in Tulsa's Pre-K Programs," *Early Childhood Research Quarterly* 24, no. 3 (2009) 213–228. Head Start data were collected in 2014 (*N* grantees=404) in Office of Head Start, *A National Overview of Grantee Class Scores in 2014*, https://eclkc.ohs.acf.hhs.gov/hslc/data/class-reports/docs/national-class-2014-data.pdf).

   The eleven-state preK data were collected in six states in 2002 and in five additional states in 2004 (*N*=671 classrooms) in Andrew J., Mashburn et al., "Measures of Classroom Quality in Prekindergarten and Children's Development of Academic, Language, and Social Skills," *Child Development* 79, no. 3 (2008): 732–749. The study reported results using an older version of the CLASS than the other studies included here. Data from this study accordingly are approximately but not exactly comparable to those of the other studies shown.
8. Christina Weiland et al., *Impacts of the Boston Prekindergarten Program Through Third Grade. Under review.*

9. Pamela Morris, "Strengthening School Readiness in New York City's Pre-K for All," *Education Week*, November 17, 2017, http://blogs.edweek.org/edweek/urban_education _reform/2017/08/strengthening_school_readiness_in_new_york_citys_pre-k_for_all .html.

10. *School Readiness in Child Care Settings: A Developmental Assessment of Children in 22 Accredited Child Care Settings* (St. Paul, MN: Minnesota Department of Human Services, 2005); Marcy Whitebook, Laura Sakai, and Carollee Howes, *NAEYC Accreditation as a Strategy for Improving Child Care Quality: An Assessment by the National Center for the Early Childhood Work Force, Final Report* (Washington, DC: National Center for the Early Childhood Work Force, 1997).

11. Marshall and Roberts, *Boston Public Schools Early Childhood Quality Study*, 2008.

12. Jason Sachs and Christina Weiland, "Boston's Rapid Expansion of Public School-Based Preschool: Promoting Quality, Lessons Learned," *Young Children* 65, no. 5 (2010): 74–77.

13. Studies using a regression discontinuity design are increasingly used to assess the impacts of large-scale early childhood programs. When random assignment to a treatment versus control group is not feasible but programs have strict age cutoffs, researchers can assess impact by comparing the school readiness skills of children who are close in age but fall on opposite sides of the cutoff.

14. Christina Weiland and Hirokazu Yoshikawa, "Impacts of a Prekindergarten Program on Children's Mathematics, Language, Literacy, Executive Function, and Emotional Skills," *Child Development* 84, no. 6 (2013): 2112–2130.

15. For a current assessment schedule and rationale, see Boston Public Schools Department of Early Childhood, "Assessments," https://sites.google.com/bostonpublicschools.org /earlychildhood/assessments.

16. Monica Yudron, Christina Weiland, and Jason Sachs, "Public Investment in Aligning Instructional Content and Improving Quality Across Prekindergarten Auspices: Classroom Outcomes and Lessons Learned," under review.

17. Amy Checkoway et al., *Year 1 Massachusetts Preschool Expansion Grant Evaluation Report* (Cambridge, MA: Abt Associates, 2017).

Acknowledgments

This book was crafted by many hands. We thank Melissa Rivard and Jodi Doyle Krous, David Ramsey and Abby Morales, Melissa Tonachel, Christina Weiland and Jason Sachs, and Marina Boni for their contributions and continued collaboration. As we wove their inside stories and thoughtful reflections into a narrative, our coauthors generously provided additional information and careful and insightful critiques to make sure that the story as a whole remained true to the history, practice, and shared vision of the Boston Public Schools Department of Early Childhood. We are deeply grateful for their assistance.

We are all extremely grateful for the opportunity to share the stories and examples in this book beyond Boston. Many, many thanks to the children, teachers, and coaches in the Boston Public Schools' early childhood programs for sharing their insights about learning, teaching, and practice. We continue to be inspired by the DEC faculty and their unwavering commitment to making Boston's public early childhood classrooms fairer and more interesting places for children and teachers. We have followed their wishes in focusing on their work as a team, crediting individuals only if we quote their words. It is with profound gratitude that we list here all of their names and titles:

Abby Morales, Program Director
Ana Vaisenstein, Program Director
Anthony Valdez, Program Director
Blaire Horner, Project Manager
Brian Gold, Senior School Readiness Manager

Carmen Lico, Program Director
Carolyn Christopher, Program Director
Chris Bucco, Program Director
Danielle Gantt, Coordinated Family and Community Engagement
    Project Manager
David Ramsey, Program Director
Fay Ferency, Program Director
Jason Sachs, Director
Karen Silver, Senior NAEYC Accreditation Manager
Kathy Pauyo, Operations Analyst
Marie Enochty, Program Director
Marina Boni, Program Director
Mayra Cuevas, Program Director
Melissa Luc, Program Director
Melissa Tonachel, Program Director
Nicole St. Victor, Program Director
Solange Marsan, Program Director
TeeAra Dias, Preschool Expansion Grant Project Manager
Theresa Vilcapoma, Program Director
Unicia Young, Program Director

Ben and Megina deeply appreciate the opportunity to collaborate in bringing *Focus on K2* to life, and continue to follow its journey with great enthusiasm. They extend *tusen tak* ("a thousand thanks," in Megina's native Swedish) to Judith Ross-Bernstein, whose optimism and deep belief in public early childhood education played an instrumental role in turning this book from vision into reality.

Betty extends special thanks to her guides in retracing the DEC's journey: Jason Sachs, Marina Boni, Marie Enochty, Brian Gold, and Nicole St. Victor, who, despite very full plates, took time to answer questions, share stories and perspectives, locate data and documents, and correct details.

We owe a huge debt to our editor, Caroline Chauncey, for her skillful shepherding of this book from vision to actuality. Her unwavering focus on our readers' perspectives brought our writing to a new level. We also thank Monica Jainschigg for her skillful and conscientious editing and Chris Leonesio for managing the book's design and production.

About the Authors, Contributors, and Collaborators

Megina Baker has been an early childhood educator in the United States and Sweden. She is now a researcher at Project Zero at the Harvard Graduate School of Education and part of the Early Childhood Education faculty at Boston University.

Betty Bardige is a developmental psychologist and an early childhood author, advocate, foundation leader, and consultant. She focuses on language, literacy, and family engagement.

Marina Boni taught children fifteen months to six years of age for many years before coming to the Boston Public Schools Department of Early Childhood, where she focuses on coaching teachers, facilitating professional development, and developing curriculum.

Jodi Doyle Krous is in her tenth year teaching an inclusive preK classroom in the Boston Public Schools' Eliot K–8 Innovation School in the North End. She actively participates in the Making Learning Visible project through the Boston Public Schools Department of Early Childhood.

Ben Mardell has taught infants, toddlers, preschoolers, and kindergarteners. He is currently a principal investigator at Project Zero at the Harvard Graduate School of Education.

Abby Morales was a preschool and kindergarten teacher in community and public school settings. She is currently a program director in the Boston Public Schools Department of Early Childhood, where she develops curriculum, coaches teachers, and provides professional development.

David Ramsey works on Focus on K0/K1 and NAEYC accreditation for the Boston Public Schools Department of Early Childhood. David has taught preK and kindergarten in a variety of public and private settings over the past twenty years in Boston and Los Angeles.

Melissa Rivard served as a researcher and documentation specialist on the Making Learning Visible Project at Project Zero and consultant to the Documentation Studio at Wheelock College. She is currently a senior project manager at the Center on the Developing Child at Harvard University.

Jason Sachs is the executive director of Early Childhood for the Boston Public Schools. Before coming to BPS, he worked for the Massachusetts Department of Education: Early Learning Services and for Associated Early Education and Care Services, a large childcare agency serving low-income families in Boston and Cambridge.

Melissa Tonachel is an early childhood educator dedicated to progressive public education for all children. She has taught preschool through second-grade students, along with aspiring teachers, and currently develops curriculum and supports teachers as a member of the Boston Public Schools Department of Early Childhood.

Christina Weiland is an assistant professor at the University of Michigan School of Education. Her research focuses on the effects of early childhood interventions and public policies on children's development, especially for children from low-income families. She has partnered with the Boston Public Schools Department of Early Childhood for more than ten years.

Index